ECE/TRADE/165

ECONOMIC COMMISSION FOR EUROPE

Geneva

EAST-WEST JOINT VENTURE CONTRACTS

Volume I

of

Guide on legal aspects of new forms of industrial co-operation

UNITED NATIONS

New York, 1989

NOTE

This Guide, drawn up under the auspices of the Committee on the Development of Trade, was drafted by the Working Party on International Contract Practices in Industry, and finally approved at its thirty-third session (November 1988).

The designations employed and the presentation of the material in this publication do not imply the expression of any opinion whatsoever on the part of the Secretariat of the United Nations concerning the legal status of any country, territory, city or area, or of its authorities, or concerning the delimitation of its frontiers or boundaries.

ECE/TRADE/165

UNITED NATIONS PUBLICATION

Sales No. E.88.II.E.30

ISBN 92-1-116437-0

05000P

EAST-WEST JOINT VENTURE CONTRACTS

CONTENTS

PART ONE

GUIDELINES ON DRAWING UP JOINT VENTURE CONTRACTS

CHAPTER THREE

PART TWO

REGULATIONS

PART THREE

MODEL DOCUMENTS

PART ONE

GUIDELINES ON DRAWING UP JOINT VENTURE CONTRACTS

CHAPTER ONE

INTRODUCTION

I. PURPOSE AND SCOPE

This Guide deals with east-west joint ventures which are established and operate in the form of a legal person, where the liability of the legal person is limited to its statutory capital (share capital), and the liability of each of the parties is limited to the amount it has subscribed as its share in the statutory capital.

The purpose of this Guide is to facilitate the drafting of east-west joint venture contracts by drawing attention to the main legal issues involved in this kind of transaction, and suggesting ways of resolving these issues, within the framework of the applicable law, in the joint venture documents.

While reflecting practical experience obtained both from east-west joint ventures operating in east European countries and from east-west joint ventures based in western Europe, this Guide concentrates on east-west joint ventures located in the east European countries of the ECE region.

II. REGULATION OF EAST-WEST JOINT VENTURES

Six east European countries of the ECE region have issued regulations concerning the establishment and operation, in their respective territories, of east-west joint ventures as legal persons.

In ***Bulgaria,*** joint ventures are regulated by Decree 56 of 6 January 1989 on Economic Activity in the People's Republic of Bulgaria, the Regulation of 15 February 1989 on the application of Decree 56, Decree No. 2242 of 1987 on Free Trade Zones, and the Regulation on the Application of Decree 2242. Decree 56 had been preceded by Decree No. 535 of 1980 on Economic Co-operation between Bulgarian Juridical Persons and Foreign Juridical and Physical Persons. The present law allows wholly foreign-owned companies.

In ***Czechoslovakia,*** the principles regarding the creation and activities of joint ventures in that country are codified in Act No. 173 of 8 November 1988 on Enterprises with Foreign Property Participation.

In ***Hungary,*** joint ventures were authorized for the first time in 1972. The regulations were subsequently amended several times - namely, in 1977, 1978, 1979, 1982 and 1985. In the autumn of 1988 two entirely new laws on this subject were enacted - namely the Act VI/1988 on Economic Associations (the Company Act) and the Act XXIV/1988 on Investments by Foreigners in Hungary (the Foreign Investment Act). Under this legislation, not only joint ventures, but also wholly foreign-owned companies are possible.

In ***Poland,*** the Law on Economic Activity with the Participation of Foreign Parties (the Polish Foreign Investment Law), of 23 December 1988, laid down the rules on starting and conducting economic activities with foreign participation. This law had been preceded by the Law of 23 April 1986 on Companies with Foreign Capital Participation, and earlier legislation regulating the establishment of firms in small industries (1976) and banks with foreign capital participation (1982). The new Foreign Investment Law permits wholly foreign-owned companies.

In ***Romania,*** Law No. 1 of 1971 authorized the formation of joint ventures by Romanian enterprises with foreign firms. This law was followed, in 1972, by two implementing decrees: Decree No. 424 on Constitution, Organization and Operation of Joint Companies; and Decree No. 425 on Tax on Profits of Joint Companies. Decree No. 395 of 1976 refers, among other things, to duty-free imports of goods for use by joint ventures.

In the ***Soviet Union,*** east-west joint ventures are regulated by three decrees of 1987 and one decree of 1988. The first of these is the Decree of the Presidium of the USSR Supreme Soviet of 13 January 1987 on questions concerning the establishment in the territory of the USSR and operation of joint ventures, international amalgamations and organizations with the participation of Soviet and foreign organizations, firms and management bodies. The second is the Decree of the USSR Council of Ministers of 13 January 1987 on the establishment in the territory of the USSR and operation of joint ventures with the participation of Soviet organizations and firms from capitalist and developing countries (Decree 49). On 17 September 1987, the CPSU Central Committee and the USSR Council of Ministers issued the Decree on further measures on the carrying out of external economic activities in the new conditions of economic management (Decree 1074). This Decree amends the provisions of the two Decrees of 13 January 1987, regarding certain important matters. It was later incorporated in Decree 49 through Decree 352 of the USSR Council of Ministers of 17 March 1988. On 2 December 1988, the USSR Council of Ministers issued further amendments to earlier rules through the Decree on the Further Development of the Foreign Economic Activities of State, Co-operative and other Public Enterprises, Amalgamations and Organizations. Subsequent to the Decrees of January 1987 the USSR Ministry of Finance and certain other government agencies have issued a number of orders and instructions regulating in more detail the operation of joint ventures in the Soviet Union.

In this Guide, references will be made, when appropriate, to the stipulations of the above-mentioned regulations in order to illustrate the approaches which the respective governments have adopted regarding the questions dealt with here. English translations of the the basic joint venture rules of the six countries are included in Part II of this Guide. Developments in these rules have been taken into account up to the end of 1988.

It should also be noted that the respective legislations of the countries under review do not cover all questions relating to the establishment and operation of joint ventures on their territories. For instance, not all these countries have corporate laws which would form the basic legal framework for a joint venture. Such a framework must therefore be created through contractual arrangements between the parties. Moreover, in some countries a number of regulations regarding domestic enterprises are not applicable to east-west joint ventures, which further broadens the area which should be covered by the parties' mutual agreements. All this makes it very important for the parties to regulate in great detail in their contracts the various aspects of their joint venture. A set of illustrative joint venture contracts and charters, compiled by the ECE secretariat, is included in Part III of the Guide.

III. TERMINOLOGY

In this Guide the terms mentioned below will have the following meanings.

Joint venture means the legal person to be incorporated by the parties for the purpose of carrying out the agreed joint venture activities.

Joint venture contract means the agreement of the parties on the establishment of the joint venture.

Charter means the statute of the legal person, agreed upon by the parties.

Statutory capital means the aggregate amount of the respective investments by the parties as tied-up capital of the joint venture.

Host country means the east European country in which the joint venture is established.

Local party means the host country organization, firm or management body which is a party to the contract and/or to the preceding joint venture negotiations.

Foreign party means the natural or juridical person from another country which is a party to the contract and/or to the preceding joint venture negotiations.

Products means the goods manufactured, services rendered, or scientific-technical results produced by the joint venture.

Plant means the industrial or other works where the products are manufactured.

CHAPTER TWO

ISSUES RELATING TO ESTABLISHMENT AND APPROVAL

Setting up an east-west joint venture requires systematic and careful preparation. A multitude of different questions must be studied and analysed by the parties, and a number of documents drafted. Finally, the joint venture may have to be presented to the respective host country authorities for approval. An account of the main features of the preparatory work is given below.

I. INITIAL FEASIBILITY STUDY

For the parties to assess whether the projected joint venture would satisfy their requirements and expectations, an initial feasibility study should be prepared at an early stage. The study would also serve the important function of indicating whether the joint venture is in line with the objectives which the respective host country legislation stipulates for an east-west joint venture (see section II.B below), and whether it would be approved by the relevant authorities of that country, in cases when approval is required.

Each joint venture sets its own premises for the initial feasibility study. Individual host countries may also have their own requirements or preferences in this respect. For example, under Czechoslovak and Polish practice the feasibility report is prepared according to the UNIDO methodology (see Part III of this Guide).

II. HOST COUNTRY LEGISLATION AND INTERGOVERNMENTAL TREATIES

The respective host country legislation dealing with the establishment and operation of joint ventures and applicable intergovernmental treaties should also be carefully studied and analysed.

In addition to providing a general orientation to the various legal aspects involved in the setting up of a joint venture in the country in question, this kind of study is necessary in order to ascertain not only which principles are mandatory and which are optional, but also whether there are areas which are not regulated at all or are regulated only to a small degree. Another reason for the need to study local legislation carefully is the possibility that certain rules which normally bind local enterprises in the host country are not applied to joint ventures with foreign participation. The parties may therefore wish to include in the joint venture documents provisions relevant to these matters.

The host country joint venture laws regulate a number of different issues.

A. Permitted activities

Thus, several joint venture laws define the sectors in the national economy of the host country where east-west joint ventures may operate. As an example of a rather broad definition the Romanian rule can be cited, according to which joint ventures with foreign participation may be set up in the sectors of industry, agriculture, construction, tourism, transport, and scientific and technological research, with the object of producing and marketing material goods, performing services or carrying out work. The Czechoslovak rules contain an even more general provision, stating that a joint venture may be active in any branch of national economy, with the exception of those branches which are important for the defense and security of the Czechoslovak Socialist Republic.

B. Host country objectives

Most of the joint venture laws set forth some general objectives which the joint venture should promote. By way of illustration, under Soviet rules, the purpose of the joint venture should be to satisfy more fully the domestic requirements for certain types of manufactured products, raw materials and foodstuffs; to attract advanced foreign equipment and technologies, management expertise and additional material and financial resources to the USSR national economy and to expand the national export sector and to reduce superfluous imports. In addition to enunciating some of the objectives mentioned above, the Polish law makes special reference to the export of services and the Romanian law to the promotion and development of scientific research activities. In this connection special mention should be made of the Romanian requirements that the products of the joint venture should be intended particularly for export and that the joint venture should conduct all its operations in convertible currency.

C. Taxation and incentives

(1) General principles

All the joint venture regulations now under review contain rules on the taxation of joint ventures. These rules are complemented by administrative acts of the respective government bodies. Thus, for example, the USSR Ministry of Finance has issued Regulations on the taxation of joint ventures set up on Soviet territory. In addition to laying down certain general principles, the Regulations deal with the assessment and payment of the profit tax to the State budget, the taxation of that part of profits of foreign partners which is transferred abroad, exemptions from the tax, auditing and payment of taxes, and appealing against actions of finance authorities.

The rates of tax payable by a joint venture vary considerably from country to country. Thus, under Bulgarian law, companies pay profit tax at the rate of 50 per cent. However, if foreign participation in a company exceeds 49 per cent and 5 million levs in convertible currency, the tax rate is 30 per cent. Exceptionally, this lower rate may be applied to joint ventures with even smaller foreign shares. In Romania, profits made by joint ventures are subject to an annual tax of 30 per cent. Also under Soviet law joint ventures will pay taxes at the rate of 30 per cent of their profit. In Hungary, the basic corporation tax is 40 per cent of the taxable profit not exceeding three million forints, and 50 per cent on the part exceeding that amount. In Poland, income tax is 40 per cent of the taxable income. In Czechoslovakia, the prescribed contribution (corporate tax) rate is 40 per cent of assessable earnings from the activities of the joint venture.

The amount of tax payable by a joint venture depends not only on the applicable tax rate, but also on the accounting rules in force (see Chapter Three, Section VIII below).

(2) Withholding (dividends) tax, and the role of international treaties for the avoidance of double taxation

Under Romanian law, profits remaining for the partners after payment of taxes shall be taxed at a rate of 10 per cent, if transferred abroad. In the Soviet Union, the corresponding provision of the joint venture law states that the part of the profit due to a foreign partner in a joint venture shall be taxed, if transferred abroad, at the rate of 20 per cent.

On the other hand, in Bulgaria dividends received by foreign persons will be taxable at 15 per cent, and those received by Bulgarian companies with foreign participation at 10 per cent. In Czechoslovakia the tax rate is 25 per cent, and in Poland 30 per cent, irrespective of whether the dividends are transferred abroad or not.

It should be noticed, however, that international treaties for the avoidance of double taxation, concluded by the above-mentioned countries, may alter the rules just described, and possibly also provide for other advantages. Incidentally, the Czechoslovak, Polish and Soviet regulations make specific reference to the possibility that other principles may be applicable under such treaties.

(3) Automatic exemptions and reductions in income tax

In two countries certain incentives are available to all joint ventures. Under Polish law, each joint venture will be exempt from income tax during the first three years of its business activity. In the Soviet Union the tax-free period is two years from the moment of declaring profits. Declared profits means the profit indicated in the balance sheet of the joint venture.

Poland also provides for another kind of automatic tax incentive; the basic income tax rate of 40 per cent will become lower the more the joint venture exports, so that a joint venture which exports 75 per cent of its production will pay income tax at the rate of 10 per cent only.

Under the Hungarian Foreign Investment Act, all companies in which the foreign party's share is at least 20 per cent or five million forints are entitled to a 20 per cent reduction in the calculated tax. Further, if the statutory capital of the company exceeds 25 million forints and the foreign share is at least 30 per cent, the company is entitled, if it operates in one of the priority sectors defined in the law, to tax reductions of 60 or 100 per cent during the first five years, and of 40 or 60 per cent thereafter. In Bulgaria, joint ventures that are entitled to the 30 per cent tax rate are exempt from taxation for five years if they perform economic activities in specified high technology sectors.

(4) Case-by-case exemptions and reductions in income tax

Four countries offer incentives which are not automatic, but are applied in each individual case. In Poland, in addition to the three year tax-free period, available to all enterprises with foreign participation, a further period of up to three years can be granted to enterprises which are engaged in preferred sectors. Also in Hungary and in the Soviet Union, case-by-case reductions or exemptions are possible over and above the automatic incentives described above. In the Soviet Union, such exemptions or reductions may be granted not only on the income tax of joint ventures, but also with regard to the withholding tax on those profits of the foreign party which are transferred abroad. In Romania case by case exemptions and reductions are the only incentives available: a joint venture may obtain a total tax exemption for its first profitable year and a 15-30 per cent tax rate for the following two years.

(5) Other incentives

In some countries tax exemptions or reductions will be available in the event that profits are reinvested in the joint venture or another joint venture in the host country.

Most countries provide for exemptions in customs duties for goods which are imported for uses which are connected with the operation of the joint venture.

Hungary and Bulgaria have made it possible to establish joint ventures in customs-free and, respectively, free trade zones. In Hungary, joint ventures in customs-free zones are regarded as foreign enterprises from the point of view of customs, foreign exchange and foreign trade rules. In Bulgaria, imports to and exports from a free trade zone are exempt from duties, and profits from joint venture economic activities are exempt from income tax during the first five years; thereafter the applicable tax rate is 20 per cent.

In the Soviet Union, with regard to joint ventures established in the so called "Far East Economic Zone" the tax free period of two years, available as a general rule, has been extended to three years, from the moment of declaring profit. After the tax-free period, joint ventures in that zone will pay taxes only at a rate of 10 per cent.

D. Investment protection

Protection of foreign investment may be regulated on various levels. On national level, several joint venture laws contain provisions regarding the protection of the parties' investments in the joint venture against certain kinds of risks. Some of these provisions are unilateral undertakings by the respective host country relative to such risks, others refer to the possibility of the parties obtaining certain guarantees from a third party, normally the host country central bank. The bilateral treaties on investment promotion and protection which some of the host countries have concluded with western countries purport to deal, by laying down binding provisions on the treatment of foreign investment, with the most obvious risks involved in a foreign investment. Some of the risks relative to foreign investment, and the ways in which protection against them can be arranged, are discussed briefly below.

(1) Protection against expropriation and similar measures

One of the risks which might be associated with a foreign investment is that the property of the investor is for one reason or another expropriated or confiscated by the host government. This question is addressed in some joint venture laws.

Thus, under Hungarian law, the foreign investor is to be indemnified without delay and at the actual value for the damages he has sustained as a result of nationalization, expropriation or any other measure having similar effects.

Soviet law, for its part, stipulates that the property rights of a joint venture shall be protected under Soviet legislation on State-owned Soviet organizations, that the property of a joint venture shall not be requisitioned or confiscated by administrative means, and that the property of a joint venture can be seized (for the payment of its debts) only upon a decision of a USSR court or an arbitration tribunal which has, under Soviet legislation, jurisdiction over disputes involving joint ventures. Similarly, under Bulgarian law, investments made by foreign persons will not be subject to confiscation or expropriation in an administrative manner. Investments by foreign persons in real estate may not be expropriated except for state or public needs which cannot be met otherwise. The expropriated investment shall be made good to the foreign person. Should no agreement be reached on the amount of the compensation, it shall be determined by a district court.

International investment protection treaties and established principles of international public law may grant protection which goes beyond that mentioned above.

In some countries, foreign parties can obtain guarantees for the compensation of the damages they may suffer as a result of actions of host country authorities. Thus, in Poland the Minister of Finance, on application by the foreign party, issues a compensation payment guarantee in an amount equal to the value of that part of the joint venture's assets to which the foreign party is entitled in the event of a loss resulting from nationalization or expropriation, or from other actions having a result similar to that of nationalization or expropriation.

(2) Transfer of profits and return of investment

Some joint venture laws contain express provisions relative to the foreign party's right to transfer abroad the profits the joint venture distributes. According to Polish law, the foreign party has the right to transfer abroad such profits without a separate foreign exchange permit. Under Soviet law, foreign partners are guaranteed that amounts due to them as their share in profits distributed in foreign currencies are transferable abroad in foreign currency; they also have the right to return, upon liquidation of the joint venture, their contribution, in money or in kind. Bulgaria has a similar rule. According to the Romanian joint venture law the Romanian State vouches for the transfer abroad of not only the profits made, but also of the value of share quotas transferred to the Romanian party, and of dues resulting from the distribution of assets following upon a dissolution and winding up, and also of other dues, under the conditions stipulated in the joint venture contract or charter.

It should be noticed that, as a general rule, any transfer abroad can only be made out of the joint venture's own convertible currency resources. However, some joint venture rules contain provisions qualifying or attenuating this general rule.

Thus, in Hungary, the profits due to the foreign party and, in case of liquidation, the sums due to the foreign party can be transferred abroad without any limitation in the currency in which the contribution to the statutory capital of the joint venture was originally made.

Under Czechoslovak law, again, if the joint venture is liquidated or if the foreign party sells its share - or part of it - in the joint venture, he has the right to transfer abroad that part of the proceeds of his share which does not exceed his original contribution to the statutory capital. The part which does exceed the original contribution can only be transferred from the joint venture's own currency reserves. The foreign party's share of joint venture profits can also be transferred only from such reserves.

On the other hand, under Soviet law, for example, a joint venture may agree with its purchasers that these will pay for the joint venture's products in convertible currencies (see Chapter Three, Section XVII.B.(1)) from their own convertible currency funds. Therefore, a joint venture can in principle sell all of its products in the Soviet market and still be able to transfer the foreign party's profits and pay for its imports etc. in convertible currency. It may also be agreed that the foreign party takes its profits in the form of Soviet goods.

In this area international investment protection treaties and established principles of international public law may also provide further guarantees to foreign parties.

E. Other provisions

The bulk of the provisions of the joint venture and foreign investment laws of the socialist countries consist of rules of a more "technical" nature. These rules are concerned with such issues as capitalization and ownership; relations with the planning bodies and other authorities of the host country; purchase of equipment, raw and other materials, components, fuel, energy and other factors of production; marketing; foreign trade rights relative to purchases and marketing; foreign currency regulations; basic rules of taxation; accounting and auditing; management; labour and personnel aspects; applicable law and settlement of disputes, etc. Some of the regulations in these areas will be highlighted in Chapter Three of this Guide where the respective problems are dealt with.

III. RULES OF COMPETITION

When preparing for the joint venture, the parties should also take into account the national and international rules of competition which might be applicable to their planned activities.

A breach of the rules of competition may result from the obligation of the joint venture to formulate its marketing strategies (pricing, scope of the market) exclusively in view of the possible consequences of that strategy to the joint venture parties. Further, in the event that the joint venture products are similar to those manufactured by one or the other of the parties, the latter can agree on territorial restrictions for the sale of the joint venture products, or on the exclusive distribution of the products through the marketing network of one of the parties. These marketing agreements may involve violations of the rules of competition if they in fact prevent the competitors of a joint venture party from buying the products of the joint venture company.

IV. THE DOCUMENTATION

If the feasibility study and the study on the respective host country regulations and rules of competition lead the parties to an understanding that there is a common long-term interest for a mutually advantageous joint venture, full-scale negotiations can begin. At this point, the parties may wish to form various working groups to carry out some parts of the negotiations.

From this stage on, a number of documents on the economic, technical and legal aspects of the project will have to be prepared to enable the parties to come to a final understanding. Many of these documents will subsequently be submitted to the relevant authorities together with the application for the final approval of the joint venture (see Section V below).

A. Economic and technical documentation

During the course of commercial negotiations the following types of economic and/or technical documents might be prepared:

(1) **Financial studies.** These may cover such subjects as: the various sources of funding; pro-forma balance sheets and profit and loss statements; cash flow predictions; accounting and auditing principles; customs and tax implications; incentives; foreign exchange regulations, including repatriation of capital and profits; reinvestment; etc.;

(2) **Market studies.** The following subjects might be covered: the markets which will be aimed at, the demand in these markets, and growth prospects; short-, medium-, and long-term sales strategies, including market outlets, pricing, sales promotion, after-sales service, and customer feedback; trademark policies; structure and intensity of competition and the important trends in this field; etc.;

(3) **Technical feasibility studies.** These studies deal with such subjects as: machinery and equipment requirements and the sources from which they will be purchased; patent and know-how licence requirements and the respective suppliers; plant situation and plant services requirements; sources for the supply of raw materials, components and other materials, including the requirements of imported goods both at the implementation stage of the project and during operation; continuity of supply, including prices and delivery times, previous experience of main suppliers in this respect and possible implications on stock levels; factory design and layout and local factors to be taken into account in this respect; host country standards and specifications affecting production; etc.;

(4) **Organization and labour studies.** The following subjects might be treated in these studies: optimum organizational structure for the joint venture; statutory management organs, their control and liabilities; composition of statutory organs as regards representation of each party, and election of the members of these organs; term of office, quorum and manner of acting, recording and working language; names and qualifications of the individuals who will occupy key posts when operations are started, and related time schedules; necessary back-up teams at the parties' own organizations; availability of labour and its real cost; labour qualifications, requirements and recruitment policies; training; conditions of employment; etc.

B. Legal documentation

The legal documents which may be prepared in view of the joint venture project can be divided into three groups as follows:

(1) Pre-foundation documents

As early as the negotiation stage the parties may wish to prepare and sign certain legal documents, such as:

1. ***Letters of intent or protocols.*** These documents are normally used to record the steps which have so far been taken by the parties relative to the project under negotiation, and possibly to agree on the measures still to be taken by them in view of facilitating further negotiations. As a rule, when the parties prepare and sign these kinds of documents they do not intend to commit themselves to agreeing subsequently to the project, and they are well advised not to use therein any language which could be interpreted as such a commitment.
2. ***Non-disclosure agreements, agreements on non-competition.*** These documents are principally aimed at protecting the interests of the parties in the event that they disclose to their negotiating partners technical know-how, business data, or any other information which the disclosing party wishes to be kept secret. These agreements are intended to remain binding - usually for a number of years - even if no contract is concluded relative to the joint venture under negotiation.

(2) Foundation documents

These documents can include:

1. The joint venture contract; and
2. The charter.

The requirement that foundation documents include both the joint venture contract and the charter is contained, for example, in the Romanian joint venture decree. With regard to both of these documents the decree contains a list of the questions which must be regulated therein. On the other hand, the parties can include, both in the joint venture contract and in the charter, any other provisions which they wish to agree on. This latter principle is also set forth in the Soviet joint venture decree, at the end of the list of items which the charter must contain (no requirements are stated with regard to the joint venture contract).

It should be noted, however, that not all joint venture laws require the use of two separate foundation documents.

When negotiating the structure and contents of the joint venture documentation, the parties should therefore take into account the provisions of the host country legislation in this area, and, if both a joint venture contract and a charter are to be drawn up, agree, within the framework of the stipulations of the applicable law, on what provisions will be included in the charter and what will be left to be agreed in the joint venture contract or any other agreements which will be concluded for the realization of the joint venture objectives.

While agreeing on this question the parties should also take into account that the legal rules which will apply, in the event that the parties would subsequently wish to alter some of the agreed provisions, may be different depending on whether the said provision is included in the charter, in the joint venture contract or in some other agreements. A change in the joint venture contract will, as a rule, require the consent of all the parties which have signed it, while a change in the charter provisions may be possible by majority, or qualified majority, vote.

(3) Auxiliary documents

Auxiliary documents can be contracts which the joint venture company concludes with:

1. one of the joint venture parties. These can include:
   - Contracts of *sale* or *purchase,* whereby the joint venture either sells to a party products produced by it, or purchases from a party machinery, equipment, raw materials, components, energy, electricity, etc., necessary in its own production;
   - *Licence* contracts, whereby the joint venture acquires the right to use a partner's patents, know-how or trademarks;
   - Contracts for *services,* such as installation or supervision of installation, technical assistance, training, or management;
2. other entities abroad, or in the host country (for instance, specialized foreign trade organizations). These contracts can deal with the same subjects as those mentioned above; or
3. employees of the joint venture company.

This Guide deals principally with the drawing up of the joint venture contract, but references are also made to matters which may be dealt with in other documents.

V. APPROVAL AND REGISTRATION

With the exception of Bulgaria and Hungary, the parties wishing to establish an east-west joint venture in a CMEA member country must always obtain the approval of the approparaite authorities for the joint venture, and include in the application relevant supporting documentation. In Bulgaria, permission from a relevant state body is required only when the foreign party's share exceeds 49 per cent in a Limited Liability Company and 20 per cent in a Joint-Stock Company. In Hungary, again, approval is needed only if the foreign investor is to hold a majority in a joint venture, or if its wishes to establish a wholly foreign-owned company.

A. Documentation

The requirements concerning the documentation to be submitted vary from country to country.

The joint venture regulations of most of the countries contain rather general stipulations in this respect. Broadly speaking, two sets of documents are mentioned: (i) a feasibility study (or studies) on the technical and economic aspects of the project; and (ii) foundation documents, which usually include the joint venture contract and the charter.

B. Submission of the application

The submission procedure also varies from country to country. Regarding the question of who files the application, the Czechoslovak and Soviet rules stipulate, for example, that this will be done by the local party, whereas the Romanian regulations provide that the application will be submitted jointly by the parties. It is to be stressed, however, that even in the case that the application is formally submitted by the local party alone, it is in the interest of all parties concerned - including the host country authorities - that the foreign party also participates actively in the preparation of the necessary documentation.

The application is submitted to the ministry or government agency designated in the applicable regulations. In Romania, for example, this is the Ministry of Foreign Trade, and in Poland the Foreign Investment Agency. Under Hungarian law, in those cases where approval is needed, the application is submitted to the Ministry of Finance. In Czechoslovakia the appropriate body is the ministry or government agency under which the local party operates. In the Soviet Union, if the local party is a state enterprise, amalgamation or organization, it has the right to make decisions on setting up joint ventures with the consent of its superior management body (the ministry or government agency under which it operates). If the local party is a co-operative, the application is submitted, depending on the circumstances, either to the Council of Ministers of the respective Union Republic or Autonomous Republic, or to the Executive Committee of the Soviet where the local party operates, or to the Union Republic ministry or government agency which supervises the enterprise where the respective co-operative has been established.

With the exception of Romania and the Soviet Union, the bodies to which the application has been submitted (or forwarded) will discuss it with such other government bodies as are prescribed in their respective regulations. In the case of Romania and the Soviet Union, the advice of these other bodies will have to be obtained by the local party before the application is filed.

The final approval is granted in Bulgaria by the "relevant state body", in Czechoslovakia by the government agency under which the local party operates, in Hungary jointly by the Ministries of Finance and Trade, and in Poland by the President of the Foreign Investment Agency. In Romania the approving authority is the State Council. In the Soviet Union this body is the respective USSR ministry or agency to which the application regarding the consent of setting up the joint venture was submitted.

Czechoslovak, Hungarian and Polish laws set a time limit for the approval. Under Czechoslovak and Hungarian law, the appropriate decision must be made within three months from the day when the application was submitted. In Poland the corresponding time is two months.

C. Registration

Under the regulations of all of the countries now concerned, the joint venture must be registered with the authority prescribed by the law. Depending on the host country, the register may be a special register for joint ventures, or a register where all enterprises, domestic as well as those with foreign participation, are registered. Such registration has constitutive effect - that is to say, the joint venture shall become a legal entity through the registration, and at the time when the registration takes place.

The practical meaning and effect of the registration can be illustrated by some provisions of the USSR Ministry of Finance Regulations Concerning the Registration of Joint Ventures. According to these provisions, Soviet state-owned, co-operative and other public enterprises and economic organizations are prohibited from entering into any transactions or contracts with joint ventures prior to their registration; Soviet banks may open accounts for joint ventures, make monies available to them, and carry out crediting and payment operations with them only after they have been duly registered.

Under Soviet law, a certificate of registration is issued to a registered joint venture. On the basis of the certificate, the joint venture must publish a notice on its establishment. The information entered into the joint venture register and published accordingly shall be regarded as known to third parties, and no dispute concerning the issue will be considered by the USSR Ministry of Finance.

CHAPTER THREE

THE JOINT VENTURE CONTRACT

I. PARTIES

The contract should include a clear definition of the parties, with a description of the legal status, capacity and/or authorization of each of them with regard to the conclusion of the contract.

II. PREAMBLE

The purpose of the preamble is to put the transaction in question in a larger perspective. It usually describes briefly the relevant business activities of the contracting parties and the respective inputs which each of the parties is willing and capable of bringing into the joint venture, and, when applicable, relates the steps which have been taken, by the time the contract is signed, in the preparation of the contract.

Sometimes the preamble sets forth some of the assumptions under which the parties enter into the relationship regulated by the contract. However, since in different jurisdictions different legal significance may be attached to the preamble, any provision which is meant to have binding effect or to be a condition precedent to any of the undertakings agreed on in the contract should be incorporated in the contract text itself.

III. DEFINITIONS

It is customary and advisable to agree in the joint venture contract on precise definitions of the key concepts used therein, in order to ensure uniform interpretation and understanding of these terms by all parties. In east-west joint venture contracts agreement on such definitions can be of utmost importance because many of the legal and economic concepts used in east European countries may differ considerably from those used in western countries, and *vice versa*. In the event that a large number of terms is to be defined, they are usually included in a separate chapter.

IV. SCOPE OF THE JOINT VENTURE

One of the first sections of the joint venture contract, after the preamble and definitions, could be devoted to a description of the basic framework of the joint venture. The section could include provisions on such matters as the objectives of the joint venture, the corporate form to be used, the implementation schedule of the necessary investments, and the duration of the joint venture. More elaborate provisions on some of these issues may have to be included elsewhere in the joint venture contract.

A. Objectives of the joint venture

The joint venture contract should define the scope of the business activities in which the joint venture is to engage. It may be necessary to specify the products to be produced (services to be rendered) by the joint venture in a separate section (see Section XIII below). Similarly, provisions relating to the purchase of raw materials, components, etc., and marketing of the products (services) of the joint venture may require a chapter of their own (see Section XVII below).

In view of the fact that any changes in the agreed objectives of the joint venture may have to be approved by the host country authorities, it may be advisable to agree on a very broad definition of the objectives, including therein all such activities which the parties might, even at a later stage, wish to embark on. If this is done either party may, however, wish to include in the joint venture contract a provision to the effect that starting some of these activities requires mutual agreement by both parties.

B. Legal form

In some countries the parties can choose between two (Bulgaria, Czechoslovakia, Poland, Romania) or several (Hungary) corporate forms in which the joint venture activities will be carried out. In the Soviet Union the same form is used by all joint ventures. The parties should specify in the joint venture contract the appropriate form. The necessary details regarding the practical steps to be taken for the incorporation and related matters should also be agreed upon (see Section IX below).

C. Implementation schedule

In order to provide for an orderly implementation of the necessary investments the parties should include in the joint venture contract a time schedule which sets out the dates by which the various measures must be undertaken and completed. The schedule could cover such items as measures necessary for the completion of the approval procedure, incorporation of the company, conclusion of agreements accessory or complementary to the joint venture contract (such as licence, construction, lease, leasing, purchase, employment contracts, etc.), taking possession of the facilities where the company is to operate, completion of the technical layout(s) for the plant, installation of the production equipment, training of the company personnel, testing and commissioning of the plant, etc.

D. Duration

In principle, a joint venture can be established either for an indefinite period, or for a limited time only. If the legislation of the host country does not contain provisions regarding this matter, the parties can choose either alternative. Normally, a joint venture is established for an indefinite period. However, under Soviet law the period of operation of the joint venture must be specified in the foundation documents.

V. PLANNING AND CO-ORDINATION

The parties may wish to include in the joint venture contract provisions setting forth some of the basic business policies under which the company is to be operated. Here, also, the respective host country regulations should be taken into account.

A. General business principles

The Soviet Union has included in its joint venture law a provision describing the general business principles to be observed by the company. According to this provision, joint ventures shall operate on the basis of full cost accounting *("polnyj khoziaistvennyj raschet")*, self-support *("samookupaemost")* and self-financing *("samofinansirovanie")*.

In the joint venture contract, the parties may wish to refer to these or some other criteria - for example, that the company shall be operated in accordance with the principle of sound industrial and commercial management. However, in order to ensure that the contents of these kinds of general provisions are understood in the same manner by both parties, it may indeed be necessary to give them precise definitions, for example in that part of the joint venture contract where other key concepts are also defined.

B. Internal business planning

The joint venture contract should also lay down the basic principles regarding the planning of business operations of the joint venture. Such planning should, of course, be carried out in accordance with the requirements, if any, of the applicable law of the host country. For instance, under Bulgarian law, a company shall draw up its own plan for economic activity on the basis of contracts concluded, economic terms, norms and regulators, state contracts and its own marketing, technological and other projects.

On the other hand, the foreign party may wish to introduce into the planning procedure elements which are not required in the host country, but which may be useful for the management of the joint venture in a manner which satisfies both parties' legitimate interests in this respect.

Issues which can become the subject matter of internal business planning could include decisions concerning prices, the quality of output, depreciation costs, etc. Systematic planning is likely to be required in the area of purchases of raw materials and components, and sub-contracting, as well as travel abroad (see also subsection VII.B below). Planning requirements may also emerge, say, from taxation. Thus, for example, under the USSR Ministry of Finance regulations on the taxation of joint ventures, the amounts of advance tax payments for a current year will be determined by the joint venture itself on the basis of its financial plan for that year.

The parties may wish to agree on the first business plan (or a first set of short-term and longer-term business plans). If this is the case, such business plan(s) should be annexed to the joint venture contract as an integral part thereof.

C. Co-ordination with host country authorities

Joint ventures established in east European countries do not receive production assignments from planning authorities. This principle is reflected, for instance, in the Soviet joint venture law which stipulates that a joint venture developes and approves its business operation programmes independently, and that State bodies of the USSR will not fix any mandatory plans for a joint venture. On the other hand, joint ventures must in practice co-ordinate their activities with the host country economy.

In some countries such co-ordination is not merely a matter of necessary and useful practice, but a requirement prescribed by law. Under Bulgarian law, the competent state authorities co-ordinate with the respective companies their participation in the fulfilment of the state plan on the basis of mutual agreements and state contracts. In Romania, again, the joint venture develops its activities according to five-year and one-year programmes in conformity with the objectives set by the joint venture's charter. The joint venture shall communicate annually, in a timely fashion, to the ministry which supervises the Romanian party, the main economic-financial aims provided under the activity programme, in order for them to be included in the plan of economic-social development of Romania.

For these reasons, the parties should carefully study the requirements set by host country legislation and practice regarding the co-ordination of the joint venture's activities with the relevant authorities. Having done this they should consider whether provisions should be included in the joint venture contract specifying the principles which will be followed in the said co-ordination.

Host country legislation may regulate the procedure to be observed in this respect. Thus, for example, Soviet law stipulates that while the joint venture shall enter into relations with the central State authorities of the USSR and of the Union Republics through authorities superior to the Soviet partner in the joint venture, contacts with local government authorities and other Soviet organizations shall be direct.

D. Co-ordination between the joint venture company and its partners

As part of their joint venture, the parties may have to agree on the questions related with the co-ordination of the activities of the joint venture with the respective activities of each of the parties. For instance, it may be necessary to include in the joint venture contract provisions regarding the delivery by one party of goods or services to the joint venture and the respective terms to be applied thereto, or regarding the competing activities of the parties, on the one hand, and of the joint venture, on the other, in those fields of their activities which overlap. In this connection the parties may also wish to refer to some general principles, such as equality and mutual profitability, to be applied in their mutual relations. However, when providing for these issues in the joint venture contract, the parties should pay due attention to the applicable national and international rules against the restraint of competition (see Chapter Two, Section III above).

VI. REPRESENTATION

A. Representation of the company

The parties should agree in the joint venture contract (or in the charter, as the case may be) on the principles to be applied regarding the representation of the joint venture in its relations with third parties. Under Bulgarian law, when a company is registered, the names of the organs and persons who represent the company must be entered in the register, and samples of their signatures must be enclosed.

B. Affiliates, branches and representation offices of the joint venture

If the parties intend that the joint venture should at some point establish branches and/or representation offices either in the host country or abroad, they should provide for such a possibility in the joint venture contract. Under the laws of some countries, such as the Soviet Union, setting up of branches or representation offices is not possible without corresponding provision in the foundation documents. In the Soviet Union, it is also necessary to indicate in the foundation documents whether a given affiliate will be a legal person or not; as to representation offices, they are not legal persons and act in the name and on behalf of the joint venture.

C. Representation of the foreign party by the company

The parties may wish to agree that the joint venture will act as a representative of the foreign party for the marketing of the latter's products or services in the host country. If this is the case, the parties should find out whether such a representation is permitted under the host country legislation and, if it is, whether specific conditions are attached thereto.

VII. FOREIGN TRADE RIGHTS AND FOREIGN CURRENCY TRANSFERS

A. Foreign trade rights

The parties should specify in the joint venture contract whether or not the joint venture will be engaged in foreign trade activities - that is, whether the joint venture itself will import the raw materials, components, production equipment, etc. it needs to carry out its activities and/or export its products. In Czechoslovakia, a foreign trade licence can be applied for only after the establishment of the joint venture.

In Poland, if the application for a permit to establish an enterprise with foreign participation sets forth export and/or import as part of the subject and scope of its business activities, the granting of the permit amounts to a permission to engage in the foreign trade activities described in the application. Under Hungarian law, joint ventures can carry out foreign trade activities in accordance with the rules applicable to other economic organizations; foreign trade permit or registration will be required.

In Bulgaria, Romania and the Soviet Union foreign trade rights are provided for directly in the respective regulations of these countries. On the other hand, in the Soviet Union, for instance, a joint venture may use the services of a Soviet organization for foreign economic affairs (former foreign trade organization) and, for this purpose, conclude with it a commission contract.

B. Foreign currency rules

The purposes for which joint ventures usually need foreign (convertible) currencies are: transfer abroad of the profits of the foreign partner; transfer abroad, in the case of liquidation of the joint venture or the transfer by the foreign partner of its share in the joint venture, of the proceeds of the liquidation or transfer; transfer abroad of part of the salaries of foreign employees of the joint venture and contributions to their social security and pension schemes in their home countries; payment for raw materials, components, know-how, or patent licences, and other imports necessary for the production of the joint venture, payment of travel expenses for business trips abroad by the employees of the joint venture, and repayment of credits in foreign currency and their interest.

The basic rules regarding foreign currency transfers are contained in the host country legislation. On the other hand, in Romania, the parties should specify in the joint venture contract the currency in which transfers will be made to the foreign partner. Even regarding other countries, the partners may wish to include in the contract, if permitted by the applicable law to do so, a similar provision defining the currency in which transfers shall take place.

In Poland, a joint venture shall resell 15 per cent of its foreign currency export proceeds to a Polish foreign exchange bank. In economically justified cases the President of the Foreign Investment Agency may set, in the foundation permit, a lower resale rate. After resale, the joint venture may distribute, without a separate foreign exchange permit, profits in foreign currency from its surplus of export proceeds over import outlays. In economically justified cases the Minister of Finance may allow a foreign shareholder to transfer abroad an amount of profit exceeding the surplus. Such a decision may constitute part of the foundation permit.

VIII. ACCOUNTING AND AUDITING

In all the countries under review the joint venture laws contain rules dealing with accounting. However, the contents and coverage of these rules vary from country to country. Room is often left for the parties to agree on issues considered important.

A. General principles

Regarding the general principles of accounting, the Polish law stipulates that the general principles of accounting will be laid down by the Minister of Finance, in compliance with the requirements of the Commercial Code.

The Soviet joint venture decree stipulates that joint ventures shall maintain business, book-keeping and statistical accounting in accordance with the standards established in the USSR for State-owned Soviet enterprises. The forms of such accounting and book-keeping have been jointly specified by the USSR Ministry of Finance and the USSR State Committee for Statistics (GOSKOMSTAT, former USSR Central Board of Statistics). According to these specifications, for example, the accounting and book-keeping of joint ventures is carried out by accountants under the supervision of the principal accountant, whose activities, in turn, are governed by the respective Decree of the USSR Council of Ministers. When recording their economic operations in their book-keeping accounts joint ventures should follow the respective Plan of book-keeping accounts, and its implementing regulations, approved by the USSR Ministry of Finance.

B. Depreciation rates

With regard to depreciation, under Polish and Soviet rules depreciation rates applicable to domestic enterprises shall also be applied to joint ventures. However, under Soviet law a different system may be stipulated in the founding documents. In Romania, depreciation rates can be agreed upon by the joint venture partners.

C. Funds

A joint venture must, under the rules of all of the countries considered here, create a reserve fund (sometimes called the risk fund). The joint venture regulations of Romania and the Soviet Union contain a number of basic provisions regarding this fund, but the laws also direct the parties to agree more specifically on certain matters in the founding documents. Under applicable law, joint ventures may also have to create other funds. Thus, for instance, under Czechoslovak regulations the joint venture must also create other funds: the cultural and social fund and the remunerations fund. In the Soviet Union, the USSR Ministry of Finance Regulations on taxation of joint ventures provide that the foundation documents shall include a list of the funds intended for the development of production, science and technology, and shall specify how these funds will be raised and used.

D. Other matters

In addition to the issues dealt with above, the parties may wish to include in the joint venture contract provisions regulating the following matters: fiscal year of the joint venture; language in which books will be kept; whether other books will be kept than those required by the mandatory rules (if any) of host country legislation, and the accounting principles to be followed in such parallel book-keeping; who shall bear the costs of parallel book-keeping. The parties may also wish to agree on the internal control of the joint venture. Thus, for instance, in the Soviet Union joint venture parties often provide in the foundation documents for the creation of a Controlling Commission of the joint venture for the control of the joint venture's current financial and business activities.

E. Auditing

In some countries, joint venture laws contain provisions relative to auditing. Thus, in Romania, the Ministry of Finance appoints one or two members to the body (usually called the Auditing Commission) which controls the joint venture's accounts. Under Polish law the joint venture's balance sheet is audited by the appropriate organ of the Ministry of Finance or by any other entity, chosen by the joint venture, that the Minister of Finance has authorized to audit the annual balance sheet of enterprises. Under Soviet regulations, the auditing of the financial-economic activities of a joint venture will be effected as agreed by the parties.

In Hungary, the Company Act contains detailed rules on auditing. The law sets forth, among other things, the rights and obligations of the auditor, including the right to inspect the books of the company and the obligation to have, in the circumstances described in the law, the meeting of the supreme body of the company convoked to an extraordinary meeting.

Upon acquainting themselves with the provisions of host country legislation, the parties should include the necessary stipulations in the joint venture contract. Matters which might need regulation could include the following: number and nationality of the auditors; persons who cannot be auditors (e.g. members of the management or employees of the joint venture); manner of electing the auditors and their term of office; the scope of the issues to be audited; the auditors' report, when and how it is to be presented to the highest governing body of the joint venture (and possibly to the host country authorities); the auditors' duty to convene the highest decision-making organ to consider specific matters; the remuneration of the auditors.

IX. INCORPORATION

A. Practical steps

The joint venture contract should indicate which of the parties will be responsible for the incorporation of the joint venture. The local party, usually being in the best position to organize the incorporation, will often be assigned this task, but the parties may wish, for specific reasons, to adopt some other way of proceeding in this matter.

Even if only one party is made responsible for the organization it may be advisable to state expressly in the joint venture contract that the other party shall have to render him such assistance (providing information, certificates, signatures, etc.) as will be necessary for the proper incorporation of the joint venture.

As mentioned above, in order to ensure that the various measures necessary for the implementation of the joint venture investment are properly taken and synchronized, the joint venture contract should include a time schedule regarding the incorporation of the joint venture. Three deadlines could be set therein. Firstly, the joint venture contract might stipulate a date by which each party must have undertaken those steps which the applicable law or the joint venture contract obligates him to take in view of the approval of the joint venture project. A second date might be agreed on by which the joint venture must have been approved by the host country authorities. The third date to be fixed in the joint venture contract would be the date by which the joint venture must have been registered in accordance with the applicable host country regulations. As a sanction the joint venture contract could stipulate that the non-observance of these deadlines would entitle either party to rescind the contract by written notice with immediate effect (see also Section XX.F below).

It may happen that, even if the parties have tried to draft the incorporation documents so as to comply with the requirements of the applicable law, the registering authority may not approve certain provisions for inclusion therein. In view of this possibility the parties may wish to stipulate in the joint venture contract how these documents will be altered, during the incorporation process, in order to comply with the requirements of the appropriate authority.

B. Name

For a number of reasons, the name under which the joint venture will operate is often of importance to the parties. The name will also have to be included in the incorporation documents. It should therefore be agreed on. If it is not possible to ascertain beforehand whether the name preferred by the parties will be acceptable to the incorporating authority, provision should be made for alternative names.

It may be of interest to the parties to determine in advance what will happen to the name of the joint venture in the event that the joint venture contract is terminated and the joint venture dissolved. If this is the case, the appropriate provisions should be included in the joint venture contract.

C. Registered office

The joint venture contract should specify the place in which the joint venture is going to have its registered (head) office.

D. Charter

The charter of the joint venture should be drawn up in accordance with the requirements of host country legislation concerning the appropriate legal form. As a rule, such legislation sets forth the issues which must be dealt with in the charter. Usually the partners can also include in the charter provisions other than those required by law, provided they are not in contradiction with the latter.

E. Correspondence of the charter with contractual arrangements

During the life of the joint venture it may occur that the parties agree to amend the joint venture contract or some other agreement they have concluded within the framework of the joint venture, or to enter into entirely new contractual arrangements. These may also entail changes in the charter. Or it may happen that the legislation under which the joint venture is incorporated is changed so that adjustments are necessary in the charter. With these possibilities in mind, the parties might consider it useful to include in the joint venture contract provisions according to which they will, when appropriate, take all necessary steps to amend the charter to give full effect to the intent and purposes of the joint venture contract and the other agreements the parties have concluded in pursuance thereof. The relevant host country regulations should be observed in this connection. Thus, for instance, under Soviet law the joint venture must inform the USSR Ministry of Finance of any amendments to the foundation documents (see also Section XX.E below).

F. Costs of incorporation

The incorporation of the joint venture necessarily involves certain expenses. The parties should stipulate in the joint venture contract how they will be shared. Usually this is effected in proportion to the shareholdings of the parties, but other formulae can also be used.

X. STATUTORY CAPITAL AND CAPITAL CONTRIBUTIONS

A. Minimum capitalization

Hungarian legislation requires a minimum capitalization of one million forints if the joint venture is established in the form of a Limited Liability Company. In a Company Limited by Shares minimum capitaliaztion is 10 million forints. Under the corresponding Polish Law the share of the foreign party may not be less than 20 per cent of the statutory capital of the joint venture, and not less than 25 million zlotys. In Bulgaria, the rules that provide special economic conditions for joint ventures are applicable only to companies where the share of the foreign party in the statutory capital exceeds 49 per cent and 5 million levs in convertible currency.

The regulations in other countries do not impose any lower limits on capitalization.

B. Parties' shares of the statutory capital

Only under Romanian law the local party's share may not be lower than 51 per cent and, consequently, the foreign pary's share not higher than 49 per cent. In all the remaining countries, on the other hand, foreign ownership above 49 is possible. Under Bulgarian, Hungarian and Polish law wholly foreign-owned enterprises are possible.

Depending on the joint venture form used, the form of the parties' ownership in the joint venture may also vary. Thus, the ownership may be in the form of a partnership interest, without any share certificates being issued, or it may indeed be in the form of owning a given number of shares, evidenced by share certificates issued to the owner, or in yet another form.

Once the parties have agreed on the size of the statutory capital and on the ownership ratios, they should introduce the respective provisions in the foundation documents. Thus, they should indicate the total amount of the statutory capital and the way in which it is broken down into individual partnership interests or shares. If there are several classes of ownership interests or shares, these should be indicated as well as the differences, if any, which exist between such classes (for example, different voting rights)

C. Subscriptions

The joint venture contract should set out the ownership interests or the number of shares which each party will subscribe, the price of each share, when applicable, and the total price of the ownership interests or set of shares to be subscribed by each party. The joint venture contract should also state clearly in which currency the payments will be made and, if made in a currency other than that of the host country, the rate at which the payments will be converted into local currency.

D. Cash payments

The parties should agree in the joint venture contract on the manner in which cash payments for the ownership interests or shares are made. Normally they are made to a bank account opened specifically for the purpose. The joint venture contract should stipulate who will be responsible for opening such an account for the joint venture.

It may be that not all of the monies due as cash payments from the parties are needed at once. If this is the case, the parties may wish to agree in the joint venture contract that only part of the payments will be made at, or upon, the signing of the joint venture contract, and that the balance will be paid later, in accordance with the capital requirements of the joint venture. The joint venture contract should state clearly by whom the remaining payments will be called in, and within what time period from the call the respective payments should be made. When applicable, the joint venture contract could also state that, upon the agreed payments being made, the parties will be delivered corresponding share certificates or other documents certifying that they have effected the payments.

E. Non-cash contributions

In most countries either corporate law or joint venture legislation expressly allow payments for share subscriptions also to be made in forms other than cash - that is, in kind, in services, in industrial property rights, etc. Often the law which permits other forms contains stipulations on how these contributions will be assessed.

Thus, for example, under Soviet law, contributions to the authorized fund of a joint venture may include buildings, structures, equipment and other assets, rights to use land, water and other natural resources, buildings, structures and equipment, as well as other proprietary rights (including those to use inventions and know-how), money assets in the currencies of the partner's countries and in freely convertible currencies. The contribution of the Soviet partner to the authorized fund of a joint venture is evaluated on the basis of agreed prices with due regard to world market prices. The contribution of the foreign partner is evaluated in the same manner. In the absence of world market prices the value of the property contributed is agreed by the partners. By agreement between the parties to a joint venture their contributions to the authorized fund may be assessed in both Soviet and foreign currency.

Therefore, if the parties agree that part of the capital contributions will be made in forms other than cash, the joint venture contract should describe, and indicate the value of, each such contribution. The documentation which substantiates the indicated values of the contributions should be referred to in the joint venture contract, and, where appropriate, appended thereto.

Within the framework of the applicable law, the joint venture contract should also contain stipulations on how and when the different contributions will be handed over to the joint venture, who will accept them on behalf of the joint venture, and when these contributions will be entered in the books of the joint venture.

XI. FINANCING

A. Financing plan

The joint venture contract should define how, over and above the statutory capital, the setting up of the joint venture and the carrying out of its operations will be financed. This could be done in the form of a financing plan. When drawing up the financing plan the applicable host country regulations should be taken into account.

B. Sources of financing

Under Bulgarian law, a company may take credits from various banks. Relations between the company and banks shall be regulated by contract. Banks shall excercise control over the effective use of the credits granted by them. Interest rates shall be negotiated between companies and banks on the ground of the basic interest rate and depending on credit supply and demand, the solvency of the credit recipient, the term of the credit and, with regard to foreign currency credits, in conformity with conditions prevailing on international credit markets.

The Czechoslovak joint venture regulations stipulate that the joint venture may raise loans in foreign currency from a Czechoslovak foreign exchange bank; from a foreign bank it can raise loans only with the approval of the Czechoslovak State Bank.

Under Hungarian law, the raising of credits by a joint venture is subject to same regulations that apply to purely Hungarian economic organizations.

In Poland, Polish foreign exchange banks may extend credits to the joint venture. The joint venture may also raise credits from abroad without a foreign exchange permit.

In Romania, the joint venture may obtain credits in convertible currency from authorized Romanian banks or from abroad.

Under Soviet law, credits in foreign currencies can be obtained by the joint venture from the USSR Bank for Foreign Economic Relations or, with its consent, from foreign banks and firms. Credits in roubles are available from the USSR State Bank or the USSR Bank for Foreign Economic Relations. These two banks are also authorized by the joint venture decree to control whether the credits are used for the specified purposes and secured and repaid in due time.

XII. FACILITIES

A. Local legislation

Before agreeing on the details concerning the facilities which the joint venture will need in order to carry out its activities, the parties should get acquainted with the applicable host country regulations. These may greatly affect the way in which the agreement will be conceived.

Thus, for instance, in the Soviet Union, land, the interior of the earth, waters and forests are the exclusive property of the State. However, the right to use them may be agreed upon as (part of) the Soviet party's contribution to the joint venture. In Bulgaria, companies with foreign participation must obtain the permission of the Council of Ministers to build and use immovable property for a specified period of time for the performance of their economic activities. However, companies with foreign participation may not own land, sub-soil resources, forests and waters.

In Poland, joint ventures may be granted State land in perpetual use, or they may lease such land. Subject to existing laws they may also acquire and lease land and other real estate not owned by the State.

Different rules may be in force in other countries. Under Soviet law, the design and construction of the joint venture's facilities, including those intended for social needs, shall be carried out through contractual arrangements and paid for with the joint venture's own, or loaned, money. Prior to approval, the designs shall be agreed on under the procedure established by the USSR State Building Committee. It should also be noted that, under the law, orders from joint ventures shall be given priority both as regards the construction or assembly work to be carried out by Soviet organizations, and as regards material resources required for the construction. Major construction projects require the permission of local government agencies, in other cases the Soviet party only informs such agencies of the construction to be undertaken.

B. Description of facilities

The parties should agree in the joint venture contract on the requirements concerning the joint venture facilities. In the case of a production plant, the contract might define - in an appendix, if necessary - the production capacity of the plant and the margins for increase in the capacity, the required equipment, machinery, instruments, commissioning equipment and spares, and other items necessary in the production. The preliminary plant and equipment layout, corresponding to the general description of the plant, might also be appended to the joint venture contract; the contract might also stipulate by whom and within what time the preliminary layout will subsequently be developed to a final layout.

C. Plant building

When appropriate, the joint venture contract might also define the terms and conditions concerning the construction or leasing, as the case may be, of the building where the plant is going to be installed. The contract should further state who shall take care of the necessary practical steps to have the building constructed or leased, and within what time limits.

D. Other services

In order to bring the facilities of the joint venture into operative state it may be necessary that the parties render the joint venture some services other than those mentioned above, such as assistance with respect to the procurement and installation of the necessary machinery and equipment, commissioning of the plant, etc. If this is the case, the parties should include in the joint venture contract the relevant provisions to this effect.

E. Terms and conditions

The joint venture contract should clearly specify whether the services of the parties shall be rendered without or against compensation and, in the latter case, what terms will be applicable. When appropriate, the parties might attach to the joint venture contract specific conditions applicable to such services.

XIII. PRODUCTS

As was pointed out above, it may be useful and even necessary to specify in a separate section the products to be produced by the joint venture. This is particularly so in cases where the joint venture is to operate in the field of manufacture of high-technology products, or of products using such technology which is - or can be - applied, by the party from whom the technology originates, in the production of products other than those designated for the joint venture. The following discussion addresses this particular kind of situation.

A. Description, know-how and patents, national standards and technical norms

In order to define precisely the products which are to be manufactured by the joint venture, the joint venture contract should contain sufficiently detailed descriptions of each of the products in question. The contract should also stipulate, regarding each product, whether it is to be produced by the joint venture on an exclusive or non-exclusive basis. In addition to describing the technical characteristics that the products should have, the contract could, when appropriate, specify some key technical characteristics which the products should not possess, these characteristics being typical of products reserved for the exlusive production by one or the other of the joint venture parties.

If the joint venture is to use specific know-how, patents or patent applications in its production, these should be identified in the joint venture contract. Often it will also be necessary to refer to the national standards and technical norms of the host country which will have to be observed in the production.

B. Terms and conditions

If the parties, or either of them, are to make available to the joint venture their proprietary technologies to be used in the production of the products, they will have to agree on the terms and conditions of that use. This they can do either in the joint venture contract or, as is more common, in a separate patent licence or know-how contract, to be concluded between the joint venture and the grantor of the licensed rights.

If the latter alternative is used, the licence contract can be concluded only after the joint venture has been formed and the persons entitled to sign for it have assumed office. On the other hand, it is usually in the interests of both parties that the terms and conditions of the licence contract are known and agreed to at the time when the joint venture contract is signed. Also, host country authorities may require that such conditions are included in the joint venture application. Therefore, if a separate licence contract is to be concluded, it could be negotiated simultaneously with the joint venture contract, and an unsigned copy thereof could be appended to the joint venture contract. In the joint venture contract the parties would make a reference to this licence contract and agree that, as soon as the joint venture is incorporated, an identical licence contract will be concluded between the joint venture and the grantor of the licensed rights.

C. Research and development

In addition to defining the technical specifications of the products, the know-how, patents and patent applications which will be used in their production, and the terms and conditions under which such use will be possible, the parties may wish to stipulate in the joint venture contract a number of other subjects relevant to the products. Particularly in the event that the products have a high technological content and the technology used is subject to rapid development, the parties may wish to make clear what principles will be followed regarding the research and development activities which will be necessary in order to keep the products competitive.

Several approaches are possible. It can be agreed that the joint venture will have its own research and development unit which shall be solely responsible for the development work. Or the parties can decide that all development work is done by the grantor of the licensed rights, and that the terms and conditions under which the results of such work will be available for the joint venture will be defined in the licence contract. A third alternative would be that both the joint venture and the licensor will perform development work, and that the results will be available to the other party under agreed terms and conditions.

D. Product quality

Since it should be the aim of the joint venture that its products be competitive in the national and international market, the parties may wish to agree in the joint venture or licence contract on certain basic principles regarding the quality of the products. If the products are based on the technology of one of the parties, and if this party manufactures similar or corresponding products, the contract could stipulate, for example, that the composition, specifications, performance, durability and finishing of the joint venture products should correspond to those of the products manufactured by the said party.

In order for the joint venture to meet this requirement it could be agreed that that party shall furnish the joint venture with up-to-date know-how and technology, and with the documentation on quality standards and control procedures which are in force from time to time for those products. When appropriate, it may be agreed that the party which has furnished the technology will control from time to time the quality of the products produced by the joint venture. In this connection the parties may wish to agree that the representatives of that party must have free and safe access to the facilities of the joint venture where such control is to be effected.

If the parties consider that, in order to ensure that the desired quality level is reached and maintained, an expert or specialist (or several of them) from the personnel of either of the parties should occupy, at least for a certain initial period, a given key post (or a number of key posts) in the production or quality control management of the joint venture, stipulations to this effect could be inserted in that section of the joint venture contract which deals with the personnel of the joint venture (see Section XV.B below).

The parties may also wish to agree in the joint venture or licence contract on the procedure to be applied in the event that the quality of the products manufactured by the joint venture does not meet the agreed standards.

E. Product liability

In addition to being contractually liable against its purchasers for defects in the products it manufactures and sells, the joint venture may have to face claims from the users or consumers of the products, for the damage the products have caused to such users or consumers, or their property. Such product liability claims do not require as their basis a contractual relationship between the joint venture and the plaintiff, but are founded directly on the laws of the country where the products is sold.

Owing to the seriousness of the problem the parties should consider to which extent the risks involved can be covered through product liability insurance, and agree on the measures to be taken in this respect.

XIV. ORGANIZATION AND MANAGEMENT

A. Organizational structure

A central issue which the parties will have to regulate is the organization of the joint venture. This involves agreement not only on the composition and/or functioning of the statutory organs of the joint venture but also on the operational structure of the joint venture, on the functions and responsibilities of its various divisions and units, and on the allocation to these various departments of the human resources which will be available to the joint venture.

The agreement of the parties on these details should be documented in the joint venture contract. The agreed structure could also be illustrated by an organization chart. The joint venture contract could further set forth the conditions under which the organizational structure can be modified.

B. Statutory organs and their internal relations

The rules regarding the statutory organs of joint ventures are stated, depending on the jurisdiction in question, either in the general corporation laws of the host country or in the specific regulations concerning joint ventures with foreign participation, or in both. By and large, under the joint venture regulations of the various countries now reviewed the structure of the management organs of joint ventures is similar to that of western corporations. In a joint venture, there are normally two managing bodies, one being the highest decision-making organ, the other being responsible for the day-to-day management of the joint venture.

Under Czechoslovak law, the decisions regarding the matters of an Association are made by its members; in a Company Limited by Shares the General Meeting of Shareholders is vested with all powers and rights related with the management of the company.

In Bulgaria, the highest organ is called the Partners' General Meeting (in Limited Liability Companies) or the General Meeting of Shareholders (in Joint-Stock Companies), in Hungary the Members' Meeting (in Limited Liability Companies) or the General Assembly (in Limited by Shares Companies), in Romania the General Assembly of Shareholders, in Poland the Assembly of Partners, and in the Soviet Union the Board.

The day-to-day business management is carried out in Bulgaria by the Managing Director (Limited Liability Company) or the Board of Management (Joint-Stock Company), in Czechoslovakia by the members or the persons entered in the respective register as officers (Association) or by the Board of Directors (Company Limited by Shares), in Hungary by the Managing Director (Limited Liability Company) or by the Board of Directors (Company Limited by Shares), in Romania by the Managing Committee (Limited Liability Company) or the Administrative Council (Joint Stock Company), and in the Soviet Union by the Management.

With regard to some countries, certain additional remarks must be made with regard to the pattern just presented. Thus, under Polish law an enterprise that has more than 50 shareholders, must also have a Supervisory Board or a Revision Commission. In Hungary, while a Company Limited by Shares must always have a Supervisory Board, such an organ is compulsory in a Limited Liability Company only in the circumstances defined in the Company Act. Additionally, when the number of full-time employees in a Limited Liability Company or a Company Limited by Shares is, on an annual average, over 200, the employees will participate in the monitoring of the company's operations through such Board; one third of the members of the Board must be elected by the employees.

In the Soviet Union the parties may also provide for a third body, e.g. a Supervisory Commission. In Czechoslovakia, the Board of Auditors supervises all activities of a Company Limited by Shares. Under Bulgarian law, the Board of Comptrollers, or, as the case may be in Limited Liability Companies, the Comptroller, supervises the activities of the management of the company, and reports thereon to the highest decision making organ.

Before starting negotiations on the organization of the joint venture, the parties should get acquainted with the relevant provisions of the host country legislation. Once they have identified the various organs prescribed - or allowed - by the law, they should find out exactly which matters fall within the jurisdiction of each of the different organs and to what extent the rules establishing the internal division of powers and responsibilities between such organs are mandatory and to what extent the parties may deviate from this division by common agreement.

An important aspect of the division of powers and responsibilities between the various joint venture organs is the question of control of the activities of the different organs by other organs, and the principles concerning the collective and individual liabilities of the members of the organs, for the activities they have undertaken as such members. Here, also, the parties should have a clear picture of the environment in which they are to operate, and, to the extent necessary and permitted by that country's regulations, agree upon these matters in the joint venture charter.

C. Composition and election

The laws of the CMEA member countries set no nationality requirements for the persons performing management functions of the joint venture. However, according to the model joint venture charter elaborated by the Romanian Ministry of Foreign Trade the president of the Administrative Council must be a Romanian citizen residing in Romania.

Taking into account the applicable rules, the parties may include in the joint venture contract, or in the charter, as the case may be, provisions regarding the allocation of the number of management posts in the joint venture organs, or specific posts in such organs, between the parties.

D. Term of office

The company or joint venture laws of different countries have different rules with regard to the term of office of the members of the various organs of joint ventures. These rules should be studied and, if the parties want to agree otherwise and deviation from them is possible, a corresponding provision should be included in the charter.

E. Quorum and manner of acting

The parties may wish to include in the charter provisions regarding the quorum necessary for the making of decisions in the management organs. Such provisions might stipulate, for example, that the quorum necessary for the transaction of any business in the respective organs consists of a majority of the members of that organ, provided, however, that at least one appointee of each joint venture party is present.

With regard to the manner of acting, the Soviet joint venture decree stipulates that the parties must define in the charter of the joint venture the questions on which unanimous decisions are required. Additionally, the parties are bound by the provision of the Decree of 2 December 1988, stating that all basic decisions of the Board concerning the activities of the joint venture must be made unanimously by all members of the Board.

The regulations of the other CMEA countries are silent on this point, and it would seem that a requirement of unanimity can be included in the charter, if the parties so wish.

XV. EMPLOYEES AND CONDITIONS OF EMPLOYMENT

A. Qualifications

It may be in the interest of the joint venture project - particularly in cases where the joint venture uses advanced know-how and production technologies or deals with products whose sale involves sophisticated marketing techniques - that the parties stipulate not only the composition and functioning of the statutory organs of the joint venture, but agree also on the qualifications which must be met by the occupants of given posts elsewhere in the organization.

Thus it may be useful to incorporate in the joint venture contract as an appendix the work description of, and qualifications required from, all the executive officers and other key persons of the joint venture. In cases where staff at a lower level should meet particular technical or other requirements, these should also be specified in the joint venture contract.

B. Recruitment and dismissal

It may be necessary to agree in the joint venture contract on the principles to be applied when employees are recruited for the joint venture. In particular, it may be in the interest of the joint venture that the foreign party, or its nominees in the company management, also have a sufficient say in recruitment, so that a suitable and qualified work force will be engaged by the joint venture. On the other hand, the joint venture should take full advantage of the know-how, experience and contacts of the local party in this respect.

Grounds for dismissal are, as a rule, specified in the host country labour regulations. However, under present Soviet regulations, for example, questions relative to recruitment and dismissal of employees can be decided by the joint venture management.

C. Use of foreign employees

If certain posts are to be occupied by persons originating in the organization of one or the other party, the joint venture contract should specify these posts and indicate whether they shall be manned in the agreed way permanently or for a limited period only.

When agreeing about these matters, the parties should take into account that in three of the CMEA member countries the joint venture laws contain provisions dealing with the use of foreign employees in the joint venture. The Romanian law stipulates that foreign personnel may be employed in managing positions. According to the Polish law, foreign citizens and persons without Polish permanent residence card may be employed with the consent of the regional authority of voivodship level. The Soviet decree stipulates that the personnel of joint ventures shall consist mainly of Soviet citizens. According to a Soviet interpretation this means that foreign employees can be used in highly qualified posts, such as quality control.

D. Conditions of employment

The joint venture contract should contain sufficiently detailed provisions concerning the specific conditions of the employment contracts of the individual employees of the joint venture. Also regarding these matters the joint venture laws contain certain provisions.

In Romania different basic rules apply to labour relations with employees who are citizens of the host country, on the one hand, and foreign employees, on the other. Romanian personnel shall enjoy the rights and obligations provided by the legislation in force for the personnel of State enterprises. The rights and obligations of foreign personnel shall be established by the Board of Directors, or the Managing Committee, as the case may be.

The Hungarian Foreign Investment Act stipulates that the labour-law status of employees will be governed by the Labour Code and - within its limits - the company charter and employment contracts. The Labour Code and regulations based on it govern trade union rights. However, rules relative to regulation of wages and incentives for executive officers will not be applicable to companies where foreign share is 20 per cent or 5 million forints, or more.

In Bulgaria, different rules apply depending on whether the share of the foreign party in the statutory capital of the joint venture does or does not exceed the limits already mentioned above, namely 49 per cent and 5 million levs in convertible currency. If it does, conditions of employment will be regulated in the employment contract. Parties to the contract may agree, also when the employee is a Bulgarian citizen, that part of the remuneration of the employee will be paid in foreign currency. If the foreign share does not exceed the above limit, the general rules of the Decree on Economic Activity will apply.

The Soviet joint venture decree stipulates that Soviet law shall also apply to foreign citizens, except for matters of pay, leave and pensions which are regulated in the contract signed with each foreign employee. Also with regard to Soviet employees, questions concerning the form and amount of pay, as well as material incentives in roubles can be agreed upon.

Polish law stipulates that the salary system should be set out in the founding documents of the joint venture, or by the decisions of its organs. The remuneration of the employees must be set and paid in zlotys; however, employees held to be foreign persons under the Polish Foreign Exchange Law may be partially paid in foreign currency.

In accordance with the applicable host country legislation, the parties should agree on the salary levels of the various posts or employee groups in the company, and on the principles that will be applied for salary increases. With regard to employees who are not nationals of the host country the parties should specify the currencies in which their salaries will be paid: frequently part of the salary is paid in local currency, while another part is paid in foreign currency. When stipulating on these matters the parties should make sure that the foreign employees will be permitted to transfer their foreign currency earnings abroad.

The joint venture laws contain provisions regarding the social services and social insurance arrangements applicable to the joint venture employees, or at least refer to the provisions of a host country legislation in this respect. These provisions should be studied when conditions of employment are agreed upon.

As a rule, labour disputes involving nationals of the host country will be covered by that country's legislation. On the other hand, other principles may often be applicable to labour disputes with employees who are not citizens of the host country. The parties should agree on these principles so that they can be reflected in the respective employment contracts.

E. Visas, work permits, accommodation

The parties may wish to include in the joint venture contract provisions regarding the steps to be taken by either party in order to secure that foreign employees are granted expeditiously all necessary authorizations, such as visas and work permits, which will be necessary for them to exercise in the host country those functions which have been agreed upon in the contract. Similar provision may be included regarding the arrangements to be made with regard to accommodation, schooling and other social services for the foreign employees and their dependants.

XVI. TRAINING

A. Need for training

It may be that some of the persons to be engaged by the joint venture as employees need to receive special training in order to meet the qualifications agreed on by the parties. If this is the case, the joint venture contract should set forth the necessary details concerning such training.

B. Places where training is to take place

Usually the training is carried out at the foreign party's plant or at the plant of the joint venture, or at both places. The joint venture contract should specify where training is to be effected.

C. Persons to be trained

With regard to trainees, the following details might be specified in the joint venture contract: (a) the aggregate number of persons to be trained; (b) the number of host country trainees, and that of trainees originating from the foreign party's organization; (c) maximum aggregate length of training; (d) maximum length of training for each trainee; (e) maximum number of trainees to be trained at any one time; (f) the general professional qualifications to be met by the trainees; (g) the training language and the level of knowledge of that language which must be possessed by the trainees.

D. Aims, training programme

The parties should stipulate in the joint venture contract the general and specific aims of the training. A training programme should be agreed upon, indicating the subjects in which training will be given, the training methods, and the procedure for evaluation of progress made by the trainees.

E. Visas, work permits, accommodation

As is the case with the employees of the joint venture the parties may wish to include in the joint venture contract stipulations concerning the measures to be taken by the parties in order to ensure that the trainees and their instructors may carry out the training programme as agreed.

F. Cost, insurance

The joint venture contract should specify how the costs, including travelling expenses, of the training will be covered, i.e. whether they will be divided between the parties in a specified way, or whether they will be borne by one of the parties only. When applicable, provisions should also be included regarding holidays. Further, the contract should stipulate how the trainees and their instructors will be insured, and who will cover the respective costs.

The parties may wish to stipulate that the persons to be so trained are committed, in their respective employment contracts, to stay with the joint venture for an agreed minimum period or, if permitted by the host country legislation, to reimburse the company for all or part of the training costs.

XVII. PURCHASES AND MARKETING

A. Purchases

Several joint venture laws contain provisions regarding the purchase of raw materials, components, etc. necessary for the operations of the joint venture. In this respect, a distinction must be made between the purchases necessary for the joint venture operations which are made in the host country, on the one hand, and purchases from abroad, on the other.

(1) Domestic purchases

As regards domestic purchases, in a number of countries the joint ventures operate under the same conditions as local enterprises. This is the case in Hungary, Czechoslovakia and Poland. Under Polish regulations, the joint venture may also purchase goods and services for foreign currency from licensed entities.

In Bulgaria, there are two sets of rules on domestic purchases. One applies to companies where foreign participation exceeds 49 per cent of statutory capital and 5 million levs. The other concerns companies below these limits. Companies of the former group are free to negotiate the prices of goods and services that they buy from the local market, and they may also conclude deals with Bulgarian companies in convertible currencies. With regard to the latter group, prices of goods and services shall be established in conformity with prices on the international markets, and with the supply and demand on the home market; specific prices will be negotiated between companies.

Under Romanian regulations, purchases from local sources must be made in the convertible currency agreed upon in the joint venture contract. However, for petty expenses and for supplies of products for which no prices can be established in foreign currency, payment can be made from the joint venture's Romanian currency account at the Romanian Foreign Trade Bank. Also in Bulgaria, local enterprises may agree in their contracts with the joint venture that payments for goods or services are to made in foreign currency.

In the Soviet Union, joint ventures may, upon agreement with Soviet enterprises and organizations, determine both the currency which is used in the purchase of goods from the Soviet market and the manner in which they are purchased. In practice, this means that the supply of raw materials, energy and similar factors of production can be realized either through the so-called wholesale trade, or through the distribution system of the particular branch used by the Soviet joint venture party, or through the Soviet foreign economy organizations. Payments can be made in roubles at Soviet wholesale or agreed prices, or in foreign currencies at prices based on world market prices.

The joint venture contract should specify the manner in which the necessary raw materials, components, etc. will be purchased within the framework of host country legislation. When applicable, the contract should also include stipulations regarding the supply of water, electric power and other basic factors of production to the joint venture. When finalizing their agreement in this respect, the parties may have to approach host country authorities in order to obtain their assent to the arrangement, and to have the appropriate provision included in the establishment permit.

(2) Purchases from abroad

Joint ventures are entitled to make direct purchases from abroad in convertible currencies. In Hungary, however, foreign trade permit or registration is required (see also Section VII.A. above). As a rule, the convertible currencies used to pay such imports must originate from the joint venture's own resources. In Poland, foreign currency export proceeds can be used for this purpose only after the resale of 15 per cent of such proceeds have been sold to a Polish foreign exchange bank.

B. Marketing

The parties should agree on the basic principles which will be applied in the marketing of the joint venture's products both domestically and abroad. One of the questions to be agreed in this connection is to what extent the existing distribution networks of the parties will be used for the marketing and sale of the joint venture products. The principles can be incorporated in the joint venture contract or appended to the joint venture contract as (a) model commercial agency or distributorship contract(s) to be concluded between the joint venture and the respective commercial agent or distributor once the joint venture has been incorporated. To the extent that either of the parties would act as a commercial agent or distributor, the joint venture contract should contain a commitment by both parties that they will cause such agreement to be concluded upon incorporation of the joint venture. With regard to contracts with third parties it may become necessary to deviate from the principles agreed between the parties, but even here the principles would serve as guidelines for those who negotiate the contracts on behalf of the joint venture.

The joint venture laws of the countries under review contain certain provisions regarding the marketing of the joint venture products. Here, too, it is useful to distinguish between domestic and foreign markets.

(1) Domestic marketing

In the Soviet Union, joint ventures can agree with Soviet enterprises and organizations on the currency to be used and on the manner in which sales are to be realized on the domestic market. Joint venture products can be sold to the Soviet market in the form of wholesale trade, by way of direct contracts with consumers, or by way of contracts with intermediary trade organizations. Payments can be made in roubles at Soviet wholesale or agreed prices, or in foreign currencies at prices based on world market prices.

Under Bulgarian, Polish, Czechoslovak and Romanian regulations the joint venture is entitled to sell its products directly to the domestic market. In Romania, moreover, the sale must be in the convertible currency agreed upon in the joint venture contract. In Poland, the joint venture may sell, within the scope of its business, goods and services wholly or partially for foreign currency, after obtaining a foreign exchange permit. In Bulgaria, the two sets of rules, discussed above with respect to domestic purchases, are also applicable to domestic sales.

(2) Marketing abroad

Joint ventures can export their goods directly, without going through foreign trade organizations. In Hungary, foreign trade permit or registration is required (see also Section VII.A. above). It should be noted, moreover, that under Romanian law, all exports, including those to countries with non-convertible currencies, must be effected in convertible currencies.

XVIII. TRANSFER OF SHARES

The parties may wish to include in the joint venture contract provision concerning the transfer of the joint venutre's shares from one party to the other, or from a party to third parties.

A. Restrictions on ownership

A basic framework for the drafting of the contract provisions regulating the transfer of shares is set by those rules, if any, of the host country limiting the share of foreign ownership of joint venture shares to a certain maximum. Thus, in Romania contract provisions allowing the foreign party to acquire a majority of the shares of the joint venture would be in contradiction to the express stipulations of the respective joint venture regulations limiting foreign ownership to a maximum of 49 per cent, and would therefore be unenforceable.

B. Approval by authorities

Two countries - namely Poland and the Soviet Union - require that permission is obtained from host country authorities for any transfer of shares. In Poland, a permission is also required if Charter provisions regarding the parties equity shares are changed. Under Bulgarian law, when the foreign share exceeds 49 per cent in a Limited Liability Company, and 20 per cent in a Joint-Stock Company, permission from the relevant state body is required.

C. Consent by other shareholders or by the company; pre-emptive rights

Under the Bulgarian Decree on Economic Activities, in a Limited Liability Company the approval of the Partners' General Meeting is necessary for a transfer of shares. In Hungary, if a business share in a Limited Liability Company carries an obligation to make a subsidiary contribution, approval of the company is required for a transfer. In the Soviet Union, the consent of other joint venture parties is required for the transfer of shares; such a consent is also required if new parties are to join the joint venture. However, no consent is necessary in the case of a reorganization of one of the parties, or if a general succession takes place. In Romania, the approval of the joint venture (i.e its corporate bodies having jurisdiction in this matter) is required.

When appropriate, the parties might agree in the joint venture contract on the conditions which a third party, to whom shares are transferred, should fulfil. Such conditions might either be positive (for example, that the third party must be active in a specified field relevant for the joint venture) or negative (for example, that it must not be a competitor of the joint venture), or both.

The parties may wish to include in the joint venture contract provisions to the effect that a party who wishes to transfer its shares must first offer them to the other party of the joint venture, or that, once the shares have been offered to a third party, the other joint venture party will have a priority right to purchase them at the price at which they have been offered to the third party. Under Soviet law, Soviet parties have a right to acquire the foreign party's shares which are to be transferred; this right is valid also against new joint venture parties. In a Hungarian Limited Liability Company, other members, the company, or the person designated by the Members' Meeting have - in this order - an option to buy business shares offered for sale.

The joint venture contract also might provide for a specific mechanism for settling disputes that may arise in connection with the transfer of shares. This mechanism might be simpler and quicker than the system which would be applicable to other disputes (see section XXII below).

D. Transfer of shares and the joint venture contract

The joint venture contract should contain provisions regarding the role of the joint venture contract in the event of a transfer of shares. The contract might stipulate that all the terms and provisions of the contract must be made binding upon, and shall also be to the benefit of, and be enforceable by, the respective transferee. The joint venture contract should further provide whether the transfer of the shares will release the transferor from his obligations under the contract.

XIX. TERMINATION AND LIQUIDATION

Most of the joint venture regulations reviewed herein contain provisions relative to the termination and/or liquidation of the joint venture.

A. Statutory grounds for termination

The Bulgarian Decree on Economic Activity stipulates that a company is to be considered insolvent if it fails to meet a liability for more than 60 days due to lack of funds on its accounts in the serving banks, which then declare the insolvency. After insolvency is declared a procedure of agreement will be initiated between the company and its creditors. In the event that no agreement is reached, the company will be declared bankrupt by a district court. In addition to this general rule, a specific provision regarding Joint-Stock Companies stipulates that the company must be terminated if its statutory capital falls below one million levs.

Under the Hungarian Company Act, a company will cease to exist when the period of duration set forth in the Charter has expired or another condition of termination has been fulfilled; or the company decides upon its discontinuance without a successor; or it merges with another company, dissociates therefrom or is transformed into another company form; or the Court of Registration declares its termination; or the court dissolves it in the course of winding-up procedure; or termination is prescribed by the provisions of the Company Act relating to the particular forms of association. The company shall cease when it is struck off from the Trade Register.

The Polish Foreign Investment Law stipulates that if the joint venture conducts an activity which is contrary to the terms laid down in the permit authorizing the establishment of the joint venture, the authority that issued the permit will request this to be corrected within a specified period; non-compliance will result in the authority restricting the scope of, or withdrawing, the permit.

The Soviet joint venture law stipulates that the joint venture may be liquidated by a decision of the USSR Council of Ministers if its activities are not consistent with the objectives defined by the foundation documents of the joint venture. The liquidation of a joint venture must be registered at the USSR Ministry of Finance.

B. Agreed grounds for termination

In addition to the Hungarian Company Act, Romanian and Soviet laws also expressly stipulate that a joint venture can also be wound up on the basis of the provisions included in the foundation documents of the joint venture. While the Bulgarian, Czechoslovak and Polish regulations do not contain any provisions in this respect, grounds for termination of the joint venture can also be agreed under their respective laws.

The parties should therefore include in the charter (or the corresponding founding document) provisions regarding the agreed grounds for termination. The provisions should also define, with due regard to the provision of the applicable law in this respect, the corporate organ which takes the decision, and the manner in which a decision on the termination is to be made (unanimity or qualified majority).

C. Liquidation

Some joint venture laws include provisions regarding the liquidation of the joint venture's assets in the case of winding up. For example, Bulgarian and Czechoslovak laws contain detailed provision on the functions of the liquidator of the joint venture.

In Poland, in the event of liquidation of the joint venture, Polish partners enjoy the right of pre-emption of the property and rights constituting the joint venture's assets, unless the founding documents of the joint venture provide otherwise.

Under Romanian law the procedure to be applied in the liquidation of joint ventures, the obligations and responsibilities of the liquidators, and the distribution among parties of the assets resulting after liquidation, are to be established by the joint venture charter.

The Soviet joint venture law stipulates that in the case of liquidation of a joint venture the foreign party has the right to the return of his contribution in money or in kind, *pro rata* to the residual balance value of his contribution at the moment of liquidation, after discharging his obligations to the Soviet parties and third parties.

When drawing up the foundation documents, the parties may wish to consider whether these should contain, to the extent permitted by the applicable law, provisions that would complement the provisions of the law dealing with liquidation.

The matters that might be covered could include: the methods of evaluating the joint venture's assets and liabilities, including intellectual property rights; the methods of selling joint venture property; the allocation and transfer of joint venture convertible currency reserves; repatriation of liquidation proceeds. When agreeing on these matters due attention should be paid to the respective provisions of host country legislation.

XX. MISCELLANEOUS PROVISIONS

As with almost any international contract, a joint venture contract usually contains a number of provisions which are often grouped under the heading "miscellaneous". A short account is given below of some of the most important of these provisions.

A. Relief from liability

The parties may wish to provide in the joint venture contract for those circumstances which might bring relief from liability for consequences of failure to perform contractual obligations. Where the parties fail to make such provision, the circumstances prompting relief from liability for consequences of failure to perform contractual obligations result from the law applicable to the contract.

The parties might stipulate that a party is not liable for failure to perform any of its obligations if it can prove that the failure was due to an impediment occurring after the signing of the joint venture contract, and which was beyond its control, and that it could not reasonably have been expected to have taken the impediment into account at the time of the conclusion of the contract, or to have avoided or overcome it or its consequences. Examples of such situations are: war, civil strife, interference by public authorities, fire, natural disasters, etc. A party may not rely on a failure by the other party to perform contractual obligations to the extent that such failure was caused by the first party's act or omission.

In addition to the circumstances prompting relief from liability for failure to perform contractual obligations, the contract should also specify the procedure in the event of a party invoking relief. The following items constitute the most important provisions in this respect: the party which fails to perform and which is claiming relief should, without undue delay, give notice to the other party of the commencement of the impediment and of its inability to perform its obligations; the parties should specify the consequences for failure to give such notice (for example, payment of damages); and the right to terminate the contract in the event of a protracted impediment.

The parties should specify in the contract that relief from liability may also be granted in the case where one party's failure to perform has been caused by an act or important omission of the other party.

B. Confidentiality of information

The joint venture contract should specify which information is to be treated as confidential and state that both parties are precluded from revealing such information. Both parties should also bind to confidentiality all persons concerned with the execution of the joint venture contract, including their employees. The parties should further agree on how long confidentiality should be maintained. Normally, confidentiality provisions go beyond the term of the contract - often for an unlimited period. Finally, the joint venture contract should provide for the consequences entailed by violation of the confidentiality provisions.

C. Right of inspection

The parties may wish to stipulate in the joint venture contract that each party will, by their duly authorized representatives, have the right at any time during office or business hours to inspect, copy or obtain copies of any and all books of accounts, records, statements, contracts, minutes and other documents of the joint venture. They may also want to provide that each party will be furnished with audited financial statements of the joint venture within an agreed period from the end of each fiscal year.

D. Incorporation and survival of the joint venture contract

Joint venture contracts sometimes contain provisions stipulating that the contract shall survive the incorporation of the joint venture and shall be effective and binding upon the parties and their successors and assigns for as long as either party or its successors or assigns shall have any shares (or equivalent) in the joint venture, unless the contract is terminated in accordance with its respective provisions.

E. Amendment of the joint venture contract

The joint venture contract should stipulate the conditions under which it can be amended or supplemented. It could state that this is possible only by an instrument in writing executed by and between the parties (and with any necessary government approvals, see Chapter II, Section V).

F. Effectiveness of the joint venture contract

Joint venture contracts normally contain a clause stipulating that the contract shall become effective only upon the parties securing the respective permission of the authorities of the host country and, when applicable, of the foreign party's country. The contract should also provide that if such permissions are not obtained within an agreed period, each party has the right to rescind the contract.

G. Languages

The joint venture contract should specify the language(s) which will be used for different purposes within the joint venture and in its outside connections (meetings of the various organs of the company, minutes of such meetings, contacts with local authorities, correspondence with joint venture parties, etc.). The contract could also specify how translation and interpretation will be provided for in the event that they are needed, and how the resulting costs will be covered.

XXI. APPLICABLE LAW

Some of the joint venture regulations now reviewed contain express references to the general application of host country legislation to the relations between the parties. Such a reference can be found in the Bulgarian and Czechoslovak regulations.

The same is true for the Soviet joint venture decree; the charter of the joint venture and the legal capacity of the joint venture are to be construed in accordance with Soviet law. However, since the joint venture contract is considered to be a foreign trade transaction, the rights and obligations agreed on therein are to be governed, failing agreement on the law applicable thereto, by the law of the place of the conclusion of the contract. Similarly, the mere fact that the parties have agreed on arbitration (see Section XXII) in a third country, does not in itself mean that the law of that country would be applicable; if applicable law has not been agreed upon, the relationship between the parties will be determined by the conflict of laws - rules applied by the arbitrators.

Under Polish law, the parties may freely arrange their mutual relations, unless provisions of the Polish Commercial Code or the joint venture law state otherwise.

The joint venture law of the Soviet Union stipulate that Soviet law shall be applicable to the relationship between the joint venture, as a Soviet legal person, and other Soviet legal persons.

As pointed out above (see Section XV) the joint venture regulations of most of the countries now under review contain provisions regarding the law applicable to the relations between the joint venture and its employees. As a general rule, the relationship between the joint venture and the employees who are citizens of the host country is governed by the laws of that country, whereas other principles may often be agreed on relative to foreign employees of the joint venture.

XXII. SETTLEMENT OF DISPUTES

Within the framework of the provisions of the applicable law, the joint venture contract should provide for the settlement of the disputes relative to the joint venture.

A. Amicable settlement

Experience in international joint ventures indicates that, as the joint venture evolves, disagreements and disputes are likely to arise between the joint venture partners. If this happens, all parties should make every reasonable effort to settle such differences amicably.

With regard to disputes between the joint venture parties, in the joint venture contract a number of different mechanisms can be devised to help to settle differences in a constructive way at an early stage, before they have deteriorated to a conflict which could be solved only through formal proceedings.

Thus, a provision can be inserted in the joint venture contract stipulating that, if a party considers that the other party is guilty of a breach of his obligations under the contract, he must give that other party written notice indicating the reasons why, in his opinion, the contract has been breached; the other party will then have an agreed period (e.g. 30 days) to answer to the charges, and/or make good the breach.

The joint venture contract could also provide for a special body, composed of agreed representatives of the parties (e.g. their respective Chief Executive Officers or Chairmen of Boards of Directors), which would deal with the differences that cannot be solved by the appropriate organs of the joint venture.

A third mechanism that could be used is a conciliation procedure, whereby the dispute is submitted to an outside third party which subsequently proposes a settlement to the dispute, such a proposal not, however, being binding upon the parties, but merely a recommendation.

B. Settlement in arbitration or through general courts of law

Under the Soviet joint venture decree, disputes among parties in a joint venture over matters related to its activities are settled either by the USSR courts or, by common consent of both sides, by an arbitration tribunal.

The Bulgarian Decree on Economic Activity stipulates that disputes between foreign persons, subsidiaries and companies with foreign participation, and Bulgarian companies and other legal and natural persons, shall be settled by Bulgarian courts. However, by agreement between the parties, disputes between foreign persons, their production and trade subsidiaries, companies with foreign participation, and Bulgarian companies and other legal persons, may be settled in a court of arbitration chosen by the parties. It is advisable to include in the joint venture contract stipulations delimiting the jurisdiction of the arbitration court and to define which provisions of the contract the arbitration court will be allowed to amend or modify in case of dispute.

With regard to the relationship between the joint venture company and third parties, the Soviet principles described above also apply to disputes between a joint venture and Soviet state-owned, co-operative and other public organizations and disputes amongst joint ventures. A similar rule is contained in the Romanian joint venture decree under which litigation arising from contractual relations between joint ventures and Romanian corporate bodies can, if the parties so agree, be settled in arbitration, instead of courts of law.

Only the Romanian joint venture decree contains express provisions regarding the way in which disputes between a joint venture company and its employees are to be settled. According to these provisions, litigation between joint ventures and Romanian natural persons shall be brought before the law courts. It should be understood, however, that under the labour laws of all the countries under review, disputes between joint ventures and their host country employees are within the exclusive jurisdiction of the respective national courts of law.

If permitted by the applicable law, the parties may wish to agree on the language to be used in the court or arbitration procedures.

PART TWO

REGULATIONS[1]

1 Unofficial translations into English

BULGARIA

DECREE 56

ON ECONOMIC ACTIVITY

(9 January 1989) [2]

Issued by the State Council of the People's Republic of Bulgaria

Chapter One

GENERAL REGULATIONS

Art. 1. (1) This decree shall apply to the implementation of economic activities in all sectors and branches of the national economy.

(2) Economic activity shall be carried out on the basis of all forms of ownership: state and municipal property transferred for management; property of co-operative and public organisations, of citizens, foreign legal and natural persons and property under joint forms of ownership.

Art. 2. (1) The main form of carrying out economic activity shall be the company.

(2) Publishing, advertising, promotion, exhibition and other houses may be founded in the cultural sphere to operate as companies.

(3) Individual citizens and groups of citizens may carry out economic activity without registering companies.

Art. 3. Foreign legal and natural persons carry out economic activities in this country under the provisions of this decree.

Art. 4. (1) All companies shall be granted equal conditions for economic activity.

(2) The economic activities and investments of foreign legal and natural persons shall be under the protection of the state. The state shall ensure equal economic and legal conditions for economic activities and investments in the country to all foreign persons.

(3) The Council of Ministers may order that the stipulations of this decree be not applied in whole or in part to the economic activities of foreign persons from countries where discriminatory measures are applied with respect to Bulgarian companies.

Art. 5. Economic activities shall be carried out by combining the state's planning and regulating functions on the strategy and objectives of socio-economic development with the indpendence of companies, the operation of market mechanisms, and in compliance with the law.

Art. 6. Economic activities in the country may not be carried out without observance of the requirements of environmental protection.

Art. 7. The state shall not be liable for the obligations of companies nor shall the companies be liable for the obligations of the state or other companies.

Art. 8. Companies and other legal persons may set up joint companies or join to form unions.

Art. 9. Annually, by March 31 of the following year, companies shall submit to local tax authorities an accounts report and a balance sheet endorsed by a qualified person.

2 Corrections: 24 February 1989

Chapter Two

COMPANIES

Section I

GENERAL PROVISIONS

Art. 10. (1) A company is a proprietarily, socially and organisationally autonomous participant in economic activity with a name of its own, and it operates on a cost-benefit account principle. A company is a legal person, with the exception of one-person and collective companies of citizens.

(2) Companies may be state-owned, municipal, co-operative, of public organisations, joint companies and companies of citizens.

Art. 11. (1) The initiative to form, reorganise or close down a company can be taken by: a state organ, a public organisation, a bank, an existing company, or citizens.

(2) The constitution, reorganization and termination of a company shall be registered at the local distric court. The decision of the court shall be published in the State Gazette, the date of which is operative with regard to the setting up, reorganization or termination of the legal person.

(3) The court shall register a company on the basis of:

1. An act of constitution which, depending on the type of company, can be:
   (a) for a state owned company - a decision by the Council of Ministers or a minister or head of another government body appointed by the Council;
   (b) for a municipal company - a decision by the Municipal People's Council;
   (c) for a co-operative company - a decision by the co-operative's constituent assembly;
   (d) for a subsidiary - a decision by the board of management of the existing parent company;
   (e) for a joint company - a constituent contract;
   (f) for the company of a public organisation - an act of the body specified by the the charter of the public organisation;
   (g) for a company of citizens - a written application, respectively a constituent contract.
2. The charter of the company and other documents envisaged by the regulations for the application of this decree.

(4) Entered into the register shall be: the name, seat, subject of activity, statutory capital, divisions, bodies and persons that represent the company and the changes that have occurred; samples of the signatures of the persons representing the company shall be enclosed.

(5) The entries shall be made under the conditions and in the order established by the Civil Procedure Code.

Art. 12. A company shall be terminated by decision of the respective body or persons under Art. 11, para. 3 or, in case of bankruptcy, by decision of the district court.

Art. 13. The Council of Ministers may transfer, gratuitously or non-gratuitously, specific items of state-owned property between state companies. Unfavourable consequences shall be settled by the transfer deed.

Art. 14. This decree shall be applied to the economic activities of co-operative and public organisations.

Art. 15. (1) Companies may establish, reorganise or close down subsidiaries under Art. 11. A subsidiary is a legal person.

(2) An independent company, upon the consent of the institution which provided the capital to set it up, may assume the status of a subsidiary under contract with the parent company. This change shall be entered into the register as stipulated by Art. 11.

(3) Half plus one of a subsidiary's board of management members are named by the board of management of the parent company.

Art. 16. (1) Companies shall determine for themselves:

1. The internal organisational and production structure of the company (institutes, plants, factories, shops, workshops and other divisions);
2. The rights, obligations and responsibilities of the individual divisions and the mode of interaction between them;
3. The internal management of the company.

(2) The divisions of a company are formed and operate according to the principles of self-management, self-financing, and autonomous account.

Art. 17. (1) A company shall carry out its activities in accordance with its designated object of activities. It may carry out any other activity except activities prohibited by a law, decree or act of the Council of Ministers.

(2) Companies which are legal persons carry out foreign economic activity under the conditions of this decree on their own, through a society of which they are partners, or through another company.

(3) The foreign economic activities of a company, including the foundation and participation in overseas companies and other investments abroad, shall be carried out freely, without applying for permission from a state institution, except in the cases specified in this decree.

Art. 18. The Council of Ministers may specify import and export conditions and quotas and prohibit the import and export of certain goods and services.

Art. 19. The Council of Ministers may establish a regime of permission for foreign economic transactions and activities specified by it, and introduce export fees.

Art. 20. (1) The property of a company consists of the right to ownership, respectively to management, use and other titles, titles to intellectual property, securities, shares in companies, outstanding claims and other rights and obligations.

(2) Companies may lease items of their property to citizens and other companies in the order established by the regulations for the application of this decree.

(3) Companies may issue bonds under the conditions and in the order established by the regulations for the application of this decree.

Art. 21. (1) Companies may issue staff shares in the order established by the regulations for the application of this decree.

(2) Staff shares may be acquired by persons who have been in the company's employment for at least a year.

(3) Staff shares shall be registered shares, the face value of a share being 50 levs. They entitle holders to dividends from the annual profit and shall be bought back by the company at their face value upon request by the owner or upon termination of the employment contract.

(4) The board of management of the company shall determine the maximum number of staff shares which can be owned by a member of its personnel; it may not exceed 200 shares.

(5) Retired persons may keep their staff shares, provided they have worked at least ten years for the company before their retirement.

(6) Staff shares may be inherited. The share of heirs who are not employed by the company shall be bought by the company at their face value.

Art. 22. The bodies of a state, municipal or public-organisation company are: the general assembly of employees (the assembly of representatives), the board of management, the supervisory board, and the managing director.

Art. 23. (1) The general assembly of employees (the assembly of representatives) shall be considered legitimate if attended to by at least two-thirds of its members. It takes decisions by a show of hands and with simple majority.

(2) The general assembly examines the overall plan of the company and votes guidelines for the social development of the personnel.

Art. 24. (1) Half plus one of the members of the board of management and the supervisory board shall be named by the bodies and organisations which have provided the capital to constitute the company; the rest shall be elected by the general assembly (the assembly of representatives).

(2) The board of management, the supervisory board and the managing director shall be elected for a term of up to five years.

(3) The board of management shall:

1. Adopt the company's regulations;
2. Define the strategy and approve the company's development plans and the rules for the organisation and management of economic activity;
3. Elect and dismiss the chairman of the board of management, the managing director and his deputies;
4. Set the remuneration, grant incentives and impose penalties on the officers it has elected;
5. Take decisions on founding, reorganising or terminating subsidiareis;
6. Approve the annual account of the company's economic activities, the annual balance sheet and the distribution of incomes;
7. Decide on issuing bonds and staff shares.

Art. 25. (1) Persons who are not employed by the company, except officers specified by the Council of Ministers, may also be elected members of the board of management or to the post of chairman of the board.

(2) The chairman of the board of management and the company's managing director may be foreign nationals.

Art. 26. (1) Members of the board of management receive an annual remuneration from the company's wage fund, and its amount shall depend on the final results of the performance of the company.

(2) Members of the board of management shall be liable for the damage they have caused to the company through their fault.

Art. 27. (1) The company's managing director shall:

1. Organise, direct and supervise the company's activities on the principle of one-man management and see to the proper use and protection of its property.
2. Represent the company and perform the functions entrusted to him by statutory acts or by the board of management.

(2) The board of management shall not interfere with the managing director's operative work.

(3) The managing director is member of the board of management by virtue of his office.

(4) If necessary, an operative buro shall be set up to assist the managing director; the buro shall include his deputies and other persons appointed by him.

(5) The managing director may be dismissed before the expiry of his term by the board of management or the respective body under Art. 11, para. 3 if he violates statutory acts, allows mismanagement of company property or runs the company inefficiently.

(6) The decision to dismiss the managing director may be appealed before the county court within whose jurisdiction the company's seat is.

Art. 28. The supervisory board shall control the fulfilment of the decisions of the general assembly and the board of management and the protection of the company's property. It shall account for its activities before the general assembly.

Art. 29. Not eligible as member of the board of management or supervisory board, as comptroller or managing director of a company shall be any person who:

1. Has been convicted for an intentional crime;
2. Is prohibited to hold a position involving financial liability;
3. Has been member of a board of management or managing director of a company terminated because of bankruptcy, if unsatisfied creditors have remained;
4. Is a spouse or relative to third degree, direct or collateral line of descent included, of a member of the board of management or supervisory board, or of the company's managing director.

Art. 30. (1) Companies may form commercial groups to implement their policy in a given area, to draw up major investment decisions, for marketing, management of innovation processes and other.

(2) Companies shall determine by contract the specific objectives and competence of the group and its bodies.

Art. 31. Companies and their unions may be members of the Union of Industry and Commerce. The bodies of the Union shall be elected at a congress which also approves its statutes.

Section II

JOINT – STOCK COMPANIES

Art. 32. A joint-stock company is one which has its statutory capital distributed in shares.

Art. 33. (1) A joint-stock company shall be formed on the basis of a constituent contract and a charter.

(2) The bodies of a joint-stock company are the general meeting of shareholders, the board of management, the supervisory board and the managing director.

Art. 34. (1) A company's statutory capital and shares shall be fixed at their face value in levs. The minimum face value of a company's statutory capital shall be one million levs.

(2) Shares may be registered or bearer shares. Bulgarian citizens may acquire only registered shares in an order established by the Council of Ministers.

(3) The minimum face value of one share shall be 1000 levs.

(4) One share shall entitle its holder to one vote at the shareholder's meeting, the right to dividends and a liquidation quota proportional to the face value of the share.

Art. 35. A joint-stock company may be founded by two or more legal persons.

Art. 36. For the registration of a joint-stock company it is necessary that:

1. Its charter has been adopted;
2. All shares have been subscribed for;
3. 30 per cent of the statutory capital has been deposited;
4. The board of management and the supervisory board have been elected;
5. The specific requirements set forth in this decree and the regulations for its application have been met.

Art. 37. The company charter shall specify:

1. The name and seat of the company;
2. The subject of its activities;
3. The statutory capital;
4. The number and face value of shares, including the number of registered and bearer shares;
5. The mode of decision-making by the company's collective bodies;
6. The terms and procedure of depositing the entire face value of shares and the consequences of failing to fulfil this obligation;
7. The ways of distributing the profit, covering losses and calculating dividends, and the conditions and mode of their payment;
8. The procedure of convening the general meeting of shareholders and its competence;
9. The procedure of electing and convening the board of management and the supervisory board, and their mandate and competence;
10. The procedure of reducing and increasing the statutory capital.

Art. 38. (1) The general meeting of shareholders shall:

1. Change and amend the charter;
2. Set the guidelines of the company's activities;
3. Decide on re-organising or terminating the company;
4. Determine the number of members of the board of management and the supervisory board, elect and dismiss them, and determine their remuneration;

5. Approve the balance sheet, the distribution of income and the account of the board of management on the company's performance and decide on discharging its members from liability;
6. Approve the account of the supervisory board;
7. Decide on issuing bonds and staff shares;
8. Decide on reducing or increasing the statutory capital;
9. Appoint the liquidators, except in the event of company bankruptcy.

(2) The decisions of the general meeting under items 1, 3, 8 and 9 of the preceding paragraph shall become effective after they have been entered in the company register at the district court. These decisions shall be taken by a majority vote of the holders of no less than three-quarters of all shares.

Art. 39. (1) The board of management shall:

1. Draw up the annual report and the balance sheet and submit them for approval by the general meeting of shareholders;
2. Draw up plans and programmes for the company's activities;
3. Put before the general meeting of shareholders proposals to increase or reduce the statutory capital;
4. Elect and dismiss the managing director and his deputies and set their salaries.
5. Elect a chairperson from among its members;
6. Approve the rules of organisation of the budget, salaries and the other company rules and regulations;
7. Decide on opening or closing down subsidiaries, divisions and representation offices and on the company's participation or termination of participation in associations in the country or abroad;
8. Decide on forming funds and determine the procedure for raising and spending them;
9. Decide on acquiring and alienating immovable property rights, using investment credits, giving guarantees and warranties, acquiring and transferring licences, participation in auctions and tenders;
10. Examine and settle all matters except those which are within the competence of the general meeting of shareholders.

(2) The decision under items 1, 3, 4, 7 and 9 of the preceding paragraph shall be taken by a majority vote of two-thirds of the members of the board of management;

(3) The board of management may take decisions *in absentia* by a protocol, signed by all its members.

Art. 40. The managing director of a joint-stock company shall be elected for the current tenure of the board of management and become its member by virtue of his office.

Art. 41. The board of management shall be obliged to publish in a central daily paper the balance sheet for the preceding year by 31 March of every year. Published together with the balance sheet shall be:

1. A profit and loss account for each of the preceding 5 years;
2. The dividends paid during each of the preceding 5 years.

Art. 42. (1) A shareholder may request the district court to repeal decisions of the general meeting of shareholders, or of the board of management, that are unlawful or contrary to the company charter, within two weeks from learning about such decisions.

(2) The court shall hear the case in the presence of a public prosecutor. The court's decision shall be final.

Art. 43. Besides the general terms and conditions for company termination and the ones envisaged in the charter, a joint-stock company shall be terminated when its statutory capital falls below one million levs.

Section III

LIMITED LIABILITY COMPANIES

Art. 44. (1) A limited liability company has a statutory capital in which the partners hold shares.

(2) The liability of the partners for the company's debts shall be limited to the amount they have paid for shares, or are due to pay to the statutory capital.

(3) Shares are indivisible. The statutory capital shall be at least 50,000 levs.

Art. 45. (1) A limited liability company shall be formed by at least two legal persons on the basis of a charter adopted by the partners.

(2) The charter shall specify:

1. The name and seat of the company;
2. The subject of its activities;
3. The statutory capital and the shares of each partner;
4. The conditions or time limit for the company's termination.

Art. 46. The governing bodies of a company shall be the shareholders' general meeting, the managing director, and the supervisory board or comptroller.

Art. 47. (1) The general meeting shall consist of one representative of each partner and a representative of the company's personnel who has an advisory vote.

(2) The company's managing director and the chairperson of the board of comptrollers shall have advisory vote at the general meeting.

(3) The partners' general meeting shall:

1. Amend and supplement the charter;
2. Admit new partners, approve the transfer of shares to other partners or new members and expell partners;
3. Approve the annual report and the balance sheet and distribute the profit among the partners;
4. Decide on increasing or reducing the statutory capital;
5. Elect the managing director for a term of up to five years and discharge him of office;
6. Elect members of the supervisory board or a comptroller for a term of up to five years and set their remuneration;
7. Decide on opening or closing divisions and representations and on participation or termination of participation in companies located in Bulgaria or abroad;
8. Decide on acquiring and alienating immovable property and titles to it, and on the use of investment credits;
9. Decide on issuing bonds and staff shares.

(4) Each partner shall be entitled to votes in the general meeting in proportion to his share in the statutory capital.

(5) Decisions under paragraph 3, items 1 and 2 shall be taken by unanimity, and under items 3-9[3] by simple majority unless the charter stipulates otherwise.

(6) The representative of a partner to be expelled shall have no voting rights when the expulsion decision is taken.

Art. 48. (1) A partner shall be expelled from the company for failure to deposit the agreed share within the term set in the contract or to fulfil other obligations under the charter.

(2) If, by unanimous decision of the general meeting, the expelled partner's share is not bought by the remaining partners or by a newly admitted partner, the statutory capital shall be reduced by its value.

(3) The expelled partner shall be entitled to receive the share's nominal value or its real value according to the balance sheet, depending on which value is lower.

---

3 As corrected on 24 February 1989.

Art. 49. The partner shall be dismissed from the company under the terms of the constituent contract. The provisions of paragraphs 2 and 3 of the preceding article shall be applied.

Art. 50. Any partner may demand the setting aside of unlawful decisions of the general meeting or of decisions at variance with the charter as stipulated by Art. 42.

Art. 51. A company shall be terminated by unanimous decision of the general meeting.

Section IV

UNLIMITED LIABILITY COMPANIES

Art. 52. (1) An unlimited liability company is one in which one or several partners have unlimited liability for the obligation of the company while the remaining partners are liable up to the amount of their contributions.

(2) The partners of unlimited liability shall be jointly liable. The relations between them are settled by contract.

(3) Shares may be issued to the amount contributed by the partners of limited liability.

Art. 53. (1) The company charter shall specify:

1. The name and seat of the company;
2. The subject of its activities;
3. The statutory capital;
4. The partners of unlimited liability and their part of the statutory capital.
5. The part of the statutory capital that shall be taken by the partners of limited liability and how it is divided; if shares are issued - their number, kind and face value;
6. The manner in which the company is represented;
7. The procedure of profit distribution;
8. The procedure of withdrawing from the company and terminating it.

(2) Unless the charter provides otherwise, partners having limited liability may transfer their shareholdings or registered shares to third persons upon written notice to the company.

Art. 54. Partners having unlimited liability must deposit at least one third of the statutory capital.

Art. 55. The economic activity of the company shall be carried out by the partners of unlimited liability.

Art. 56. For matters not settled in this section the stipulations concerning limited liability companies shall be applied.

Section V

COMPANIES OF CITIZENS

Art. 57. (1) Citizens may set up one-person, collective, or joint companies.

(2) Companies of citizens may carry out any activity within their registered subjects of activities, except those prohibited by a law, a decree or act of the Council of Ministers.

(3) Joint companies of citizens must have a statutory capital of no less than 10,000 levs and shall be registered upon depositing at least 75 per cent of the declared statutory capital. One-person and collective companies shall not be required to register statutory capital.

(4) Citizens are obliged to work personally in the companies registered by them.

(5) One-person and collective companies shall not be levied a profit tax but their members shall be taxed under Art. 13 para 2 of the Law on Total Income Tax.

Art. 58. (1) The joint company of citizens shall be a legal person. It shall be established through a constituent contract which specifies:

1. Its name and subject of activities;
2. Its statutory capital and the partners' shares in it;
3. Its governing bodies and the manner of decision making;
4. The partners' rights and obligations;
5. The manner of income distribution;
6. The procedure and conditions of admission of new partners, withdrawal or expulsion from the joint company.

(2) Unless agreed otherwise, property contributions shall be assessed in the order established by the regulations for the application of this decree.

(3) The individual incomes of partner shall be taxed under Art. 13 para. 2 of the Law on Total Income Tax.

(4) Partners shall be jointly liable for the company's obligations to the amount of contributions made or due to be made to the statutory capital, or, if this should prove insufficient, with their personal property, but not in excess of its value by the date of discontinuing payments, including the increase until the termination of the bankruptcy procedures.

Art. 59. (1) Any citizen may participate in a company of citizens and work for other companies by contract.

(2) The following persons may not be founders or participate in companies of citizens:

1. Persons who have been convicted for crimes against socialist or personal property;
2. Persons deprived of the right to hold posts of financial liability;
3. Persons who have participated in companies closed down for bankruptcy, if unsatisfied creditors have remained;
4. Persons on whom administrative penalties have been imposed for systematic offences in practising the respective activities.

Art. 60. (1) No distraint or prohibition shall be imposed on the property of companies of citizens for partners' debts. No compensation shall be made on a partner's debt against outstanding claims of the company or on debts of the company against a partner's outstanding claims.

(2) If the creditors of one of the partners[4] are not satisfied with his personal property, they may claim the debtor's share in the company. The other partners may pay the debt to the amount of the said partner's share within 3 months from the date of filing the claim. If they fail to do so, the company shall be terminated by a court at the creditor's request.

Art. 61. (1) A one-person company shall be terminated upon the person's death or interdiction.

(2) A joint company shall be terminated upon a partner's death or interdiction, unless agreed otherwise.

(3) Any partner may leave the joint company on a one-year notice, unless agreed otherwise.

Art. 62. A company of citizens shall be registered at the district court in accordance with Art. 11.

Art. 63. (1) A company of citizens may employ by labour contract up to 10 persons in observance of the stipulations of the labour legislation. The individual labour contract may provide for an employee's participation in the profits and losses of the company.

(2) For seasonal jobs, the companies of citizens may conclude temporary labour contracts with an unlimited number of workers.

Art. 64. Companies of citizens, as well as individual producers, may establish unions to protect their economic and social interests.

---

4 As corrected on 24 February 1989.

Chapter Three

INSOLVENCY AND LIQUIDATION OF COMPANIES

Art. 65. (1) An insolvent company shall be declared bankrupt.

(2) An insolvent or bankrupt company may be granted assistance by the state or by arrangement with its creditors.

(3) If the bankruptcy may not be avoided as provided under para. (2) hereinabove, the company shall be liquidated as herein provided.

(4) The liquidation of companies in all other cases of termination shall be settled by the regulations for the application of this decree.

Art. 66. (1) A company shall be considered insolvent if it fails, for more than 60 days, to pay a specific monetary obligation due to lack of funds on its accounts in the serving banks, which then declare the insolvency.

(2) After insolvency is declared, a procedure of conciliation shall be initiated between the company and its creditors.

(3) The procedure of conciliation shall be initiated at the request of the company or one[5] of its creditors, filed with one of the serving banks. Within 14 days from the initiation of the procedure the managing director of the company must notify its creditors of executable outstanding claims by registered mail.

(4) In the course of the procedure of conciliation, the creditors and the debtor may take steps to restore the debtor's solvency by way of financial or other assistance, by deferring or extending the repayment of the liabilities.

(5) The procedure of conciliation shall be chaired by the president of the bank concerned with the procedure, or by an employee of the bank authorised by him.

(6) A representative of the state, appointed by a competent state body, may also take part in the procedure of conciliation.

(7) The procedure of conciliation must be concluded within one month of its initiation. This term may be extended by agreement between the creditors and the debtor.

Art. 67. (1) If no agreement is reached as provided under the preceding article, the president of the bank who chairs the procedure of conciliation must, within three days, notify in writing the district court where the company is registered.

(2) On the basis of the notification as provided under the preceding paragraph, the court shall initiate bankruptcy proceedings. The proceedings may also be initiated at the request of the company, the creditors or the public prosecutor.

(3) The court shall specify a deadline by which the debtor must submit:

1. A balance-sheet up to the date of initiation of the proceedings;
2. A statement of the company's outstanding claims and liabilities;
3. An inventory of the company's property and its book value.

Art. 68. (1) On the basis of the data made available as hereinabove provided, the court, having heard the debtor and the creditors who have joined the proceedings, shall declare the company bankrupt and the date of termination of payments.

(2) In its decision under the preceding paragraph, the court shall:

1. Appoint a liquidator - one or more persons;
2. Impose a distraint or prohibition on the debtor's property;
3. Set a time period during which the liquidator shall be required to submit a detailed balance sheet of the debtor's property taking into account the three month deadline within which the creditors must submit their claims to the liquidator.

(3) The court's decision may be appealed by the debtor within 14 days. The appeal does not stay its execution.

Art. 69. (1) The court's decision of bankruptcy shall be entered in the district court's company registers, published in the State Gazette, and copies of it shall be posted at designated posts at the court and at the Union of Industry and Commerce.

(2) Within a period of three months from the publication of the court's decision in the State Gazette as provided under the preceding paragraph, the creditors must notify the liquidator in writing of their claims.

---

[5] As corrected on 24 February 1989.

Art. 70. As of the date of the court's decision of bankruptcy:

1. All economic activities of the company and the competence of its bodies shall be terminated;
2. All liabilities of the company shall become due;
3. The accrual of interest on all liabilities of the company shall cease.

Art. 71. (1) Persons with appropriate qualifications shall be appointed as liquidators.
(2) The liquidator shall execute the decision of the court.

Art. 72. The creditors shall be invited by the liquidator to appoint their representative to audit the books of account and the liquidator's activities.

Art. 73. (1) The liquidator must establish, irrespective of the creditor's claims, all the debtor's liabilities on the basis of available data and additional inquiries, as well as his outstanding claims, and undertake immediate measures for their prompt collection.

(2) The liquidator may agree to the termination of all valid contracts, transfer the rights and obligations under these contracts to other persons with the consent of the other party, and sell all the debtor's perishable or quickly depreciable assets.

Art. 74. (1) Upon receipt of the data under Art. 67, para. 3, the court shall invite the creditors to conclude the bankruptcy by conciliation. The draft conciliation agreement shall be prepared and sent to the creditors by the liquidator.

(2) Within 14 days from the sending of the draft agreement, the court shall summon the creditors for adopting an agreement on concluding the bankruptcy. Should they fail to reach agreement, the court shall decide that the debtor's property will be liquidated.

Art. 75. All the debtor's movable and immovable property and property rights thereof shall be sold in the established order, or if such order has not been established, through a specialised trading firm, or at a public auction. State-owned land, forests, waters or subsoil are not eligible for sale.

Art. 76. (1) After converting the debtor's assets into money, the liquidator shall draw up a liquidation balance sheet containing:

1. The collected dues;
2. The proceeds of the liquidation of the property;
3. The remaining property and its market value;
4. The debtor's liabilities;
5. The liquidation costs.

(2) The liquidator shall submit the liquidation balance sheet to the court and to the creditors, together with a proposal as to the way in which they are to be satisfied.

(3) The creditors may appeal in court within 14 days from the receipt of the distribution proposal.

Art. 77. (1) Should one of the creditors contest a claim by another creditor, the former must file an appeal against him and the liquidator. Should he fail to appeal within two weeks of the date of the session under Art. 74 para. 2, the claim shall be considered uncontested. The filing of an appeal shall stay the transfer of the sum to the creditor whose claim is contested.

(2) In the distribution, the funds for the contested liabilities shall be provided in proportion to the claims of the other creditors.

(3) All claims filed after the expiry of the time period as provided under Art. 69 para. 2 hereinabove, shall be repaid from the assets remaining after distribution.

Art. 78. (1) Having heard the creditors, the debtor and the liquidator, the court shall confirm the liquidation balance sheet and the final distribution of the sums among the individual creditors.

(2) The decision under para. 1 herein above may be appealed within 14 days from the date of issue. The ruling of the court of appeals is final and binding and may not be contested or repealed.

(3) Should the debtor's assets prove insufficient for satisfying all creditors, the liquidator shall propose a distribution scheme in which priority shall be given to repaying dues pertaining to remuneration of individual citizens, indemnities for tort, sums for the

state budget,[6] liabilities covered by security or mortgage, while the remainder shall be distributed proportionally among the remaining creditors.

Art. 79. (1) Following the distribution of the assets and the repayment of sums the court shall issue, *ex officio* or on request by the liquidator, a decision of temination of bankruptcy, to be published in the State Gazette.

(2) With the entering into force of the court decision on termination of bankruptcy:

1. The bankruptcy proceedings shall be terminated;
2. All the liquidator's functions shall be terminated;
3. All unclaimed or unpaid dues shall be considered precluded.

Art. 80. (1) Should a company of citizens other than a legal person be declared bankrupt, the liquidator's functions shall be performed by a bailiff and the respective provisions of the Civil Procedure Code shall be applied.

(2) In the event of a bankruptcy of a company of citizens the court may impose, on request by the creditors, distraints or prohibitions on the partners' personal property by force of Art. 68 hereinabove.

Art. 81. The state shall provide for the re-allocation or retraining of the released workforce following a company's termination or liquidation as well as social assistance for a period of time in the order established by the Council of Ministers.

Chapter Four

STATE REGULATION OF ECONOMIC ACTIVITY

Art. 82. The state shall regulate economic activity through: a system of taxes, duties and subsidies, interest rates, currency regulations, rules on labour remuneration, depreciation rates, price-formation rules and state contracts.

Art. 83. (1) State plan and state budget shall define the main goals, rates and proportions; the material, financial, currency and other balances, the objectives of social development, the macrostructural changes, the overall development of territorial entities and the guidelines for the country's participation in the international division of labour and socialist integration; as well as the economic conditions, standards and regulators.

(2) The competent state authorities shall co-ordinate with the respective companies their participation in the fulfilment of the state plan on the basis of mutual agreements and state contracts.

Art. 84. (1) State contracts may be placed only for the performance of internationally contracted obligations, for implementing the tasks of social policy, for achieving strategic, technological and market objectives, as well as for guaranteeing national security and major national balances.

(2) State contracts shall be awarded by contract, on a competitive basis. They shall not engage more than two thirds of the company's capacity.

Art. 85. The company shall draw up independently its plan for economic activity on the basis of concluded contracts, economic conditions, standards and regulators, state contracts and its own marketing, technological and other projects.

Art. 86. (1) The prices of goods and services shall be established in conformity with prices on international markets and with the supply and demand on the home market. Specific prices shall be negotiated between companies.

(2) For certain goods and services which are vital to the population's living standards the respective state bodies shall set fixed or maximum retail prices.

(3) Wholesale maximum prices shall be established for raw and prime materials and for transport services according to a list endorsed by the Council of Ministers.

Art. 87. (1) Companies shall pay value added tax, excise duties, leasing duties, customs duties, profit tax and payroll tax.

---

6 As corrected on 24 February 1989.

(2) Companies shall pay profit tax at the rate of 50 per cent. The taxable profit shall be determined in accordance with the rules for the application of this decree.

(3) Companies shall make contributions to the budgets of the municipal people's councils. Their size and procedure of payment shall be determined by the Council of Ministers.

Art. 88. (1) The profit remaining after taxation and payment of other liabilities shall be used by the company for development, for dividends and other purposes. The minimum allocations for development purposes shall be fixed by the Council of Ministers.

(2) A company shall decide what kind of funds to set up, and determine the number of its bank accounts.

Art. 89. (1) Companies shall obtain their foreign currency from receipts from export of goods and services, foreign currency credits from Bulgarian and foreign banks, purchase of foreign currency from the state and at foreign currency auctions.

(2) Companies shall sell part of their foreign currency receipts to the state under a procedure established by the Council of Ministers.

(3) Companies may buy or sell foreign currency through currency auctions organised by the banks.

Art. 90. (1) Companies may be granted bonuses and receive subsidies from the state budget; their amount shall be determined by the Council of Ministers under conditions announced in advance. Bonuses shall be paid for realized production.

(2) For certain industries and other activities determined by the Council of Ministers, instalments and interest on investment credits shall be paid out of the profit before taxation.

(3) Companies may be fully or partially exempted by the Council of Ministers from the payment of taxes for stated activities and industries or territories.

Art. 91. (1) The Council of Ministers together with the Central Council of the Bulgarian Trade Unions shall set general rules for labour remuneration and fix starting salaries according to categories of personnel and qualification levels, the amount of minimum wages etc.

(2) Basic salaries of workers, specialists and managers shall be fixed in three qualification levels: beginners, skilled and with higher qualifications.

(3) The salaries of all categories of personnel shall depend on the immediate final results (output, foreign currency, profit, profitability and others).

(4) Depending on concrete conditions, wages shall be paid by the hour, day, week or month.

Art. 92. (1) A company shall determine independently about the means to be allocated for salaries on the basis of its rules for labour remuneration in conformity with the regulators laid down in the technological and technical projects and with the stipulations of the preceeding article.

(2) A company shall pay payroll tax in a manner established by the rules for the application of this decree.

Art. 93. (1) A company may be serviced by, and receive credits from, various banks. Relations between the company and the banks shall be regulated by contract.

(2) Banks shall exercise control through the lev for the effective utilisation of the credits granted by them.

(3) Interest rates shall be negotiated between companies and banks on the grounds of the prime interest rate, and depending on credit supply and demand, the solvency of the credit recipient, the term of the credit etc., and for foreign currency credits - in conformity with the conditions on the international credit markets.

(4) The rates of exchange of foreign currency to the lev shall be determined by the Bulgarian National Bank in accordance with changes on the international money markets.

Art. 94. Companies may agree that payments for deliveries and services be done according to company (commercial) credit terms at negotiated interest.

Art. 95. (1) State authorities shall create appropriate conditions for competition between companies and prevent monopolism and unfair competition on domestic and international markets.

(2) In the event of infringement on the interests of a Bulgarian company as a result of unfair competition from the part of other Bulgarian or foreign companies and

companies of foreign persons, or through joint activities of Bulgarian and foreign companies on the domestic and international markets, the Bulgarian company concerned may apply to the Union of Industry and Commerce, or ask the relevant state authority to take measures to stop the unfair competition, or sue in courts for compensation of the damage caused to it.

Art. 96. The regional and municial people's councils may participate in joint-stock companies and issue bonds according to a procedure established by the rules for the application of this decree.

Art. 97. Statutory acts and decisions of the Council of Ministers and other state bodies contravening this decree shall be repealed by the Supreme Court upon request by the parties concerned or on a motion from the public prosecutor.

Art. 98. Property disputes related to economic activities may be assigned for settlement to a voluntary arbitration body made up of one or three members, provided agreement to this effect has been stated in writing. The ruling of the voluntary arbitration body shall be final and subject to enforcement.

Chapter Five

ECONOMIC ACTIVITIES OF FOREIGN AND MIXED COMPANIES WITHIN THE COUNTRY

Section I

GENERAL PROVISIONS

Art. 99. (1) Foreign persons may perform economic activities within the country independently, through a subsidiary (company) or through a company in the order established by this decree.

(2) This decree shall also apply to the international economic activities of foreign persons, subsidiaries and companies with foreign participation.

Art. 100. (1) Foreign persons may perform economic activities independently with permission by the relevant state body. The latter shall determine the activities for which no permission is required.

(2) Before beginning operations under the preceding paragraph foreign persons must submit a declaration. When the activities are carried out jointly with a Bulgarian company or other legal person, the permission shall be obtained and the declaration submitted by the Bulgarian participant.

Art. 101. (1) Foreign persons may establish subsidiaries with permission of the relevant state body.

(2) A subsidiary shall be a legal person and may perform independently the activities specified in the permission. Any change in the subject of activities shall require a new permission.

(3) A bank's subsidiary shall be set up in accordance with the procedure of para. 1 with a minimum statutory capital of 10 million levs.

(4) A subsidiary shall be registered with the local district court within whose jurisdiction the subsidiary's seat is located on the basis of an application by the foreign person containing:

1. The name and seat of the subsidiary;
2. Its subject of activities;
3. Information about the foreign person: name, address, registration, subject of activity and capital;
4. The amount of statutory capital and the property which is part of it;
5. The persons representing it.

(5) Registration of the subsidiary shall be done in accordance with Art. 11. The legal person shall come into existence on the date of the registration decision is published in the State Gazette.

(6) A subsidiary's accounts report and the balance sheet shall be certified by a qualified person.

Art. 102. (1) Foreign persons may open trade representations in the country with the permission of the relevant state body. At least half of the staff of a representation should be Bulgarian citizens.

(2) A representation shall not be a legal person.

Art. 103. (1) Foreign persons may constitute, or acquire shares in, a limited liability company.

(2) When the foreign participation exceeds 49 per cent a permission from the relevant state body shall be required.

(3) In the sense of para. 2, participation by companies with a higher than 49 per cent share of foreign persons shall also be considered foreign participation.

Art. 104. (1) A limited liability company shall be constituted and registered in accordance with the provisions of this decree.

(2) When the foreign participation in a company under the preceding article exceeds 49 per cent and 5 million levs in convertible currency or 50 million transferrable roubles, the provisions of Section Two of this chapter shall be applied.

(3) The relevant state body may allow a company to carry out its activity as stipulated by this chapter also in cases of smaller foreign participation.

Art. 105. (1) Foreign persons may acquire registered shares and constitute join-stock companies in the country in accordance with the provision of this decree. When the foreign participation exceeds 20 per cent, a permission from the relevant state body shall be required. Foreign persons must pay the full value of the shares for which they have subscribed.

(2) Companies under Art. 103 para. 3 and joint-stock companies with foreign participation exceeding 20 per cent may constitute or acquire shares in joint-stock companies with the permission of the relevant state body.

(3) The stipulations of Art. 104 paras. 2 and 3 shall be applied to economic activities of a joint-stock company with foreign participation.

(4) Foreign persons may participate in the board of management of a Bulgarian joint-stock company in which foreign persons have shares.

Art. 106. (1) Investments made by foreign persons shall not be subject to confiscation or expropriation through administrative procedure.

(2) Foreign persons' investments in real estate cannot be expropriated except for state or public needs which cannot be met otherwise.

(3) An expropriated investment shall be made good to a foreign person by agreement. Should no agreement be reached, the amount of compensation shall be determined by the district court.

Section II

ECONOMIC CONDITIONS

Art. 107. The profit of companies with foreign participation and subsidiaries of foreign persons shall be taxed at the rate of 30 per cent.

Art. 108. The profit from the independent economic activity of a foreign person under Art. 100 shall be taxed at the rate of 40 per cent.

Art. 109. (1) Income from dividends, shares, interest, royalties, fees for technical services and rents arising in Bulgaria for foreign persons shall be taxed at the rate of 15 per cent.

(2) Subject to tax exemption will be:

1. Dividends received on the condition that they are used for buying shares and bonds in this country;
2. Interest on loans concluded by the government of the People's Republic of Bulgaria or the Bulgarian National Bank with international financial organisations;
3. Interest on loans granted by foreign banks to Bulgarian banks at preferential interest rates;

4. Royalties for transferring industrial property into priority sectors under a list endorsed by the Council of Ministers;
5. Fees for technical services related to the supply of complete plants, technological, scientific, industrial or commercial equipment.

Art. 110. Companies with foreign participation that receive dividends from shares and profit from share capital in the order established by this decree shall be taxed at the rate of 10 per cent of the gross amount of dividends.

Art. 111. Profit from economic activity in free trade zones shall be exempt from taxation for the first five years; after the expiry of this period it shall be taxed at the rate of 20 per cent.

Art. 112. Profits of companies with foreign participation under Art. 104, paras. 2 and 3 and Art. 105, para. 3, and subsidiaries of foreign persons shall be exempt from taxation for a period of five years after registration if they perform economic activity in high technology sectors specified by the Council of Ministers.

Art. 113. Losses from economic activity during a fiscal year may be deducted from the profit over the next five fiscal years.

Art. 114. Exempt from taxation shall be the part of the profit granted under contract as donations to Bulgarian cultural, research and educational institutes, foundations, higher educational establishments and funds for relief to victims of natural disasters or for the restoration of historical monuments in Bulgaria.

Art. 115. Companies with foreign participation, subsidiaries and foreign persons under Art. 100 must keep books of account under rules endorsed by the relevant state body. Annually, and whenever requested by the relevant tax authority, they shall submit to the latter reports on accounts and economic information about their activity.

Art. 116. (1) Annual profit shall be declared within a month from the day of endorsement of the annual balance of accounts but not later than 31 March of the next fiscal year.

(2) The taxation act shall be issued by the tax authority within a month from submitting the tax return.

(3) The act may be appealed before the district court within two weeks of its announcement.

Art. 117. Companies with foreign participation shall pay value added tax, local taxes and fees.

Art. 118. When the foreign person imports for the needs of the economic activity raw and prime materials and equipment intended for production for export, they shall be exempt from import duty.

Art. 119. (1) The prices of goods and services bought and offered by companies with foreign participation, production or commercial subsidiaries and foreign persons on the internal market or for export shall be freely negotiated.

(2) Foreign persons, subsidiaries and companies with foreign participation may conclude deals in convertible currency with Bulgarian companies and other persons in this country.

(3) Goods and services for mass consumption for which the Council of Ministers has set fixed or maximum prices shall be sold at these prices.

(4) The Council of Ministers may introduce additional conditions for foreign persons as regards the prices of some raw material and energy resources.

Art. 120. (1) A foreign person may remit abroad the profit earned in foreign currency and the foreign currency part of the liquidation quota.

(2) The Bulgarian National Bank shall allow the exchange and change Bulgarian levs for the currency of investment when the foreign person:

1. Takes out of the People's Republic of Bulgaria the compensation for expropriated investment;
2. Takes out his liquidation quota from a terminated company with foreign participation to the amount of the foreign currency contribution;
3. Has earned profit in Bulgarian levs from economic activity by contract with the relevant state authority.

(3) The amount of money shall be converted from Bulgarian levs into foreign currency and from foreign currency into Bulgarian levs at the rate at which the Bulgarian National Bank buys foreign currency from companies and citizens.

Art. 121. (1) Relations of employment with subsidiaries and companies with foreign participation under Art. 104, paras. 2 and 3 Art. 105, para. 3 shall be regulated by a contract of employment.

(2) The parties to a contract of employment may agree on paying part of the labour remuneration in foreign currency irrespective of whether either party is a foreign or Bulgarian citizen. The foreign currency part of the labour remuneration paid to Bulgarian citizens shall be remitted to their bank accounts.

(3) Labour disputes with subsidiaries and companies with foreign participation under Art. 104, paras. 2 and 3 and Art. 105, para. 3 shall be settled, when one of the parties is a Bulgarian employee, by Bulgarian courts, and when one of the parties is a foreign citizen, as stipulated by the contract of employment.

(4) The provisions of Bulgarian labour laws shall be applied to matters not settled by the contract of employment.

(5) Employees of subsidiaries and companies with foreign participation under Art. 104, paras 2 and 3 and Art. 105, para. 3 shall be insured for temporary or lasting disability under Bulgarian insurance security legislation.

(6) Subsidiaries of foreign persons and companies with foreign participation[7] under Art. 104, paras 2 and 3 and Art. 105, para 3 shall pay social security installments to the amount of 30 per cent of the labout remuneration to their employees.

(7) This article shall also apply to contracts of employment between foreign persons and employees of representations under Art. 102.

(8) The Council of Ministers may introduce additional conditions for the labour remuneration of Bulgarian citizens employed at subsidiaries, companies with foreign participation and representations of foreign persons.

Art. 122. The stipulations under this section shall apply to foreign persons, subsidiaries and to companies with foreign participation under Art. 104, paras. 2 and 3 and Art. 105, para. 3. In all other cases the general rules for companies under this decree shall apply to the companies with foreign participation.

Section III

ACQUISITION OF IMMOVABLE PROPERTY AND TITLE TO IT

Art. 123. Companies with foreign participation and subsidiaries of foreign persons may be allowed, with a permission from the Council of Ministers, to build and use immovable property on this country's territory for a definite period in view of performing their economic activities.

Art. 124. Upon the termination of a company, the Bulgarian partner has the right to buy with priority the immovable property and the respective title to it. Should the Bulgarian partner refuse to do so, or upon the termination of a subsidiary or company with no Bulgarian participation, the right to buy this property shall belong to the state.

Art. 125. The price of the immovable property and the title to it, transferred under the stipulations of this chapter, shall be negotiated freely between the parties.

Art. 126. Companies with foreign participation and subsidiaries of foreign persons may not own land, sub-soil resources, forests and waters.

---

[7] As corrected on 24 February 1989.

ADDITIONAL ORDINANCES

Para. 1. Persons guilty of concealing data and entering false data in a tax return shall incur criminal liability under Art. 313 of the Criminal Code.

Para. 2. (1) For concealing a taxable revenue, tax authorities shall draw up an act. Failure to submit a tax return within the period mentioned in Art. 116, para. 1 shall also be treated as tax evasion.

(2) Based on the act the chairperson of the municipal people's council executive committee shall impose on the guilty person a fine of five times the amount of the tax due on the concealed income. If the guilty person cannot pay the full amount of the fine, the remainder shall be paid by the company.

(3) The fine ordinance may be appealed against in the order established by the Law on Administrative Violations and Penalties.

Para. 3. (1) The civil relations between foreign persons, subsidiaries and companies with foreign participation and Bulgarian companies and other legal and natural persons shall be regulated under general Bulgarian civil law. Disputes between them shall be settled by Bulgarian courts.

(2) By agreement between the parties, disputes between foreign persons, their production and trade subsidiaries, companies with foreign participation, and Bulgarian companies and other legal persons, may be settled in a court of arbitration chosen by the parties.

Para. 4. The competent authorities under this decree, unless named by a law or decree, shall be named by the Council of Ministers.

PROVISIONAL AND FINAL ORDINANCES

Para. 5. Existing enterprises and associations shall be reorganised into companies in the order of Art. 11.

Para. 6. The following decrees and articles shall be repealed:

1. Articles 1-15 and 17-24 of the Law on Foreign Trade (State Gazette, No 94 of 1969, revised and amended, No. 60 of 1974 and No. 63 of 1975).
2. Decree No. 3420 on the taxes levied on economic organisations (SG, No. 99 of 1987).
3. Decree No. 535 on economic co-operation between Bulgarian legal persons and foreign legal and natural persons (SG, No. 25 of 1980, amended No. 26 of 1988).
4. Art. 19, paras, 2, 3 and 7; Art. 20, para. 2 and Art. 42 of the Law on Total Income Tax (SG, No. 132 of 1950; revised and amended No. 104 of 1952; No. 60 of 1953; No. 15 of 1954; No. 64 of 1955; No. 91 of 1957; No. 90 of 1958; No. 91 of 1960; No. 105 of 1962; SG, No. 99 of 1963; No. 52 of 1965; No. 16 and 52 of 1966; No. 15 and No. 100 of 1967; No. 69 of 1968; No. 60 of 1970; No. 101 of 1972; No. 53 of 1973; amended No. 54 of 1973; No. 36 and No. 93 of 1979; No. 7 of 1982; No. 44 of 1984; No. 79 of 1985 and No. 33 of 1988).
5. Art. 13, para. 4 of Decree No. 2242 on free trade zones (SG, No 55/1987).

Para. 7. Art. 19, para. 1 of the Law on Total Income Tax has been amended as follows:

> The profit of public organisations derived from their economic activity shall be taxed at the rate of 20 per cent, unless otherwise provided by law or decree

Para. 8. The figure "42" in Art. 43 of the Law on Total Income Tax shall be deleted.

Para. 9. The words "and taxes" in Art. 3, para. 1 of Decree No. 2242 on free trade zones shall be deleted.

Para. 10. Pending the introduction of the value added tax, the turnover and profit tax shall be applied at rates fixed by the Council of Ministers.

Para. 11. The stipulations of the Law on Deals in Foreign Currency Valuables and Currency Control (SG, No. 51 of 1966, amended No. 26 of 1968 and No. 92 of 1969) shall not be applied in the cases of free settlements in foreign currency and a free movement of securities envisaged by this decree.

Para. 12. The partnerships formed under Decree No. 535 of 1980 on economic co-operation between Bulgarian legal persons and foreign legal and natural persons shall continue their activities in the established order unless they decide to re-register themselves in accordance with the provisions of this decree.

Para. 13. In the case of discrepancy between existing statutory acts and the provisions of this decree, the latter shall be applied.

Para. 14. The Council of Ministers shall be responsible for the implementation of this decree and shall issue regulations for its application.

Issued in Sofia on 9 January 1989 and stamped with the state seal.

The State Council of the People's Republic of Bulgaria, on the grounds of Art. 94, pt. 2, para. 2 of the Constitution of the People's Republic of Bulgaria, issues the following

DECREE No. 2242

ON FREE TRADE ZONES

(Published in State Gazette No. 55 of 17 July 1987)

Chapter One

GENERAL PROVISIONS

Art. 1. This Decree establishes the regime for setting up free trade zones on the territory of the People's Republic of Bulgaria and the conditions for carrying out productive, commercial and other economic activities in them.

Art. 2. (1) Free trade zones are created to encourage economic initiatives in the manufacture of goods, the performance of services, commercial and other activities necessary for diversifying and increasing export.

(2) The activities listed in para 1 can be effected by foreign juridical and physical persons. These activities may be performed also by Bulgarian self-managing economic organisations through association with foreign juridical and physical persons.

Art. 3. (1) A free trade zone is a part of the territory of the People's Republic of Bulgaria set aside for economic activity which is exempted from customs duties and taxes.[8]

(2) The zone is fenced in and marked with signs in the established order.

(3) If the zone consists of several separate sectors, each sector must be separately fenced and marked.

Art. 4. (1) Zones can be set up in sea or river ports, international airports, transport and forwarding centres, along main highways and railways, as well as in separate industrial and other economic areas.

(2) In the sphere of tourist services, zones can be set up also in other parts of the territory of the People's Republic of Bulgaria.

Art. 5. All payments relating to the activities carried out on the territory of the zones are effected in free convertible currency.

Art. 6. The property of foreign juridical and physical persons in the zones is not subject to any seizure or confiscation by administrative order.

Art. 7. The laws of the People's Republic of Bulgaria and the orders issued in accordance with them are binding on the foreign citizens temporarily residing or working in the zone, except when a law, decree or act of the Council of Ministers provides otherwise.

Chapter Two

SETTING UP FREE TRADE ZONES

Art. 8. (1) Free trade zones are set up by the Council of Ministers on the initiative of state bodies or interested self-managing economic organisations.

---

8 The words "and taxes" were repealed by Decree 56 of 9 January 1989 on Economic Activity.

(2) The Act of the Council of Ministers defines the site and the boundaries of the zone, approves its statute and forms the enterprise which will organise the construction of the zone and will take up its management.

(3) The Act on setting up a zone determines its mode of administrative management by which the administrative services and control are to be effected, including gate, taxation and customs control concerning the performed activities, to ensure observance of the free trade zone regime and the general legislation of the People's Republic of Bulgaria.

Art. 9. (1) The economic enterprise which organises the construction and management of the zone is a juridical person on full self-financing, including in foreign currency.

(2) The enterprise as per para. 1 organises the construction of the basic infrastructure of the zone - transport, power-supply, communications, etc., as well as of facilities of economic, social, living and cultural character, doing it on its own or through Bulgarian economic organisations and banks, on a contractual basis.

Art. 10. (1) The site, buildings and other facilities are used on a lease basis or in any other form of temporary use by contract between the zone-managing enterprise and the interested foreign juridical and physical persons, joint ventures and Bulgarian self-managing economic organisations.

(2) The rent, charges and prices of services are quoted in convertible currency and collected by the zone-managing enterprises.

Art. 11. The workers - Bulgarian citizens - required to perform the activities in the zones are conceded by the zone-managing enterprise.

Art. 12. The enterprises, joint ventures and banks set up on the territory of the zones are registered with the zone administration.

Chapter Three

RULES FOR ECONOMIC ACTIVITY IN FREE TRADE ZONES

Art. 13. (1) Encouraged in the free trade zones is productive, trading and other export-oriented economic activity.

(2) Imported and exported goods and services from and for foreign countries, subject of productive, trading and other economic activity in the zones are exempted from duty. This applies also to the exchange of goods and services between the free trade zones on the territory of the country.

(3) Goods in the sense of para 2 are subject to customs supervision as long as they are stationed in the zones.

(4) The profit from productive, trading and other economic activity in the zone is exempted from taxes.[9]

Art. 14. (1) The import of goods and services from the zone into the country is done on a contractual basis in convertible currency and in accordance with the customs laws of the People's Republic of Bulgaria.

(2) In the events of para 1, the profit from the sale of goods and performance of services is subject to taxation:

1. by 30 per cent for the portion which is transferred abroad;
2. by 20 per cent for the portion which is invested in economic activity within the zone or in joint ventures in the country.

Art. 15. Exports and imports from and into the zone are subject to mandatory declaration at the customs house.

Art. 16. The following activities are prohibited in free trade zones:

---

9 Paragraph (4) was repealed by Decree 56 on Economic Activity.

1. activities prohibited by the laws of the People's Republic of Bulgaria or contradictory to international law and customs;
2. activities incompatible with sanitary requirements or the requirements for protecting the natural environment in the People's Republic of Bulgaria, or with the international conventions of which the People's Republic of Bulgaria is a party, and the recommendations of international organisations in the humanitarian and ecological fields adopted by the country.

Chapter Four

TYPES OF ECONOMIC ACTIVITY

Art. 17. Productive, trading and other related economic activities may be carried out in the free trade zones, namely:

1. organising the manufacture of goods and services on an up-to-date technical and technological level, intended for export;
2. loading, unloading and handling of duty free imported goods earmarked for export;
3. storage and safeguarding of duty free imported goods earmarked for export;
4. handling of duty free imported goods earmarked for export (sorting out, marking, packing, parcelling, etc.);
5. commercial activity, agency and mediation;
6. bunkering ships and other transport vehicles which perform international transport;
7. banking, crediting and other financial operations, insurance and re-insurance of property.

Art. 18. Temporary duty-free import of goods from the zone into the country is allowed in the events of overhaul, processing and other specialised services, as well as for the organising of exhibitions and publicity events.

ADDITIONAL PROVISIONS

Para. 1. The labour relations and social insurance of Bulgarian citizens employed in the zones are subject to the Bulgarian Law.

Para. 2. Permits for the sojourn and the working of foreign nationals in the zones are issued by the competent authorities with priority, as a matter or urgency and under the conditions of the Law on Aliens' sojourn in the People's Republic of Bulgaria.

FINAL STIPULATIONS

Para. 3. The Council of Ministers adopts Regulations on the application of this Decree.

Para. 4. The overall management, coordination and supervision of activities in the free trade zones is entrusted to the Minister of Trade and the Minister of Finance.

Para. 5. The Minister of Trade, the Minister of Finance and the Minister of Transport determine the order of current activity in the free zones.

The implementation of this Decree is entrusted to the Minister of Trade and the Minister of Finance.

CZECHOSLOVAKIA

ACT No. 173/1988

ON ENTERPRISES WITH FOREIGN PROPERTY PARTICIPATION

(8 November 1988)

The Federal Assembly has adopted the following Act:

PART I

GENERAL PROVISIONS

Section 1

The purpose of this Act is to set forth conditions relative to the founding of enterprises where foreign persons participate, and to regulate their status as they carry out economic activities on the territory of the Czechoslovak Socialist Republic.

Section 2

(1) An enterprise with foreign property participation (hereinafter referred to as "enterprise") is a legal person which has its registered office on the territory of the Czechoslovak Socialist Republic and is established by means of a contract concluded between at least one Czechoslovak and one foreign participant.

(2) Only legal persons which are established under Czechoslovak law and have their registered office on the territory of the Czechoslovak Socialist Republic may be Czechoslovak participants in an enterprise.

(3) For the purpose of the present Act, foreign person shall mean a legal person whose registered office is, or a physical person whose domicile is, outside the territory of the Czechoslovak Socialist Republic.

Section 3

The founding, legal form, legal relations and liquidation of the enterprise, the relations arising out of the contract establishing the enterprise (hereinafter referred to as "the contract"), and the settlement of legal issues related therewith, shall be governed by Czechoslovak law. [10]

Section 4

(1) The enterprise is liable with its own assets for the breach of its commitments and other obligations.

(2) The enterprise is not liable for the commitments of the State nor for the commitments of other legal persons, and other legal persons are not liable for commitments of the enterprise; this does not exclude liabilities which arise in accordance with appropriate general rules of law.

10 Act No. 242 of 1949, Coll. on Companies Limited by Shares. Act No. 101 of 1963, Coll. on Legal Relations Arising in International Business Transactions.

PART II

AUTHORIZATION OF CONTRACTS ESTABLISHING AN ENTERPRISE

Section 5

(1) Czechoslovak participants may conclude or amend a contract only on the basis and within the limits of an authorization granted for this purpose.

(2) The authorization to conclude or to amend a contract (hereinafter referred to as "the authorization") shall be given by the central authority of State administration having jurisdiction over the proposed basic line of business of the enterprise. In the area of banking operations the authorization shall be granted by the Czechoslovak State Bank.

(3) If the granting of an authorization lies within the jurisdiction of a central authority of State administration on a Republic level, and the prospective participant has its registered office on the territory of one Republic while the prospective enterprise will have its registered office on the territory of the other Republic, then the decision to grant authorization shall be made by the central authority of State administration of the Republic on whose territory the prospective enterprise will have its registered office.

(4) The establishment of an enterprise does not require authorization under specific rules of law. [11]

Section 6

(1) In the application for an authorization the Czechoslovak participant shall set forth:

(a) its name, location of registered office, and line of business;

(b) the purpose and aims pursued by the founding of the enterprise;

(c) the line of business of the enterprise, its legal form, location of registered office, and name;

(d) the amount of the statutory capital of the enterprise, the amount of the contribution of each participant in the statutory capital, the form and currency in which the contribution will be made, the principles concerning profit distribution and loss coverage, as well as the minimum amount of the reserve fund;

(e) the representation of participants in the organs of the enterprise;

(f) data on the foreign participant;

(g) a technical and economic analysis of the proposed activities of the enterprise.

Section 7

(1) When decisions are made on applications for the authorization under Section 5 hereof, it shall be examined whether conditions exist for the prospective enterprise to effectively contribute to the development of the Czechoslovak national economy and to properly carry out its economic activities. In addition, the proposed ratio between the Czechoslovak and foreign contributions shall be taken into consideration.

(2) Authorization may be granted for economic activities in any branch of national economy, with the exception of those branches which are important for the defence and security of the Czechoslovak Socialist Republic.

(3) The respective central authority of State administration (Section 5 paragraph 1 hereof) shall make a decision on an application, in accordance with the principles of administrative procedures, [12] no later than three (3) months from the date when the application was filed in accordance with Section 6 hereof.

---

11 Act. No. 142/1970, Coll. Section 20 on Foreign Currencies.

12 No. 71 of 1967, Coll. Administrative Procedure Act.

Section 8

The authorization granted under Section 5 hereof shall replace all authorizations necessary for the enterprise under specific rules of law for the carrying out of its economic activities, provided that the authorization under Section 5 is granted by an authority which has the right to grant authorizations to engage in economic activities, and that the authorized type of economic activity of the enterprise includes such activities.

PART III

MANAGEMENT OF THE ENTERPRISE

CHAPTER I

ECONOMIC ACTIVITIES

Section 9

No obligations may be imposed on the enterprise in the State Plan of Economic and Social Development.

Section 10

Legal relations arising out of cooperation between the enterprise and Czechoslovak legal persons shall be governed by the Economic Code, with the exclusion, however, of those provisions which set forth an obligation to conclude, modify or cancel a contract without the consent of the parties, or a right to create, modify or cancel obligations, as well as of those provisions which, by their contents, are not relevant considering the nature of the enterprise, or are inconsistent with its legal standing as defined hereunder. This does not affect the scope of the International Trade Code.

CHAPTER II

FINANCIAL MANAGEMENT

Section 11

The enterprise shall be assessable only for taxes provided for in a law.

Section 12

(1) The enterprise shall establish:

(a) a reserve fund, both in Czechoslovak and foreign currencies, for the covering of losses and risks, and for the financing of fluctuations in the economy of the enterprise,

(b) a cultural and social fund in accordance with general rules of law;

(c) a remunerations fund in accordance with general rules of law.

(2) After the expiration of each calendar year, no less than five (5) per cent of the profits after payment of taxes shall be allocated to the reserve fund until it reaches the amount set forth in the contract.

(3) The use of the cultural and social fund and remunerations fund shall be governed by general rules of law.

(4) After paying taxes and allocating means to the funds under paragraph (1) hereof, the enterprise shall be free to establish a development fund and other funds.

(5) The enterprise may not be deprived of the funds it has established; the enterprise shall independently use the funds for the purposes for which they have been created.

Section 13

Upon payment of the taxes due and allocation of the necessary sums into the funds (Section 12, paragraph 1), the enterprise may use the profits for distribution amongst the participants.

Section 14

(1) The annual balance sheet of the enterprise and its financial statement shall each year be subject to approval by two auditors.

(2) The auditors shall exercise their activities in an independent way, using appropriate professional expertise.

(3) Specific rules governing the functions of the auditors, and their appointment by the respective authority of State administration, shall be enacted by the Federal Ministry of Finance as general rules of law.

CHAPTER III

FOREIGN EXCHANGE MANAGEMENT

Section 15

The enterprise shall be exempt from the duty to offer its own foreign currencies for sale to a foreign exchange bank under specific provisions [13] and, within its approved line of business, it shall have the right freely to dispose of them.

Section 16

The enterprise shall be free to open accounts in foreign currency at a Czechoslovak foreign exchange bank or at a foreign bank.

Section 17

The conversion of Czechoslovak currency into foreign currency and vice versa shall take place at rates fixed by the Czechoslovak State Bank.

Section 18

The enterprise may raise loans in foreign currency from a Czechoslovak foreign exchange bank; from a foreign bank it can raise loans only with the approval of the Czechoslovak State Bank.

13 Section 15 paragraph (1) (b) of the Foreign exchange Act. No. 142 of 1970, Coll.

CHAPTER IV

SOCIAL – ECONOMIC INFORMATION

Section 19

The enterprise must

(a) set up, in compliance with the respective general legal rules applicable to Czechoslovak organizations whose line of business is similar to that of the enterprise, a system of social-economic information;

(b) keep accounts in Czechoslovak currency in compliance with the respective general rules of law; possible exceptions from these rules, based on the different nature of the enterprise or its legal standing under this Act, may be granted to the enterprise by the Federal Ministry of Finance;

(c) supply the respective authorities with the accounting and statistical data in the extent and manner and within the time periods set forth in general rules of law.

PART IV

TRANSFER OF FUNDS ABROAD

Section 20

(1) In the event that the enterprise is liquidated or the foreign participant's share in the enterprise is terminated or reduced, the foreign participant has the right, up to the amount of his share in the statutory capital, freely to transfer abroad, in the currency in which the share was contributed, the proceeds of his share.

(2) From the currency reserves of the enterprise, the foreign participant may transfer abroad its share in the profits of the enterprise and, if the enterprise is liquidated or the foreign participant's share in the enterprise is terminated or reduced, that part of his share in the assets of the enterprise which exceeds his share in the statutory capital.

Section 21

(1) Persons employed by the enterprise whose domicile is abroad shall be free to transfer abroad their incomes earned in connection with their employment with the enterprise.

(2) The enterprise shall be free to transfer abroad sums destined to cover social insurance contributions in favour of such persons on its staff whose domicile is abroad, or to transfer these sums in accordance with the instructions of such persons, provided that the insurance is not contracted in the Czechoslovak Socialist Republic. For the purposes of this Act social insurance shall mean insurance covering illness or pregnancy, insurance for child benefits, accident and old age insurance, and unemployment insurance.

(3) The enterprise shall contract abroad retirement pension insurances for those persons on its staff whose domicile is not in the Czechoslovak Socialist Republic.

(4) All payments under the preceding paragraphs may be made only from the currency reserves of the enterprise.

Section 22

(1) The property of the enterprise on the territory of the Czechoslovak Socialist Republic may be expropriated or its property rights may be restricted only on the basis of law.

(2) If measures under paragraph (1) hereof are taken, the foreign participant shall receive a prompt compensation corresponding to the actual value of its property at the time when the property was affected by these measures; the compensation shall be freely transferable abroad in the currency in which the foreign participant paid its contribution to the statutory capital of the enterprise or, in other cases, in the currency of the country in which the foreign participant has its registered office or domicile.

PART V

LIQUIDATION OF THE ENTERPRISE

Section 23

(1) The enterprise shall be terminated through liquidation. The purpose of the liquidation is to make a balance of the property relations of the enterprise being liquidated.

(2) If the debts of the enterprise exceed its assets, it shall be liquidated in accordance with Sections 352-354 of the Civil Procedure Code. [14]

Section 24

(1) The enterprise shall solicit that an entry be made in the Enterprise Register of its liquidation and of the appointment of a liquidator. During the time when it is being liquidated it shall add to its name the words "in liquidation".

(2) The organs of the enterprise shall cease to exercise their functions on the day when the name of the liquidator is entered in the Enterprise Register. The liquidator shall have the right to act in the name of the enterprise in matters connected with the liquidation.

Section 25

(1) The enterprise shall prepare a balance sheet up to the date of the commencement of the liquidation, and shall remit it to the liquidator and to the respective authorities.

(2) Within thirty (30) days from the date when his name was entered in the Enterprise Register, the liquidator shall prepare an initial financial statement up to the date of the commencement of the liquidation, and shall remit it to the participants, together with a liquidation plan, a liquidation budget, and an inventory list made at an extraordinary inventory of the assets of the enterprise on the date of the commencement of the liquidation.

(3) During the liquidation, the liquidator shall, among other things,

(a) transfer all available financial means to one Czechoslovak banking institution;

(b) bring current business matters of the enterprise to completion;

(c) pay all taxes and dues;

(d) settle all obligations and claims;

(e) sell the assets of the enterprise in the most economic and speedy manner, or dispose of them, in accordance with the decision of the participants, in another way;

(f) present to the participants quarterly and annual reports on the progress of the liquidation, with accompanying quarterly and annual balance sheets.

---

14 Civil Procedure Code Act No. 99 of 1963, Coll., as amended on later occasions.

Section 26

(1) The liquidator shall prepare a balance sheet up to the date of completion of the liquidation, and shall submit it, together with the final report on the carrying out of the liquidation, for the approval of the participants.

(2) Upon examination and approval of the balance sheet by the participants, and upon paying the taxes due, the liquidator shall:

(a) dispose of the balance left in accordance with the decision of the participants;

(b) place all written records and written accounting materials in safe custody;

(c) inform the court of the completion of the liquidation, together with an application on the removal of the name of the enterprise from the Enterprise Register.

PART VI

GENERAL, TRANSITIONAL AND FINAL PROVISIONS

Section 27

The provisions of this Act shall apply only if an international treaty binding the Czechoslovak Socialist Republic does not provide otherwise.

Section 28

The Government of the Czechoslovak Socialist Republic may determine cases where a contract establishing the enterprise may be concluded, amended or modified without an authorization provided for in Section 5 hereof, or may set up different rules governing the procedures on granting such an authorization.

Section 29

Enterprises established in accordance with rules in force prior to the entering into force of the present Act shall be deemed to have been established hereunder.

Section 30

Section 389a of the Economic Code is hereby repealed.

Section 31

This Act shall enter into force on 1 January 1989.

ACT No. 243/1949

ON COMPANIES LIMITED BY SHARES

(17 November 1949)

The National Assembly of the Czechoslovak Republic has adopted the following Act:

Section 1

(1) Where the basic capital of a company is divided into shares (stocks) and the shareholders are not responsible for its liabilities, the company shall be a company limited by shares (hereinafter referred to as "the company").

(2) The company shall have the capacity to acquire rights and to enter into obligations.

Section 2

(1) The shares may be either in the name of a holder or on the bearer.

(2) Unless the articles of the company provide otherwise, the shares in the name of a shareholder cannot be transferred to another person.

(3) Transfers by endorsement shall be governed by the provisions of the Bills of Exchange Act.

Section 3

In order that a company is validly created, the following conditions shall be fulfilled:

a) an authorization by State shall be obtained;

b) its articles shall be approved; and

c) the company shall be entered into the register of companies.

Section 4

(1) The Minister concerned, according to the stated objectives of the company, acting in agreement with the State Planning Authority, shall have the power to grant authorizations and to approve articles of a company under Section 3 hereof.

(2) The same shall apply to approvals of the articles of a company, if the objectives clause of the articles is to be modified.

(3) For other modifications of articles, a mere approval by the Ministry concerned shall suffice.

Section 5

The articles of the company shall contain (but shall not be limited to) the following data, to wit:

(i) name and seat of the company

(ii) objectives of the company

(iii) basic capital and individual shares as well as the manner of payment thereof

(iv) statement of the rights and duties of the shareholders

(v) constitution of, and composition of, the bodies of the company as well as statement of their respective powers

(vi) representation of the company and signing on its behalf

(vii) manner and place of publication of notices by the company

(viii) convocation of the general meetings, voting on such meetings and adopting of resolutions thereon

(ix) distribution of profits

(x) appointment of liquidators of the company in case the company is wound up

(xi) affiliated companies

(xii) supervision by State authorities.

Section 6

The name of the company shall mention the fact that a company limited by shares is involved.

Section 7

Until the enactment of a new Companies Register Act, companies limited by shares shall be entered into the Commercial (Business) Register. The following data shall be entered into the Register: name and seat of the company, its objectives, its basic capital and individual shares, persons authorized to act on behalf thereof and manner of such representation, procuration and affiliations.

Section 8

(1) A shareholder shall have a *pro rata* share in the assets of the company.

(2) During the existence of the company, no shareholder can claim that the paid-in sums be returned to him. He has only the right to a share in the profits of the company as determined in the articles thereof.

Section 9

(1) The following bodies shall be constituted in every company, to wit: board of directors, board of auditors and general meeting of shareholders.

(2) The articles of the company may provide for the constitution of other bodies.

Section 10

(1) The board of directors shall be the managing and representing body of the company.

(2) The powers of the board of directors may be devolved by the latter, either wholly or partially, onto bodies constituted under Section 9, paragraph (2) hereof.

Section 11

The board of auditors shall supervise all activities of the company.

Section 12

(1) The shareholders shall exercise their powers and rights of members on the general meetings.

(2) Unless vested in other bodies hereunder or under the articles of the company, the general meeting of shareholders shall be vested with all powers and rights relating to the management of the company.

(3) In order to be valid a resolution of the general meeting adopting a modification of the articles of the company, shall be approved by the respective State authorities (Section 4, paragraphs 2 and 3 hereof). In addition, such modification shall be entered into the register.

Section 13

(1) A company may be wound up:

(a) by a resolution passed by the general assembly

(b) by a measure taken by the State authority (Section 4, paragraph 1 hereof), if taken in the interest of public policy

(c) by declaration of bankruptcy.

(2) When passing a resolution on the winding up of the company, the general meeting of shareholders may determine at the same time that the assets of the company be transferred onto another company or a peoples cooperative in consideration of shares in that company or cooperative. The merger can take effect at once, provided the creditors of the company agree. If no agreement is given, the merger shall not take effect unless and until the debts of the creditors of the company to be wound up are settled or otherwise secured.

(3) If a company is to be wound up under paragraph (1) (a) and (b) hereof, an authorization by the State authority under Section 4, paragraph (1) hereof shall be required.

Section 14

(1) Except as stated in Section 13, paragraph (1) (c) and paragraph (2) hereof, a liquidation of the assets of the company shall follow its winding up. Such liquidation shall be attended to by liquidators appointed in accordance with the respective provisions of the articles. If the company is dissolved on hand of a measure taken by the respective authority (Section 13, paragraph 1 (b) hereof), the same authority may, at the same time, appoint liquidators to carry out such liquidation.

(2) No monies must be distributed to the shareholders prior to the settlement of the liabilities or giving security in respect of such liabilities, of the company.

(3) Upon application by the board of directors, the winding up of a company shall be entered into the register of companies. In addition, the name of the liquidators and the manner in which they shall represent the company and sign on its behalf shall also be entered.

(4) Upon completion of the liquidation, the liquidators shall apply for the company to be struck off the register.

Section 15

Members on the board of directors or board of auditors and in other bodies (Section 9 hereof) or liquidators (Section 14, paragraph 1 hereof) shall exercise due care in conducting the business of the company. They shall be jointly and severaly liable for damage, if any, caused by their negligence.

Section 16

Any company shall be subject to supervision by State authorities. The supervision shall be exercised by the ministry concerned, in accordance with the objects of the company.

Section 17

(1) Companies limited by shares, created under the State Organization on Foreign Trade and International Forwarding Act, No. 119 of 28 April 1948 shall be considered as companies limited by shares created hereunder.

(2) Other companies limited by shares shall apply for a State authorization under Section 3 (a) and (b) hereof and for the approval of their articles, modified so as to meet the requirements hereunder, within a term to be fixed by a Governmental Decree.

(3) Companies limited by shares which fail to do so or which do not obtain the necessary authorizations and/or approvals, shall be wound up under Section 13, paragraph (1) (b) hereof.

Section 18

Private companies limited by shares may be transformed into companies limited by shares hereunder, provided they apply for such transformation and obtain a State authorization and approval of their articles under Section 4, paragraph (1) hereof within six months of the date of effectivity hereof; in other cases, private companies limited by shares shall be dissolved. Their liquidation shall be governed by the statutory provisions valid until now.

Section 19

(1) Upon the present Act acquiring effectivity, the following statutory provisions shall be abolished or their provisions contrary to any provision hereof shall become not applicable, more particularly:

(i) Articles 173 to 249 of the Commercial Code of 17 December 1862 No./1, Imperial Acts of 1863

(ii) Sections 147 to 222 of the Statutory Article XXXVII of 1875 (Commercial Code)

(iii) Sections 97 to 100 of the Private Companies Limited by Shares Act of 6 March 1906, No. 58, Imperial Acts

(iv) Section 3 and 4 of the Decree of the Government of the Czechoslovak Republic of 27 July 1920, No. 465, Collection on the formation of companies limited by shares, on the increase of basic capital thereof and the creation of affiliated companies thereof, as well as provision of Chapter II of the Act No. 82, Slovak Collection of 19 May 1942 on the compulsory acquisition of State debentures and on the creation of special reserve funds, provided they apply to companies limited by shares and private companies limited by shares

(v) Decrees by the ministries of interior, finance, trade, justice and agriculture of 20 September 1899 No. 175, Imperial Acts (Share Regulation)

(vi) Governmental Decree of 16 October 1924, No. 211, coll. modifying Section 44 of the Share Regulation

(vii) Decree of the Minister of Justice of 23 May 1944 No. 134, Coll., on the restriction of general meetings of companies limited by shares.

(2) Provisions of the Imperial Patent of 26 November 1852, No. 253, Imperial Acts (the so called old Associations Act) cannot apply to companies established hereunder (Sections 3, 17, paragraphs 2 and 18).

Section 20

The present Act shall acquire effectivity upon its publication. All members of the government shall implement same.

ACT No. 101

ON LEGAL RELATIONS ARISING IN INTERNATIONAL BUSINESS TRANSACTIONS

(International Trade Code)

(4 December 1963)

Excerpts

CHAPTER II

JOINT PROVISIONS

PART I

Persons

Section 8

(1) Legal persons are enterprises and other organizations, if the law under which they have been incorporated confers upon them the capacity to enjoy rights and to have obligations.

(2) Foreign trade corporations and other economic organizations that are entered into the corporate register are deemed *inter alia* to be Czechoslovak legal persons. They are considered as merchants within the meaning of this Act.

(3) The State also has the capacity to enjoy rights and to have obligations.

Section 9

(1) The legal status of legal persons is governed by the provisions of the law under which they have been incorporated, or by their articles and or memoranda of association promulgated under such provisions; they shall *inter alia* set the corporate name, designate the persons authorized to act on their behalf and indicate the manner in which such legal person will cease to exit.

Section 10

Unless otherwise provided in this Act or in special regulations, members of a legal person, if it is composed of members, are not personally responsible for its obligations.

Section 11

Czechoslovak legal persons, particularly foreign trade and international forwarding corporations, are liable for the breach of their obligations with their assets and the State is not liable for the obligations of such jurisdic persons; these legal persons are not liable for the debts of the State or of another legal persons.

Section 12

Data entered into the corporate register in which a legal person has been inscribed shall be effective *erga omnes*. If an indication, which had to be recorded under the law of the country where such register is kept, is omitted, it cannot be pleaded against third parties, unless such third parties knew or at least should have known of it. [15]

CHAPTER IV

SPECIAL PROVISIONS RELATING TO CERTAIN OBLIGATIONS

PART XIX

Contract of Association

Section 625

Basic provision

Under a contract of association two or more persons undertake to combine their activities or property values to achieve a certain economic purpose.

Section 626

Every partner is bound to exercise activities aiming at the achievement of the economic purpose of the association. Mutual rights and obligations of the partners in exercising their activities shall be governed *mutatis mutandis* by the provisions relating to the mandate where the activities are exercised for remuneration.

Section 627

Every partner in the association must refrain from any activity which would prevent from or obstruct the achievement of the economic purpose for which the contract of association was concluded.

---

15 Under Czechoslovak law, legal persons must be entered in the corporate register (Section 8 paragraph (2)). The register is kept in accordance with the provisions of the Ordinance of the Ministry of Justice concerning the corporate register No. 114/1964, C. of L. of June 14th, 1964. According to the said Ordinance, the following data should be entered into the register: the mode of establishment of the legal person, the day of its establishment, its corporate name, its registered office, the subject of its activity, its authorized agents, the names of officers who were granted procuration, as well as the manner in which these persons sign for and on behalf of the legal person.

Section 628

Damage which a partner caused to the association (to the partners) by committing a breach of his obligations, may not be set off against the gains he has realized fo achieving the economic purpose of the association.

Section 629

Every partner has the right to inspect the economic standing of the association.

Section 630

Insofar as the nature of the matter admits it, a partner shall be liable for the defects in his things brought into the association in the same way as the seller. The provisions relating to lease shall govern *mutatis mutandis* cases where things let for gratuitous use are defective, as well as to the determination of rights and obligations in respect of the maintenance and use of such things.

Section 631

The partners in the association shall distribute their gains in proportion to their shares and contributions and the extent of their activities with which they contributed to the achievement of the economic purpose of the association. Losses shall be borne by all partners in proportion to their shares or contributions.

Section 632

A contract of association shall cease to exist:

(a) upon the achievement of the economic purpose for which it was concluded or if the achievement of such economic purpose has become impossible;

(b) if all property values which were to serve the achievement of the purpose of the association have been lost;

(c) upon the lapse of time for which the contract was concluded;

(d) by agreement of all the partners.

Section 633

(1) Every partner may withdraw from the association; however, he may not do so at an inconvenient time or if by doing so he would frustrate or substantially hinder the achievement of the economic purpose of the association by the remaining partners.

(2) A partner may withdraw from the association for serious reasons regardless of the agreed term for notice. However, in such event the provision of paragraph 1 shall be applicable.

Section 634

(1) When the associaition ceases to exist, every partner shall be entitled to the return of the things which he made available for gratuitous use for the purpose of the association.

(2) The property claims of the partners in the association may not be settled prior to settling or securing the creditors' claims.

Section 635

The obligations of the partners in the association, which were established during their membership in such association, shall continue to exist even after withdrawal of such partners from the association or after the association has ceased to exist.

Association as a legal person

Section 636

An association becomes a legal person if this is stipulated in the contract and if the association is entered in the register where legal persons are registered. The entry must contain at least the name of the association, its registered office, the shares of the individual members, and the officers authorized to act on behalf and for the association.

Section 637

(1) The shares of the members, if consisting of money or other things determined generically, shall become the property of the association. Shares consisting of things determined individually shall be in the gratuitous use of the association.

(2) The value of the share in the case of things given for gratuitous use to the association shall be assessed according to the amount which the member of the association would obtain when leasing such things at the place where they are used for the purpose of the association.

Section 638

Unless otherwise indicated in the register in which the association is entered, the members of the association shall be liable for the association's obligations only to the extent of their respective shares.

Section 639

Property acquired in the course of the exercise of the common activities belong to the association.

Section 640

The association acts through its members or the person entered in the register as officer of the association. The majority of members decides on matters of the association; in case of doubt, it shall be presumed that each member has one vote.

Section 641

An association shall cease to exist only when it has been struck off the register in which it was entered.

Section 642

(1) When the association ceases to exist, every member shall be entitled to the restoration of the property values he had brought into the association and which became the property of the association, or to the repayment of their price, or, if the property of the association is not sufficient, to the repayment of a proportionate share of such price. After the settlement of all claims in accordance with the shares brought into, the remaining money will be distributed in accordance with the principles set out in Section 631.

(2) The provisions of paragraph 1 shall apply *mutatis mutandis* in the assessment of claims of a member who withdraws from the association.

ACT No. 99

CIVIL PROCEDURE CODE

(4 December 1963)

Excerpts

PART FIVE

EXECUTION OF A DECISION

CHAPTER SIX

LIQUIDATION OF PROPERTY

Liquidation Order

Section 352

(1) The court shall order the liquidation of the property of the liable party on the motion of an entitled party, if the liable party is insolvent.

(2) In the liquidation order, the presiding judge shall invite all those who have a claim against the liable party to register for the distribution of the proceeds.

(3) A liquidation order voids the community of property of husband and wife.

Carrying out the Liquidation

Section 353

The court shall liquidate the property of the liable party by selling all of his property, applying, where appropriate, the provisions governing assignment of claims (Sections 303 to 320) and the sale of movable and immovable property (Section 321 to 338).

Distribution of the Proceeds

Section 354

(1) The presiding judge shall order a session to be held for the purpose of distributing the proceeds of the liquidation of the property of the liable party.

(2) Individual claims shall be successively satisfied from the proceeds of the liquidation in the following order:

(a) claims to the reimbursement of the costs of the liquidation;

(b) claims with respect of which restriction of the transfer of immovable property was registered with a state notarial office;

(c) claims to arrears in alimony;

(d) other claims.

(3) If the total amount of the claims in the individual categories (paragraph 2 (a) to (d)) exceeds the sum left for distribution, such claims shall be satisfied proportionately; only in the case of claims with respect of which restriction of the transfer of immovable property

was registered, the order of such claims shall be decisive and shall be governed by the day of the registration of the restriction; if restriction of the transfer of immovable property was registered on the same day with respect of several claims, such claims shall be of the same order and shall be satisfied proportionately.

HUNGARY

ACT VI of 1988
ON ECONOMIC ASSOCIATIONS

(Company Act)

Excerpts

PART ONE

INTRODUCTORY PROVISIONS

CHAPTER I

GENERAL PROVISIONS

Section 1

(1) The present Act shall regulate the foundation of economic associations, their organization, the functioning of their bodies, and the rights, obligations and responsibilities of the members of associations, as well as the termination of associations.

(2) Economic associations may, in their own name, acquire rights and enter commitments; in particular, they may acquire property, conclude contracts, bring actions and actions may be brought against them.

Section 2

(1) An economic association may not be established except in the manner and form described in the present Act.

(2) Economic associations not qualifying as legal entities are: the unlimited partnership and the deposit partnership. Economic associations possessing legal entity are: the union, the joint enterprise, the limited liability company and the company limited by shares.

Section 3

Not included under the purview of the present Act are: the co- operatives, the specialized groups (teams), the water management associations, the economic working communities (worktemas) having legal entity, the social associations, as well as other personal unions by natural persons oriented towards a purpose not requiring economic activity; to all these special statutory rules shall apply. The provisions of the Civil Code shall govern civil-law associations.

Section 4

(1) An economic association - apart from exceptions listed in the present Act - may be founded by the State, by legal entities, by economic associations not possessing legal entity as well as natural persons (both nationals and foreign) for carrying on a businesslike, common economic activity or for promoting same; the said persons and entities may join an acting economic association as members.

(2) Inasmuch as a definite activity is reserved by an Act, law-decree or decree of the Council of Ministers for the State, a State-organ or State-owned economic entity, an economic association shall not pursue such activity unless at least one of its members is authorized thereto.

(3) Of economic associations only those operating in the form of a company limited by shares may carry on banking and insurance activities.

(4) For the purpose of the present Act the term natural person shall denote a human being regardless of his/her citizenship; and a foreigner shall be a natural person or legal entity declared a foreigner by the statutory rules relating to foreign exchange management.

Section 5

Unless an Act provides otherwise: the foundation of an economic association requires at least two members.

Section 6

(1) A natural person shall be a member with unlimited liability in not more than one economic association.

(2) A civil-law association may not be member in an economic association and may be not founder of a company limited by shares.

(3) An unlimited partnership or a deposit partnerhsip may not be a member with unlimited liability in another similar association.

(4) Only legal entities may be members of a union or joint enterprise.

Section 7

(1) Foreigners may be founders of an economic association or members of it only if they control a firm (corporation) under their national laws, or else they have been entered, according to their national laws, in a company (or other economic) register. Any foreign natural person or legal entity may be a shareholder.

(2) Conditions as to the participation of foreigners, differing from this Act, may be stipulated by international agreement.

Section 8

(1) The joint permit of the Minister of Finance and the Minister of Trade is required for the foundation of an economic association that has foreign majority or is fully foreign-owned, for the conversion of an entity into such company, or to the acquisition of a majority foreign interest in the association. The said permit shall include the permission of the foreign exchange authority. Inasmuch as the corresponding application is not rejected within 90 days from filing, the permit shall be considered as granted.

(2) In case of a foreign participation lower than that contained in para (1) neither the permit of the foreign exchange authority nor any other permit shall be required for the foundation of an economic association or for the participation in same.

Section 9

(1) The foreign interest in an economic association enjoys full protection and safety.

(2) The part due to the foreigner from the profit of the company, as well as the sum due to the foreigner in case of liquidation of the association or of partial or total sale of the foreigner's share, shall be freely transferable abroad, without the permit of the foreign exchange authority, subject to the money cover available with the company the transfer is to be effected according to the foreigner's relevant instruction and in the paid in currency.

(3) Special benefits and particular economic terms in favour of foreigners will be established by a special Act.

Section 10

(1) An economic association which has exclusively natural persons as members may not employ more than five hundred people.

(2) The provisions of para (1) shall not apply to economic association owned in full or in majority by foreigners.

Section 11

(1) The Court of Registration shall exercise supervision of legality of economic associations.

(2) In the framework of supervision of legality, the Court of Registration will control, whether the deed of association (rules and regulations), as well as the other instruments relating to the organization and operation of the company are in conformity with the statutory rules; and whether the resolutions of the bodies of the association do not infringe the norms governing the organization and operation of such associations, or the deed of association (rules and regulations), as well as the contents of the said other instruments.

(3) The supervision of legality does not cover such matters which come within the purview of other court or public administrative proceedings.

(4) The proceedings of the Court of Registration regarding economic associations shall be governed by the rules relating to the registration of firms by the court, with the additions contained in the present Act.

Section 12

In the economic associations the trade union's rights shall be applied according to the Labour Code and to the provisions of the statutory rules issued on the strength of the former.

Section 13

(1) In every joint enterprise, limited liability company and company limited by shares, where the number of full-time employees is above two hundred persons on an annual average, the employees of the association shall participate in the monitoring of the association's operation through the Supervisory Board.

(2) In the cases defined in para (1) above, one-third of the members of the Supervisory Board shall be elected by the employees from among themselves. Election is to take place at the next session of the Board of Directors' Meeting of the Members (Assembly) or General Assembly. This rule shall be applicable in a corresponding manner also when the number of full-time employees has become less than two hundred.

Section 14

It is forbidden to embody the membership rights in any security - except in the case of companies limited by shares. Any security drawn up in defiance of this prohibition shall be null and void and its authors shall be jointly and severally liable for any damage arising therefrom.

Section 17

The provisions of the Civil Code shall apply to the material and personal relations of the companies and their members, provided these are not regulated by the present Act.

Section 18

In the legal disputes relating to the deed of association the Permanent Arbitration Court, attached to the Hungarian Chamber of Commerce, shall have competence, provided the parties have so stipulated in the deed of association (or articles of association).

CHAPTER II

COMMON RULES RELATING TO ALL ECONOMIC ASSOCIATIONS

Title 1

The foundation of an economic association

Section 19

(1) The foundation of the economic association requires the existence of a deed of association (in the case of a company limited by shares: Memorandum or Articles of Association).

(2) The deed of association shall be incorporated in a deed to be signed by all members and endorsed by an attorney-at-law or legal counsel. This rule shall also apply to any amendment of the deed.

(3) The necessity of endorsement as per para (2) shall also apply to companies limited by shares.

Section 20

The members are free to determine the contents of the deed of association - within the limits set by the present Act and other statutory rules. In the case of uniform consensus, they may depart from the provisions of the Act relating to the deed of association, except when such departure is prohibited by the present Act.

Section 21

(1) The deed of association shall determine the following:

(a) the name and seat of the company,

(b) the members, including their names (name of firm) and domiciles (seats),

(c) the range of activity of the company,

(d) the size of the company's assets, the date and manner when they must be made available,

(e) everything else prescribed by the present Act in a binding manner for the individual forms of association.

(2) When any of the conditions listed in para (1) is missing such deed of association shall be null and void.

(3) When the deed of association fails to make a provision concerning the duration (time) of the economic association, such company is deemed to have been formed for an indefinite period.

Section 22

(1) The assets of the economic association are made available by the members who will jointly share the profit, or the increment of the property (hereinafter: profit) and jointly bear the losses, or the decrease of the property (hereinafter: loss) in the manner determined by the present Act.

(2) Upon foundation, the assets of the association (company) consist of the money deposits (cash contributions) of the members as well as of the non-monetary deposits (contributions) made available by them. The non-monetary contribution may consist of any negotiable thing having a property value, intellectual creation or valuable right (title).

(3) A member making a non-monetary contribution shall bear liability, during five years from the date of such contribution, that the value of his contribution equalled, at the time of deposit, the value indicated in the deed of association.

Section 23

(1) The Court of Registration must be notified of the foundation of the association (company) within thirty days from the conclusion of the deed of association, or of the adoption of the articles of association, for the sake of registration and publication.

(2) The notification filed with the Court of Registration shall contain all data prescribed by the statutory rules on the registration of firms by the Court. The notification must be accompanied by the documents mentioned in the said statutory rules.

(3) The Court of Registration must be equally notified of any change in the registered data within thirty days of such change.

Section 24

(1) The company is deemed to have been established by virtue of its registration in the Trade Register - with retroactive effect to the date of the conclusion of the deed of association, or the adoption of the articles of association in the case of a company limited by shares. Registration may not be denied except in case of infringement of law.

(2) The fact of registration, the data so registered as well as any change of the latter are published in the official gazette - unless the present Act provides otherwise.

Title 2

Executive officers, Members of the Supervisory board, Auditors

Section 28

Executive officers are: in case of a union and a joint enterprise: the director; in case of a limited liability company: the managing directors; in case of a company limited shares: the members of the board of directors.

Section 30

The executive officers, the members of the Supervisory Board (in the following: S.B.) and the auditors shall be appointed for a definite period of not more than five years; they may be re-elected and re-called at any time.

Section 36

(1) The S.B. controls the management of the company. In the framework of such control it may request the executive officers and other leading functionaries of the company to provide a report or information; it may examine the books and other documents of the association or entrust an expert with such examination.

(2) The S.B. is held to examine every major report submitted to the supreme body of the association (company), further the balance-sheet and the inventory of property. The chairman shall disclose the findings of such examination; without such report no valid decision may be taken on the said reports, or the balance-sheet and the distribution of the profit.

Section 39

(1) It may be provided in the deed of association that the control of the management be entrusted to an auditor(s), instead of, or in addition to, the S.B.

(2) The appointment of auditor(s) in addition to the S.B. is compulsory in the case of a company limited by shares, a one-man company and in a limited liability company having a primary capital in excess of fifty million forints.

Section 41

(1) The auditor may inspect the books of the company, may request information from the executive officers and the employees of the company, may check the cash, the stock of securities and goods, as well as the contracts and the bank account of the company. He may be present at the meetings of the supreme bodies of the company and of the S.B.; he must be present at the General Assembly of the company limited by shares.

(2) The auditor shall examine every report - in particular the balance-sheet and the inventory of property - submitted to the supreme body of the company from the aspect whether they contain truthful data, or whether they meet the provisions of statutory rules, and he shall make his opinion known. Without his declaration to this effect, no valid decision can be taken on such document.

Title 5

Termination of the company; final account

Termination of the company

Section 46

(1) The company will cease to exist when

(a) the period of duration in the deed (articles) of association has expired or another condition of termination has been fulfilled;

(b) the company decides upon its discontinuance without a successor;

(c) it merges with another company, dissociates therefrom or is transformed into another company form;

(d) the number of the members has declined to one (with the exception of limited liability company and the company limited by shares) and no new member is announced to the Court of Registration within 6 months;

(e) the Court of Registration has declared its termination;

(f) the court dissolves it in the course of a winding-up procedure;

(g) termination is prescribed by the provisions of the present Act relating to the particular forms of association.

(2) The company shall cease by cancellation from the Trade Register. Cancellation is made public in the official gazette.

Final account

Section 47

When a company is terminated without a successor, a final account (liquidation) must take place with the exception of the winding-up proceedings initiated because of permanent insolvency. The liquidation shall be carried out according to the statutory rule on winding-up procedure - unless the present Act provides otherwise.

Section 48

(1) The liquidation is carried out by the executive officers of the company - with the exception of the cases defined in paras. (2) and (3) hereunder.

(2) Members representing at least one tenth of the votes may petition the Court of Registration to appoint another person as liquidator.

(3) When the termination of a company is declared (by court), the liquidator is appointed by the Court of Registration.

(4) With the exception of the cases defined in para. (2) - (3) above, the company must notify the Court of Registration of the start of the liquidation procedure, and of the person of the liquidator - for the sake of entry and publication.

Section 49

When appointing a liquidation, the Court of Registration

(a) may only appoint a natural person who meets the requirements set by the present Act in respect of executive officers;

(b) may not appoint a natural person or legal entity against whom (which) the majority of the company members raises objection.

Section 50

Upon designation (appointment) of the liquidator, the right of the company's executive officers, representatives and employees to sign the firm's name ceases: their rights and duties are exercised by the liquidator.

Section 51

(1) The liquidator assesses the financial situation of the company, prepares the list of creditors, compiles the company's final balance-sheet and submits all these to the supreme body of the association for approval.

(2) If, in the liquidator's judgement, the company assets do not even cover the claims of the known creditors, he is under obligation to initiate a winding-up procedure.

(3) In a winding-up procedure started due to of the economic association's lasting insolvency, the creditors of the company shall enjoy priority concerning the company's assets *erga* the creditors of the members.

Section 52

(1) The liquidator shall

(a) draft a final balance-sheet and submit it to the economic association's supreme body for approval, next

(b) announce the termination of the procedure to the Court of Registration and request the cancellation of the company from the Trade Register.

(2) The balance-sheet shall be accompanied by the report of the Supervisory Board or one auditor, if there is any.

Section 53

Any dispute between the liquidator and the company-members shall be adjudged by the Court.

Section 54

The claims against economic association or its members, arising from the liabilities imposed on the company, shall expire within five years from the termination of the association or of the membership, - unless a statutory rule fixes a shorter statutory limitation for a claim.

PART TWO

THE PARTICULAR ECONOMIC ASSOCIATIONS (COMPANY FORMS)

CHAPTER IV

THE LIMITED LIABILITY COMPANY

Section 155

(1) The limited liability company (hereinafter: LLC) is an association constituted with a primary stock consisting of predetermined primary stakes, in which the member's liability towards the company is limited to providing his primary stake and other material contributions - if any - defined in the deed of association. The member is not liable for the obligations of the company.

(2) The denomination "limited liability company" or its abbreviation (in Hungarian: *kft*) must be indicated in the company's firm-name.

Foundation of the company

Section 156

(1) An LLC may be founded by a single member (one-man-company).

(2) It is prohibited to recruit members through public appeal.

Section 157

(1) In the deed of association - in addition to the matters listed in Section 21, para. (1) - the following shall be defined:

(a) the amount of the primary stock and each member's primary stake;

(b) if any money stake is not fully paid: the manner and date of payment;

(c) the extent of the voting rights and the procedure to be followed in case of equality of votes;

(d) the first managing director; in case of several managing directors, the system of management, representation and the manner of signing the firm's name;

(e) when the constitution of a Supervisory Board is compulsory, the members of the first Board;

(f) when the appointment of an auditor is compulsory, the person of the first auditor.

(2) Depending on necessity, the deed of association may define the following:

(a) the non-pecuniary contribution and their values;

(b) other valuable performances to be made by the members (subsidiary contributions), the terms thereof, as well as the amount of liquidated damages payable in case of non-performance or not suitable performance of the subsidiary contributions;

(c) powers for the meeting of the members to prescribe additional payments;

(d) prohibition of the devolution of the business share in case of succession; prohibition of dividing the business share;

(e) permission of the withdrawal of the business share;

(f) vesting each member with the powers of management and representation;

(g) limitation of the powers of representation of the managing partners;

(h) creation of a Supervisory Board, when such is not mandatory;

(i) appointment of an auditor when such is not mandatory.

(3) The foundation of a one-man LLC requires the issue of a deed of foundation. As to the contents of the deed of foundation, the rules relating to the deed of association are applicable - in a corresponding manner. Wherever the present Act mentions "deed of association", the deed of foundation is meant to be included.

Section 158

(1) The primary stock of the company consists of the primary stakes of the individual members.

(2) The primary stock shall not be less than one million forints.

Section 159

(1) The primary stakes of the members may differ, however they may be not less than a hundred-thousand forints per member. Each primary stake must be expressed in forints and exactly divisible by ten thousand.

(2) Each member has one primary stock; however, a primary stock may be owned by several persons.

Section 160

The amount of money stakes when founding a LLC shall not be less than thirty per cent of the primary stock, and not less than five hundred-thousand forints.

Section 161

(1) The foundation of the LLC must be announced to the Court of Registration - for the purposes of entry and publication. The announcement must be made jointly by all managing partners. In case of a one-man company the Court must be notified that the company has a sole founder.

Section 167

(1) In addition to providing their primary stakes, the members of the company may undertake to supply other valuable contributions (subsidiary contributions). The personal collaboration performed by a member - except by the elected officials - is deemed to be such a subsidiary contribution.

(2) The member is entitled to a remuneration for his/her subsidiary contribution; this shall be booked among the liabilities in the LLC's balance-sheet.

Section 168

(1) Subject to a corresponding provision of the deed of association, the meeting of the members may prescribe an obligation of additional payment for the members. The ceiling of such an additional payment shall be defined in the deed of association. The additional payment does not increase the member's primary stake.

(2) The additional payments shall be determined and performed in proportion to each member's primary stake. Additional payments may be prescribed even before the primary stakes have been fully paid up.

Section 169

(1) Following the registration of the LLC the rights of the members and their share in the assets of the company are incorporated in the business share. The size of the business share is proportional to the member's primary stakes.

(2) Each member may own only one business share. When a member acquires further business shares, his (initial) business share increases in proportion to the shares acquired by him/her.

(3) A business share may be owned by several persons. These will count as one member in respect of the LLC. They may excercise their rights through their common representative and they are jointly and severally liable for the member's obligations.

Section 170

The business share may be freely transferred to any member of the LLC. When the business share carries the obligation of a subsidiary contribution, the company's approval is requested.

Section 171

(1) The business share cannot be assigned to an external person (non-member) until the member has fully paid up his primary stake. The other members, the company or the person designated by the members' meeting have - in this order - an option to buy the business share offered for sale.

The organization of LLC

The members' meeting

Section 183

(1) The members' meeting is the supreme organ of the LLC; it can also decide on matters belonging to the competence of other organs. The members' meeting shall be called at least once a year.

(2) The following matters belong to the exclusive competence of the members' meeting:

(a) approval of balance-sheet and distribution of the profit,

(b) decreeing additional payments and repayment of the same,

(c) division and withdrawal of a business share,

(d) exclusion of a member,

(e) election and recall of managing directors as well as their remuneration; exercise of the employer's rights in respect of managing directors,

(f) election and recall as well as the remuneration of members of the S.B., except the case defined in Section 209 para. (2),

(g) approval of the conclusion of contracts where the value of the contract exceeds one-fourth of the primary capital of the LLC, and of contracts about to be concluded between the LLC and one of its own members, its managing director or one of their close relatives (Civil Code art. 685, para. (b)), except where the conclusion of such contract is within the habitual activities of the company,

(h) approval of contracts concluded on behalf of the LLC prior to its registration,

(i) claims for damages against members responsible for the foundation, and the managing directors and members of the S.B.; further: disposition on the representation of the company in law-suits filed against the managing directors,

(j) decision on the termination, transformation, merger or association of the LLC,

(k) amendment of the deed of association,

(l) all matters referred to the exclusive competence of the members' meeting by law or the deed of association.

(3) No departure from the provisions contained in para. (2) clauses (a) to (k) in the deed of association shall be valid.

Section 184

In a one-man company (LLC) no members' meeting shall function and the founder exercises the latter's competencies.

The managing director

Section 197

(1) The administration of the LLC's business is carried out and the representation of the company is provided for by one or more managing directors elected for a definite period from among the members (their representatives) or from among external, natural persons. The deed of association may also provide that every member (representative) is entitled to management and representation; in such a case these are to be deemed as managing directors.

(2) The first managing directors shall be appointed in the deed of association, and any contrary stipulation in it is invalid.

(3) If the company has several managing directors, these are jointly entitled to represent the company - unless the deed of association provides otherwise. If any declaration has to be made to the company, a single managing director is sufficient thereto.

Section 198

In the case of a one-man company (LLC) - provided the founder is a natural person - the deed of foundation may provide that the founder is also entitled to management and representation. In such a case the founder is deemed to be the managing director.

Section 199

(1) The managing director represents the company *erga* third parties as well as before the courts and other authorities. For a determined class of affairs the managing director may transfer this right to the employees of the company.

(2) The powers of representation of the managing director may be limited by the deed of association; however, such a limitation shall have no effect in respect of third parties.

(3) The managing director exercises the employer's rights in respect of the employees of the company. When there are several managing directors, this right belongs to the one appointed for this purpose.

The Supervisory Board (S.B.)

Section 208

(1) Whenever it is warranted by the size of the membership, the importance or character of the LLC's activities, the deed of association may provide for a Supervisory Board consisting of at least three members.

(2) The establishment of an S.B. is mandatory when

(a) the primary capital of the LLC exceeds twenty million forints, or

(b) the number of its members exceeds twenty-five, or

(c) the number of its full-time employees exceeds two hundred persons on an annual average.

(3) In a one-man company (LLC) the establishment of an S.B. is mandatory only in the case defined in clause (c), para. (2) above.

Section 209

(1) The members of the S.B. are elected by the members' meeting - except in the case defined in para. (2) hereunder.

(2) The members' meeting shall not elect any employee of the LLC for a member of the S.B.

(3) The recall of a member of the S.B. elected by the members' meeting requires a majority of at least three-fourths; a provision contrary to this rule in the deed of association shall be invalid.

The auditor

Section 215

In a one-man company (LLC) the appointment of an auditor is compulsory.

Termination of the company

Section 227

The decision to terminate the LLC must be taken by the members' meeting with a majority at least three-fourths. Any provision contrary to this in the deed of association shall be invalid.

Section 228

If the company ceases to exist without a successor, the rules of final account shall be applied with the additional provisions of Sections 229 and 230.

Section 229

Simultaneously with the approval of the closing balance-sheet, the members' meeting decides about the release of the liquidators (managing directors), the auditor and the S.B.

Section 230

(1) From the residual property remaining after the satisfaction of the creditors, first the additional payments must be refunded; next remainder must be divided among the LLC members in proportion to the primary stakes of each.

(2) The property may not be distributed until after six months following the third publication of the invitation addressed to the creditors in the Official Gazette.

Section 231

If the number of the LLC members has been reduced to one, and no new member has been announced to the Court of Registration within six months, the company does not cease but will continue to function as a one-man company, according to the rules relating to the latter. This fact shall be announced by all managing directors to the Court of Registration, for the purpose of entry and publication.

CHAPTER VII

COMPANY LIMITED BY SHARES

Title I

General rules

Section 232

(1) The company limited by shares is an economic association formed with a registered capital consisting of shares of predetermined amount and nominal (face) value, in which the member's (shareholder's) liability towards the company is limited to supplying the face value or value of issue of the share. The shareholder has, otherwise, no liability for the obligations of the company limited by shares.

(2) The denomination "company limited by shares" (hereinafter: Co. Ltd.) or its abbreviation (in Hungarian *rt*) must be included in the company's firm name.

Section 233

No departure from the provisions relating to Co.-s Ltd. is possible except if permitted by the present Act. Any legal statement contrary to this shall be null and void.

The share

Section 234

(1) The share is a security embodying the membership rights.

(2) Each share carries identical membership rights. Nevertheless, the issue of shares ensuring different membership rights is possible, if so provided by Law, or - under the powers granted by the latter - by the articles of association (Statutes).

(3) The share providing identical rights constitute a single type of shares (cf. Section 242 to 245). The Statutes shall state the rights attaching to the given type of the share, further the number and face value of the shares to be issued within the same type. Shares belonging to a definite type must have identical face values.

Section 235

(1) The face value of a share must not be less than ten-thousand forints or a multiple thereof divisible by ten-thousand.

(2) The emission of shares below nominal value is null and void; the emitters are jointly and severally responsible for any damage arising therefrom.

(3) The total amount of the nominal value of all shares constitutes the Company's registered capital.

Section 237

The minimum contents to be shown on the share includes the following:

(a) the firm name of the Co. Ltd. and its seat;

(b) the serial number and nominal value of the share, the fact whether it is a bearer's share or a registered share; in the latter case: the owner's name;

(c) the type of the share and the rights attaching to it as defined in the Statutes;

(d) the date of issue; the size of the registered capital and the number of shares at the time of issue;

(e) the signatures of the board of directors in accordance with the relevant rules;

(f) in the case of a share warrant and a temporary share: the paid up amount.

Section 240

(1) Bearer's shares are freely transferable.

(2) The transfer of registered shares is governed by the rules relating to the transfer of bills of exchange with the proviso that the transfer becomes effective in regard of the company when the name of the new owner has been entered in the Book of Shares.

(3) A foreigner may only acquire registered shares. In the case of inheritance by a foreigner, his/her bearer's share must be converted within a year into a registered share.

Section 242

(1) Subject to the corresponding provision of the Statutes, shares may be issued which entitle the holder to a dividend from the divisible profit in precedence of other types of shares (preference share). The Statutes may limit or exclude the voting rights attached to the preference share.

(2) The rules of dividend-precedence are set down in the Statutes.

(3) The Statutes may also decree the emission of other types of preference shares.

(4) The value of emitted preference shares may not exceed half of the company's registered capital.

Section 249

(1) The share may be owned by several persons who are deemed to impersonate one shareholder in relation to the company. They may exercise their right through their common representatives (proxy) and are jointly and severally liable for the obligations of shareholders.

(2) If a registered share is in joint ownership, the name of the common representative must also be entered in the Book of Shares.

Title 2

Foundation of the Co. Ltd.

Section 250

The founder of the Co. Ltd. is the emitter of the draft of the deed of foundation (hereinafter: Draft). A Co. Ltd. may also have but a single founder.

Section 251

(1) The registered capital of the Co. Ltd. shall not be less than ten million forints.

(2) The pecuniary contribution upon foundation may not be less than thirty percent of the registered capital and five million forints.

The Subscription of shares

Section 252

(1) The registered capital of the Co. Ltd. is secured by the subscription for shares.

(2) The subscription is based on the draft of the deed of foundation (Draft). The original Draft must be included in an official document or private deed having the force of full evidence; the copies of the Draft must be certified by a notary public.

(3) The Draft shall contain the following:

(a) the firm name and seat of the Co. Ltd.; its range of activity, its duration;

(b) the intended size of the registered capital;

(c) the number and nominal value of the shares, as well as their value at issue; in the case of various types of shares, their character and the rights attaching to each type;

(d) the place, starting and final day of share subscription;

(e) the priorities granted to the founders, in particular, their right to appoint the members of the Board of Directors for the first three years;

(f) the subject-matter and value of non-pecuniary contributions and the number of shares to be given in consideration; further the name (firm) of the contributor, its domicile (seat) and the name (firm) of the auditor performing the preliminary evaluation;

(g) the proceeding to be followed in the case of over-subscription;

(h) the manner of convoking the statutory meeting.

Section 253

(1) The founders must disclose, in a written declaration, the data on the basis of which the value of the non-pecuniary contribution was established.

(2) In the Draft the value of any non-pecuniary contribution may only be based on the value previously determined by the auditor.

The Statutory meeting

Section 257

(1) The founders are held to convoke the statutory meeting within sixty days from the closing day of the successful share subscription.

Foundation in camera

Section 260

(1) There is no need to release a Draft of foundation, to subscribe for the shares and to hold a statutory meeting if the founders have agreed to acquire all shares in proportions defined by them; provided such an agreement is in writing and endorsed by an attorney-at-law or legal counsel.

The Statutes

Section 261

(1) The following shall be defined in the Statutes:

(a) the firm name and seat of the Co.Ltd.;

(b) duration of the Co.Ltd.;

(c) range of activity of the Co.Ltd.;

(d) size of the registered capital, terms of payment of the shares;

(e) number and nominal value of the shares and whether they are bearer's shares or registered ones;

(f) manner of signing the firm name of the Co.Ltd.;

(g) manner of calling the G.A. (shareholders' meeting), its quorum and the proceedings in case of a lack of quorum; terms and manner of exercising voting rights;

(h) number of the members of the B.o.D. and of the S.B., and of the auditors; the manner of their election; their powers and the duration of their offices;

(i) rules of distribution of profit;

(j) modality of publishing the Co.Ltd.'s bulletins;

(k) sanctions for failure to pay up the shares.

(2) Depending on necessity, the Statutes may provide for defining the following:

(a) separate agreements relating to the non-pecuniary contributions and the preferences, if any, ensured to the founders;

(b) if various types of shares are issued, their type, number, nominal value and the rights attaching to each;

(c) if convertible or preference bonds are issued, the rules relating to them;

(d) the possibility of withdrawing the share and the relevant procedure;

(e) terms of powers granted to the B.o.D. for the case of increase of capital (Section 306);

(f) anything else the shareholders wish to include in the Statutes.

Section 262

Announcement to be made on the Co. Ltd. to the Court of Registration

(1) The establishment of the Co.Ltd. shall be announced to the Court of Registration for the purpose of entry and publication. The members of the B.o.D. are jointly responsible for presenting the announcement.

Title 3

Rights and obligations of the shareholders

Section 264

(1) The shareholders are obliged to pay in the full value of the shares within one year from the entry of the company in the Trade Register. Within the period they are obliged to effect payment when - according to the terms of the Statutes - the B.o.D. has addressed a public appeal to the shareholders. Each owner of registered shares must receive a separate notice as well.

(2) If a shareholder delayes any due payment, he/she shall pay an interest of 20 per cent yearly.

(3) If a shareholder fails to pay the due instalment within 60 days of being summoned, the B.o.D. is entitled to re-sell the temporary share by auction; at the same time such temporary share must be voided and the shareholder's right annuled. From the amount thus received, the company's claims attaching to the share shall first be satisfied, while the remainder is due to the former shareholder.

Section 265

If the shareholder has transferred his/her temporary share to a third person before paying its full nominal value, he/she will be liable as surety for the latter's obligations.

Section 266

(1) The shareholder is entitled to a *pro rata* part of the profit shown in the balance-sheet, declared to be divisible by the general assembly, in proportion to the shares owned by him/her (dividend);

(2) In case of the termination of the Co. Ltd., without a successor, the shareholder is entitled to a *pro rata* part - in proportion to his/her shares - of the divisible property as a result of the liquidation.

Section 269

(1) The voting right attaching to the share shall correspond to the nominal value of the share, with the exception of the type mentioned in Section 242.

(2) The Statutes may limit the exercise of the voting right by putting a ceiling or/by setting a proprotion to the highest number of votes represented by the shares.

(3) The Statutes may contain a provision, according to which a State-budgetary organization or a financial institution owning at least one-third of the shares is empowered to exercise 51 per cent of the voting rights.

Title 4

Organization of the Co. Ltd.

The General Assembly

Section 277

The general assembly (G.A.) is the supreme organ of the Co. Ltd.; it consists of the totality of the shareholders.

Section 278

The following matters belong to the exclusive competence of the G.A.:

(a) establishment and amendment of the Statutes;

(b) increase and reduction of the registered capital;

(c) modification of the rights attaching to the individual types of shares;

(d) decision on the amalgamation of the Co. Ltd. with another Co. Ltd.; its merger, dissolution, termination as well as conversion into another company form;

(e) election and recall of the members of the B.o.D. and of the S.B. (with the exception defined in Section 292) and of the auditor; the remuneration of all these;

(f) approval of balance-sheet distribution of annual profit;

(g) decision on the emission of convertible or preference bonds;

(h) decision on any other question relegated by law or by the Statutes to the exclusive competence of the G.A.

The Board of Directors

(Directorate)

Section 285

(1) The Board of Directors (B.o.D.) is the managing organ of the Co. Ltd. It represents the company in respect of third parties, in court and before other authorities; it sets up and directs the working organization of the company and exercises the rights of the employer.

(2) The B.o.D. consists of not fewer than three and not more than eleven members directors. The Board elects its chairman from among its member.

(3) The directors are elected by the G.A. from among the shareholders or other persons, by the G.A.

(4) Unless the Statutes provide otherwise, all directors are jointly entitled to management.

Section 286

(1) Each director has the power to sign the firm's name of the company. Nevertheless, the Statutes may provide that several directors jointly or together with a person vested with that right by the B.o.D. are entitled to sign.

(2) The Statutes may authorize some of the directors (members of the B.o.D.), or the employees of the company with general powers or with powers limited to represent it in certain business affairs.

Section 287

The right of representation of the B.o.D. may be limited by the Statutes, or by a decision of the G.A., or by the S.B. Such limitation, however, has no effect *erga* third parties. The members of the B.o.D. are jointly and severally liable to the company for any damage arising from transgression of the limitation.

The Supervisory Board (S.B.)

Section 291

(1) Each Co. Lts. must constitute a S.B. consisting of not fewer than three and not more than fifteen members.

(2) The members of the S.B. are selected from among the shareholders or other persons (with the exceptions defined in Section 292) by the G.A. However, the G.A. shall not elect any employee of the Co. Ltd.

Section 292

In a Co. Ltd. where the number of employees exceeds - on an annual average - two hundred, one third of the members of the S.B. shall be elected by the employees.

Section 293

(1) The members of the S.B. attend the G.A. of the Co. Ltd., and may submit proposals as to its agenda.

(2) Whenever, in the S.B., the opinion of the delegates of the employees differs from that of the S.B., such minority opinion shall be made known at the G.A.

The Auditors

Section 297

(1) Every Co. Ltd. has to elect at least one auditor.

(2) The auditor fulfils the tasks defined in the present Act, in other statutory rules, the Statutes, as well as those entrusted to him by the G.A.

One-man company limited by shares

Section 298

(1) A Co. Ltd. may be founded also in such way that its sole shareholder is a State budgetary organization or a financial institution.

(2) A one-man Co. Ltd. may also come about in such a way that a shareholder acquires the ownership of all shares. A natural person cannot be a sole shareholder.

Section 299

(1) The establishment of a one-man Co. Ltd. shall be announced within thirty days to the Court of Registration - for the purpose of entry and publication. In such a Co. Ltd. the liability of the shareholder for the obligations of the company is limited to the amount of its shares.

(2) Failing such notification the shareholder shall have unlimited liability for the obligations of the Co. Ltd., from the moment of the acquisition of all the shares.

(3) If winding-up proceedings are instituted because of the permanent insolvency of a one-man Co. Ltd., the shareholder shall bear unlimited liability for all obligations of the company which have arisen after the entry of the company in the Trade Register.

Section 300

In all other respects the rules of the present Act relating to the Co. Ltd. shall govern also the one-man Co. Ltd. - correspondingly - with the proviso that the rights of the G.A. are exercised in case of Section 298, para. (1) by the founder, and in case of para. (2) by the shareholder.

Title 6

Termination of the Co. Ltd.

Section 317

In case the Co. Ltd. is discontinued without a successor, the provisions regarding the final accounting shall apply with the complementary provisions of Sections 318 to 320.

Section 318

(1) The G.A. may delegate the duties of final accounting also to other person(s) than the directors.

(2) The shareholders or creditors representing at least one tenth of the registered capital or the creditors may, by indicating the reason thereof, apply to the Court of Registration to appoint another person as liquidator. Statutes may grant this right to the shareholders representing a lesser proportion of the registered capital.

Section 319

(1) The G.A., when approving the final balance-sheet, passes a decision on relieving the liquidators, the directors, the S.B. and the auditors of their duties.

(2) The liquidators may claim that the shareholders pay up the outstanding payments, provided these are needed for the settlement of the debts of the company, or to cover the expenses of liquidation, or for another reason.

Section 320

(1) Following the payment of all debts, the residual assets shall be divided among the shareholders in proportion to their shares. Inasmuch as the Co. Ltd. has issued shares carrying special entitlements, these shall be taken into consideration when the division of the assets is carried out.

(2) If the shareholders have made unequal payments on their shares, in the first place the effective payments shall be reimbursed. The remaining divisible assets shall be distributed in proportion to the shares. If the assets to be divided do not cover the effective payments, the gap shall be covered by the shareholders in proportion to their shares.

(3) It is forbidden to distribute the assets until after six months from the third publication of the appeal to the creditors in the official gazette.

PART THREE

CLOSING PROVISIONS

Entry in force

Section 331

The present Act shall enter into force on the the 1st day of January, 1989.

ACT XXIV: 1988

ON FOREIGN INVESTMENT IN HUNGARY

Having in mind the development of international economic co-operation and in particular the promotion of the direct presence of foreign capital in our economy, and

with regard to also assisting the technological progress of the Hungarian economy in this way, and

moved by the wish to ensure foreign investors the national treatment free from any adverse discrimination,

the National Assembly has enacted the following Act:

CHAPTER I

GENERAL PROVISIONS

Section 1

(1) Investments by foreigners in Hungary shall enjoy full protection and safety.

(2) The foreign investor shall be promptly indemnified for any damage arising from any possible measure affecting his property, such as nationalization, expropriation or any measure having a similar legal effect. Compensation shall be paid at actual value.

(3) The State shall see to it that indemnification be effected by that State-administrative body which took the given measure. In case of infringement of law, revision of the decision of the State administrative body may be requested from the Court.

(4) The amount of compensation shall be paid to the person entitled to it in the currency of the investment.

Section 2

For the purposes of the present Act:

(a) the term *"foreigner"* denotes a legal entity or a natural person who (which) qualifies as foreigner under the statutory rules relating to foreign exchange control;

(b) the term *"investments of foreigners in Hungary"* covers: an economic association with foreign participation (i.e. *"joint venture"*), a company founded by a foreigner (foreigners) as well as acquisition of an interest (share) by foreigners in a company (hereinafter, collectively: *"company with foreign participation"*).

Section 3

A company with foreign participation may be founded in the manner and in the forms defined in Act VI: 1988 (Act on Economic Associations, briefly: The Company Act - hereinafter: CA).

Such companies shall be governed by the provisions of the CA - with the exceptions listed in the Present Act.

Section 4

(1) A company with foreign participation may participate in the foundation of another company, or set up such a company on its own, and acquire an interest (share) in an existing company - subject to the limitation of paragraph (2) herebelow. With the exception of the provisions of Chapter IV, the provisions of the present Act shall not apply to such companies.

(2) A company limited by shares whose majority is in foreign ownership, or is fully foreign-owned, may not acquire a majority (controlling) interest in another company limited by shares.

Section 5

The supervision of legality over a company with foreign participation is exercised by the competent Court of Registration.

Section 6

Whenever an international treaty contains provisions different from the present Act, the former shall be applicable.

CHAPTER II

FOUNDATION OF A COMPANY WITH FOREIGN PARTICIPATION, ACQUISITION OF INTEREST IN AN EXISTING COMPANY

Section 7

Foreigners may participate in the foundation of a company, or else become members in a company, only if they have a firm according to their national laws, or have been entered (incorporated) in a trade (or other economic) register according to their national laws. Any foreign natural person or legal entity may be a shareholder.

Section 8

In a company with foreign participation the following persons, or entities may become inland founders or members: the State, any legal entity, economic associations which are not legal entities, as well as natural persons, in accordance with the provisions of the CA.

Section 9

(1) A company with foreign participation may be founded for the purpose of any economic activity, except those excluded or limited by law.

(2) The joint permit of the Ministers of Finance and of Trade is required for the foundation of a company fully owned or controlled through majority by foreigners, for the transformation into such a company, and for the acquisition of a controlling majority interest in a company. The said permit includes the permission of the foreign exchange authority. If the respective application is not rejected within 90 days, the permit shall be deemed to have been granted.

(3) Neither the permit of the foreign exchange authority, nor any other permit is required for the foundation of, or participation in, a company, if the foreign interest does not amount to that stated in paragraph (2) above.

Section 10

(1) Application for a permit (Section 9, para. (2)) shall be filed with the Minister of Finance.

(2) The application shall be filed by

(a) the Hungarian founder in the case of the foundation of a new company,

(b) the foreign party, in the case of a full foreign ownership,

(c) the company, if a foreigner intends to acquire an interest in an existing company.

The application must be filed in Hungarian in five copies. It may be filed by another person entrusted therewith; in the case of clause (b) an inland person must be designated to receive documents.

(3) The application shall contain the following:

(a) the names (names of the firms) of the Hungarian and the foreign members (founders), the legal form and seat (domicile) of their firms;

(b) the legal form of the company, the place of its registration and of its seat; and the description of its range of activities;

(c) in the case of an existing company: the size of the existing property (primary stock, registered capital) at the date of the filing of the application; in the case of foundation of a new company: the corresponding planned data;

(d) the manner of distribution of the net after-tax profit;

(e) the description of the company's intended business strategy accompanied with assessable data.

(4) To be attached to the application: the deed of association (memorandum, statutes, draft deed of foundation) in Hungarian; for an existing company, the amendments to the said documents that may be necessary.

Section 11

(1) The joint decision on the application shall be issued by the Minister of Finance. A dismissing decision shall be accompanied by reasons therefore.

(2) If the application has not been submitted in the prescribed form or with the prescribed contents, a rectification of the deficiencies may be ordered - once - withing 30 days from filing. The application must be adjudged on its merits within 60 days from the date when the deficiency was rectified.

(3) A copy of the decisions mentioned in paras (1) and (2) above shall be sent to the Court of Registration.

Section 12

(1) The foreigner is obliged to pay in his cash contribution in freely convertible currency - unless an international agreement provides otherwise.

(2) A non-cash contribution may consist of any kind of negotiable assets having an assessable value, an intellectual property or right of pecuniary value.

Section 13

(1) If more shares have been subscribed for than the amount that the company limited by shares intends to issue and, for that reason, some subscribers are refused (cf. CA section 255), the subscription by a State-budget organization or a financial institution may also be refused, provided the company is one with foreign participation.

(2) A foreigner may only acquire registered shares. Whenever a bearer's share is assigned to a foreigner, such share shall be transformed to a registered one. In the case of succession (upon death) the bearer's share of a foreign heir shall be transformed into a registered share within a year from the distribution of the estate.

CHAPTER III

THE TERMS OF OPERATION OF COMPANIES

Section 14

(1) The company with foreign participation (hereinafter: the Company) is liable to pay entrepreneur's profit tax (EPT). The basis of assessment (tax base) is the company's profit earned in the respective calendar year. The company shall have no other payment obligation, on the basis of its profit, towards the State budget.

(2) The rate of the EPT amounts to forty percent on the part of the tax base not exceeding three million forints and fifty percent on the part exceeding that amount (calculated tax).

Section 15

(1) The company is entitled to every tax allowance granted to other inland business organizations.

(2) Further tax-allowances in the range of the EPT:

(a) if the foreign stake in the company's property at foundation reaches twenty percent or five million forints, the Company shall be entitled to a tax allowance of twenty percent of the calculated tax;

(b) if more than half of the Company's sales receipts originate from the production of commodities or from the operation of a hotel constructed by it, and the company's original capital exceeds twentyfive million forints out of which at least thirty percent is from foreign participation, the Company shall be entitled to a tax allowance of: sixty percent in the first five years and forty percent from the sixth year onwards, the said dates being counted from the commencement of the sales of the said commodities, or from the rendering the said services, respectively;

(c) provided that the conditions specified in clause (b) hereabove are fulfilled and provided that the Company carries out an activity of special importance for the Hungarian economy - as defined in the Annex to the present Act - the Company shall be entitled to a tax allowance of hundred percent from the calculated tax in the first five years and sixty percent from the sixth year onwards, the said dates being counted from the commencement of the sales of the said commodities, or from the rendering of the said services, respectively.

(3) The tax allowances may be availed of in the form of tax-reduction.

(4) Provided that the conditions specified in para. (2), clause (a) are fulfilled, the Council of Ministers may - by Decree - grant a tax allowance that is of a longer duration or more favourable than those provided for in para. (2), to Companies carrying out financial activities or activities of special importance - as defined in the Annex to the present Act.

Section 16

(1) Provided that the conditions specified in clauses (b) and (c) of para. (2), section 15, are fulfilled, if the foreign member (share-holder) invests partly on entirely the dividend due to him to increase the original capital, the Company shall be entitled to a tax allowance equalling to the sum of the tax due on the said sum, such tax allowance being available in the form of tax deduction.

(2) A further condition for the tax allowance according to para. (1) above is that the net profit should be at least equal to the aggregate sum of the increment of the original capital and the tax allowance attached to it.

Section 17

In the case of an investment made by the Company, hundred percent of the general turnover tax previously charged, having accrued in the year under review, shall be retainable.

Section 18

Means of production made available by the foreign member of the Company to the Company as a non-cash contribution, may be imported to the country free of customs duty.

Section 19

The Company shall be entitled

(a) to acquire property rights (ownership) and other rights on the real estate required for its economic activities defined in the deed of association (company statutes);

(b) to freely dispose of its assets within the limits of Hungarian legal rules and the deed of association (company statutes).

Section 20

(1) In the course of purchase and sale of goods, the Company shall act according to the statutory rules relating to the trade of commodities and market supervision.

(2) Rules of the market shall govern the formation of prices, within the limits, however, of legal regulations prohibiting unfair economic activity and formation of unfair prices. Whenever an official price is set by legal rules, that price shall be applied.

Section 21

The Company may exercise foreign-trade, wholesale and retail trade activities according to the rules governing domestic economic organizations.

Section 22

Statutory rules relating to the protection of quality of products and services shall also be applied to the Company.

Section 23

The Company may contract loans and transact its money turnover according to rules applicable to other domestic economic organizations.

Section 24

The Company's accountancy, the drawing up of its balance-sheet and submission of statistical data as well as state auditing shall be governed by the statutory rules relating to other domestic economic organizations.

Section 25

In the case of lasting insolvency, the rules relating to winding-up proceedings shall apply.

Section 26

(1) On the wages and salaries paid to employees, the Company shall pay a social security contribution equal to that paid by other domestic economic organizations.

(2) The Company shall be liable to pay social security contributions only for such foreign employees who wish to avail themselves of free health-care and the services of the Hungarian social insurance system. This provision shall also be applied to old-age pension contributions (paid by employees) as appropriate.

Section 27

Foreign persons may be executive officers, managing directors, members of the supervisory board and employees of the Company.

Section 28

(1) The labour-law status of the employees shall be governed by the Labour Code, and - within the framework of the former - the deed of association (company statutes) and the employment contract; their liability shall be governed by the CA and the Labour Code.

(2) Trade union rights are governed by the Labour Code and other legal regulations issued on the strength of the latter.

Section 29

Statutory rules relating to the regulation of wages and the material (financial) interest-system of those in leading position (executive officers) shall only apply to such companies in which the amount of the foreign stake is lower than 20 percent or five million forints.

Section 30

The property of the Company shall be indicated, and its books shall be kept, in forints - with the exception of Companies active in duty-free zones (off-shore companies). The value of the non-cash contribution supplied by the foreign investor shall be registered in forints on the basis of the currency valid at the foreigner's seat.

Section 31

(1) The Company's transactions in foreign currencies and foreign exchange, as well as its settlements of this type, fall under the same rules as those applicable to other domestic economic organizations.

(2) Any conversion of forints into foreign currency and *vice versa,* in connection with the foundation, operation and liquidation of the Company, shall be effected at the current, valid rate of exchange, officially quoted by the National Bank of Hungary. The same applies to the transfer of any sum by the foreigner to the benefit of the Company as well as to the transfer by the Company to the foreign member - under any title whatsoever.

(3) The Company may keep the foreign member's cash contribution made in convertible currency on its own account, in the currency of the actual payment. The Company may freely use such sums for procuring means of production, spare parts and durable assets needed for its activities. Means of production paid from this account may be imported to the country free of customs duty.

Section 32

(1) Any share due to the foreigner from the profit of the Company, and any amount due to the foreigner in the case of termination of the Company or the assignment (alienation) of the foreign share - completely or partly - shall be freely transferable abroad in the currency of the investment upon the respective instruction by the foreigner to this effect, - provided the Company possesses the proper cover.

(2) In the event of termination of the Company, the commitments that encumber the foreigner must be met before such transfer can be made.

Section 33

Foreign executive officers, managing members, members of the supervisory board and foreign employees of the Company may freely transfer abroad, in the currency of the country of their permanent domicile, fifty percent of their after-tax incomes received from the Company and paid to the Company's bank.

Section 34

Whenever a statutory rule makes an activity subject to official permit for Hungarian economic organizations, such a permit shall also be acquired by the Company - regardless of the permit defined in section 9, para. (2).

Section 35

Unless the present Act provides otherwise, provisions that are not related to the Civil Code and govern exclusively State-owned economic organizations and co-operatives in their quality as such, shall not be applicable to the Company.

Section 36

Banks may undertake a guaranty, subject to the usual banking terms, for the Company's commitments towards the foreign member, arising from his membership.

CHAPTER IV

COMPANIES OPERATING IN DUTY-FREE ZONES [16]

Section 37

(1) A company founded by a foreigner or with foreign participation may also be established in a duty-free zone, foreigners may also acquire a share in such a company. However, no union may be established in a duty-free zone.

(2) This Act shall apply - with the modifications and completions specified in the present Chapter - to the foundation of companies in duty-free zones, to the acquisition of a share in, and the operation of, such a company.

(3) The terms and conditions of the technical delimitation of a duty-free zone, of the erection of projects and carrying on activities in such zones, and the rules of passenger and goods traffic to and from such zones, are contained in the statutory rules relating to customs law and customs clearance.

Section 38

A duty-free zone shall be deemed as foreign territory from the point of view of customs, foreign-exchange and foreign-trade regulations, the latter, however, with the qualifications of section 39 hereunder. A company operating in a duty-free zone shall be deemed a foreign company from the point of view of the said statutory rules. Accordingly, the statutory rules relating to price regulation, and to State auditing are not applicable to companies operating in a duty-free zone.

Section 39

(1) The provisions of international agreements entered into by the Hungarian People's Republic relating to foreign trade, and export and import prescriptions covering certain countries or certain goods, shall also be applicable to companies operating in a duty-free zone.

(2) Inasmuch as an international agreement entered into by the Hungarian People's Republic has determined the type or volume of exported or imported goods, the permit of the Minister of Trade is required before a company operating in a duty-free zone can engage in foreign-trade activities with certain goods or with countries covered by such international agreements.

Section 40

Before a company operating in a duty-free zone can be entered in the Trade Register, it has to submit decision of the Minister of Finance confirming that the real estate at which the Company plans to display its activities has been declared a duty-free zone.

---

16 Legal rules on such zones are contained in the Decree No. 68/1988 (XII.26) of the Ministers of Finance and of Trade on the detailed regulations concerning customs-law.

Section 41

(1) A company operating in a duty-free zone shall keep its accounts - with the exception defined in para. (2) hereunder - in the convertible currency determined in the deed of association (company statutes).

(2) The Minister of Finance may decree that certain accounts shall be kept, and the balance-sheet be drawn up, in forints.

(3) Apart from the exceptions as provided for in Section 42 of this Act and granted occasionally by the Minister of Finance, a Company operatin in a duty-free zone shall make its transactions in convertible currency.

(4) A company operating in a duty-free zone.

(a) shall keep its foreign currency and foreign-exchange asssets as long as they do not exceed the amount of its property at foundation (primary stock, registered capital) with an inland financial institution; the excess assets may be kept either with an inland or with a foreign financial institution;

(b) may raise credits both from inland sources and from abroad;

(c) may freely dispose of its assets deposited in Hungary or abroad in freely convertible currencies.

Section 42

(1) A company operating in a duty-free zone shall purchase the forint amount needed for its establisment and operation from a Hungarian financial institution against convertible currency. The forint amount shall be kept on an account with a Hungarian financial institution.

(2) The following items shall be disbursed from the account mentioned in para. (1):

(a) public dues (taxes, etc.),

(b) wages and other bonuses of the employees, contributions attached to the former;

(c) fees for the use of land (rent) and for public utilities, and

(d) payments for purchases in retail trade, for construction, assembly, repair and similar works carried out in the duty-free zone, as well as the equivalent of any other acquisition and service, not within the proper functions of the Company, but necessary for its establishment and operation, paid to Hungarian private individuals and economic units not vested with foreign trade rights.

Section 43

The Minister of Finance may also grant fully or partially the benefits due to companies operating in a duty-free zone to companies with foreign participation that are not operating in duty-free zones, provided that such a company does not carry out any activity involving transit of goods across the border. Such a financial institution may be qualified as foreign.

CHAPTER V

CLOSING PROVISIONS

Section 44

Either an inland or a foreign regular court or arbitration court may proceed in legal disputes of companies with foreign participation relating to the deed of association, provided that this has been stipulated in writing by the founders, respectively members, of the Company.

Section 45

The present Act shall enter into force on 1 January 1989; simultaneously, Section 11/c of the Decision of the Council of Ministers Nr. 1016/1985 (III.20) shall be amended as per Section 5 of this Act.

Section 46

(1) The provisions of this Act

(a) shall be applicable to the companies with foreign participation, already functioning upon the entering into force of the Act, with the exception of the rules relating to the permit proceedings (Sections 10 and 11);

(b) shall also be applied in the cases already filed, with the proviso that the ninety days' deadline for the administration proceedings (cf. Section 9, para. 2) shall start on 1 January 1989.

(2) The permit deeds issued prior to the entering into force of the Act shall remain in force.

(3) The tax allowances (benefits) granted to companies with foreign participation prior to the entering into force of the Act may be retained - until their expiry - from the calculated tax, up to the amount of the latter.

Section 47

The present Act shall not affect those regulations that pertain to the establishment of banks and financial institutions with foreign participation (cf. Act II: 1979, Section 34). In the case of an establishment of such a bank or financial institution the full value of its shares shall be paid up - contrary to the provisions of Section 264, para.(1) of the CA - within three years from the registration of the company limited by shares in the Trade Registered.

ANNEX TO SECTION 15, PARA.(2), ITEM C) OF THE ACT: ACTIVITIES OF SPECIAL IMPORTANCE

Electronics and electronization :

- development and manufacture of active, passive and electromechanical components;
- production of computer peripherals;
- production of electronic telecommunication main and subexchanges;
- manufacture of robot-technology means; services related to the application of such means;
- computer-assisted designing systems (CAD);
- production of electronic equipment including electronic appliance for general consumer use.

Production of and components to vehicles.

Production of machine-tools.

Production of agricultural, food-processing and forestry machinery and equipment

Specific components for engineering industry

- production of precision prefabricates; castings, forgings and pressings;
- production of components and subassemblies of general use (high-grade fittings, valves, hydraulic and pneumatic elements, increased and high stress-resistant synthetic parts and technological materials;)
- production of up-to-date coupling elements;
- production of tools and devices;
- production of technical ceramics.

Packaging techniques

- production of packaging materials and appliances;
- production of packaging machines.

Production of pharmaceuticals, plant protective agents and intermediates

- production of new drugs.
- production of innovative plant protectives;
- production of key intermediates to the manufacturing of pharmaceuticals and plant protectives;
- production of veterinary preparations.

Production of articles - as a result of relating investments - increasing the export, or decreasing the imports against convertible currencies, for agriculture and food-processing industry.

Development of the domestic protein-basis.

Production of propagating or breeding materials.

Products, materials and devices resulting from the technological development aimed at saving materials or energy, also including the production of equipment, serving the utilization of by-products and waste-materials available in large quantities.

- development and application of technologies aimed at the production of materials of high solidity and more up-to-date constructions and of smaller volume (such as structural materials, technologies improving the quality of materials);

- production of elements used in process-control enabling the continuous measurement and checking of technological prescriptions and qualitative parameters;
- development of means for low-waste technologies improving per unit consumption of materials;
- production of equipment for recycling of massive by-products and wastes (e.g. in forestry, plant cultivation, animal breeding).

Telecommunication services

Tourism

- establishment and operation of facilities serving medical and thermal convalescence tourism, if operated by the legal person who has established them;
- reconstruction of historical castles and mansions;
- establishment and operation of hotels (or their network) of medium category, if operated by the legal person who has established them.

Biotechnology

- production of products developed on the basis of biotechnological processes.

POLAND

THE LAW
ON ECONOMIC ACTIVITY WITH THE PARTICIPATION OF FOREIGN PARTIES

(The Polish Foreign Investment Law)

(23 December 1988)

In order to create a stable environment for the further development of mutually advantageous capital cooperation between Polish and foreign parties, to guarantee foreign parties protection of their property, income and other rights, the following is proclaimed:

CHAPTER 1

GENERAL PROVISIONS

Article 1

1. This law sets forth the conditions for the commencement of, and the principles for the conduct of, economic activity with the participation of foreign parties on the territory of the Polish People's Republic.

2. For the purposes of this law - economic activity is defined as production, construction, trade and services conducted for profit.

Article 2

1. The activity referred to in Article 1 may be conducted either in the form of a limited liability company or a joint stock company, hereinafter referred to as "Companies", established jointly by Polish parties and foreign parties, or solely by foreign parties. The contribution of foreign parties may not be lower than 20 per cent of equity.

2. Unless the provisions of this law state otherwise, the provisions of Polish law, in particular the Commercial Code, shall apply to the Companies.

Article 3

1. Polish parties entitled to participate in Companies are:

(1) the Treasury and other legal persons established under the laws of the Polish People's Republic and with their registered seats in Poland;

(2) natural persons domiciled in Poland.

2. Foreign parties entitled to participate in Companies are:

(1) legal persons having their registered seat abroad;

(2) natural persons domiciled abroad; and

(3) companies established by persons referred to in points 1 and 2 which have no legal personality.

Article 4

1. The Foreign Investment Agency, hereinafter referred to as "Thee Agency", is hereby established as the bureau of the President of the Agency. The structure and operating principles of the Agency are outlined in its charter conferred by the Prime Minister.

2. The President of the Agency is the central administrative authority on foreign investment, responsible to the Prime Minister.

3. The Prime Minister, on the advice of the Minister of Foreign Economic Relations, appoints and dismisses the President of the Agency.

4. The responsibilities of the President of the Agency include:

(1) formulating the objectives and implementing the policy of the State on investment co-operation with foreign countries;

(2) stimulating and undertaking measures to increase the interest of foreign parties in pursuing economic activities in the Polish People's Republic in the areas, and within limits, corresponding with the interests of the national economy;

(3) supervising the compliance of the activities of foreign parties, operating under this Law, with its provisions and with the conditions set forth in the permit for the establishment of a Company;

(4) performing other responsibilities as provided by in the Law.

5. The Foreign Investment Council shall constitute the advisory body of the President.

The members of the Council are appointed and recalled by the Minister of Foreign Economic Relations on the advice of the President of the Agency.

Article 5

1. The establishment of the Company shall require a Permit. The issuance of the Permit authorizes the commencement of the business activity indicated therein.

2. A Permit is to be issued whenever the business activity ensures in particular:

(1) introduction of modern technologies and management methods into the national economy;

(2) provision of goods and services for export;

(3) improvement in the supply of modern and high quality products and services to the domestic market;

(4) protection of the environment.

3. A Permit is also required for:

(1) the transfer of shares or ownership interests in the Company among the shareholders;

(2) the access of a new Shareholder to the Company;

(3) the amendment of the Company's founding act, changing either the ratio of equity holdings or the related voting rights or the nature and value of contributions;

(4) the change in the object of the company's activity, as specified in the permit.

4. A Permit shall be issued, upon application by the interested parties, by the President of the Agency.

5. No separate foreign exchange permit is required for foreign exchange transactions indicated in Paragraphs 1 and 3.

Article 6

1. A Permit shall be denied whenever the conduct of the business activity is unjustified due to:

(1) a threat to State economic interests;

(2) the requirements of environment protection;

(3) State security and defense interests and the protection of State secrets.

2. The decision to deny a Permit, based on Paragraph 1, clause 1 or 3, does not require any explanation of the underlying facts.

3. The interested parties have the right to appeal to the President of the Agency to re-examine the case within fourteen days from the date of the delivery of the decision denying the Permit.

4. The decision to deny a Permit may not be appealed to the Supreme Administrative Court.

Article 7

Whenever the conduct of business activity, specified in the Permit, by virtue of other regulations requires a licence, the Permit is issued in agreement with the appropriate licensing authority.

Article 8

1. The President of the Agency may condition the issuing of a Permit upon the foreign party undertaking the business activity jointly with a Polish party, and upon the acceptance of a set ratio between the Shareholders' contributions to a Company's equity.

2. In economically justified cases the President of the Agency may agree to the raising of equity of a joint stock Company through public subscription of shares, setting the ratio of shares to be held by Polish and foreign parties. To such companies, Article 5, paragraph 3, clauses 1 and 3 of this Law do not apply; Article 10, paragraph 1, clause 1, and Article 11, paragraph 1 apply respectively.

CHAPTER 2

ESTABLISHMENT OF A COMPANY

Article 9

Parties establishing a Company may, without restriction, arrange their relationships and the internal affairs of the Company in its founding act, unless provisions of the Commercial Code or this Law state otherwise.

Article 10

1. An application for a Permit should set forth:

(1) the partners;

(2) the subject and scope of the business activity of the Company, including export and import activities;

(3) the anticipated term of the Company;

(4) the funds, required by the Company to commence business, including equity;

(5) the ratio between each Shareholder's contribution to the Company's equity, and the form of contribution;

(6) the registered seat of the Company, and the location of its production facilities.

2. The application referred to in Paragraph 1 should enclose:

(1) a draft of the Company's founding act as required by the Commercial Code;

(2) documentary evidence as to the legal status and financial conditions of prospective Shareholders; and

(3) a feasibility study of the proposed Company.

3. The documents enumerated in Paragraph 2 should be submitted in Polish, or in a foreign language, together with a certified translation thereof into Polish.

4. The decision on whether to issue the Permit should be made within two months from the date of the filing of the application.

Article 11

1. A Permit should set forth:

(1) the Shareholders, the name and the registered seat of the Company, the location of its production facilities and the object and term of the Company;

(2) the ratio between each Shareholder's contribution to the Company's equity, and the form of the contribution;

(3) other requirements that the Company should satisfy in the conduct of its business; and

(4) the duration of the Permit's validity.

2. Whenever the Company plans to change the location of its production facilities, it informs the President of the Agency of the new location. The lack of objection within one month is to be understood as an approval.

Article 12

1. The Company shall be registered in court in accordance with the regulations pertaining to the commercial register.

2. The application for registration should have the Permit attached.

Article 13

The Board of Directors of a Company, within two weeks from the date of its registration, is required to notify the President of the Agency of its registration, attaching the statement of registration and a copy of the Company's founding act.

Article 14

The authority that issued the Permit has the right to enter the Company and its production facilities and to review its books and records in order to determine whether the activities of the Company comply with the conditions of the Permit.

Article 15

If the Company engages in any activity incompatible with the conditions set forth in the Permit, the authority that issued the Permit shall request this to be corrected within a specified period, otherwise it may restrict the scope or withraw the Permit.

Article 16

1. The contribution to the Company's equity may be made both in money and in kind.

2. The contribution of the foreign parties may be made:

(1) in foreign currency, or in zlotys obtained through a documented exchange of foreign currency;

(2) in kind - either transferred from abroad or acquired for zlotys obtained through documented exchange of foreign currency.

3. The contribution of a foreign party domiciled or having its seat in a member country of CMEA may also be made in transferable roubles, or in the national currency of one of these countries, in accordance with the applicable agreements binding the Polish People's Republic.

4. The total value of foreign parties' contributions to the Company's equity shall not be less than 25 million zlotys. This amount is adjusted according to the changes in the rate of exchange of the zloty to the foreign currency in which the contribution is made.

5. The contribution of the Polish parties may be made in zlotys, in foreign currency, or in kind. The rights to the State-owned real estate may be contributed to the Company to the extent allowed, and in accordance with, the principles set forth in the regulations on the administration of the State land.

6. The value and the nature of the in-kind contributions shall be set forth in the Company's founding act and are subject to verification by independent experts at the request of the authority issuing the Permit. If such verification finds that the market value of the in-kind contribution is lower than that given in the application, the cost of verification shall be borne by the Shareholder making that contribution.

7. Only registered shares shall be issued in exchange for a contribution to a Company's equity.

CHAPTER 3

BUSINESS ACTIVITIES OF THE COMPANY

Article 17

1. To determine the profit of the Company, the depreciation of fixed assets, including those situated permanently on leased land, and non-material assets, based on the depreciation rates applicable to the State owned enterprises, should be added to total outlays.

2. The depreciation allowances are retained by the Company.

3. The profit of the Company, less the corporate tax due, constitutes the after-tax profit.

4. From the after-tax profit a contribution equal to 8 per cent of such profit shall be made to the reserve fund to cover any balance loss. The Company may cease to make such contribution when the reserve fund reaches 4 per cent of the company costs in a fiscal year.

5. The after-tax profit distribution among the Shareholders is based on their holdings in the Company. Other principles of profit distribution shall require approval of the President of the Agency.

Article 18

1. The Minister of Finance determines the general principles of accounting for the Companies, in compliance with the requirements of the Commercial Code.

2. The annual balance sheet of the Company shall be audited within three months of its filing by the competent authority of the Minister of Finance or by any other entity, chosen by the Company, authorized by the Minister of Finance to audit the annual balance sheet of companies. The cost of auditing is borne by the Company.

3. The balance sheet is considered audited if within 3 months the authority indicated in Paragraph 2 does not notify the Company of its objections. After the objections are compiled with, the balance sheet is considered audited.

4. The share of profit that can be transferred abroad by the foreign Shareholder in accordance with the provisions of this Law shall be determined on the basis of the audited profit of the Company, appearing in its annual report.

Article 19

1. The Company shall resell 15 per cent of its foreign currency export proceeds to a Polish foreign exchange bank. Proceeds from the sale of the replaced fixed assets of the Company are exempt from the obligation. In economically justified cases the President of the Agency may set in the Permit a rate of resale lower than that determined under Paragraph 1.

2. After the resale referred to in Paragraph 1 is effected, the Company may use, without a separate foreign exchange permit, the balance of its export proceeds to purchase abroad goods and services, required for its activity.

Article 20

1. The Company may distribute profit in foreign currency from its surplus of export proceeds over import outlays, without a separate foreign exchange permit.

2. The foreign Shareholder has the right to transfer abroad the amount of profit referred to in Paragraph 1 without a separate foreign exchange permit.

3. The Polish Shareholder has the right to transfer the amount of profit, referred to in Paragraph 1, to his foreign currency account in a Polish foreign exchange bank.

4. In economically justified cases the Minister of Finance may allow the foreign Shareholder to transfer abroad an amount of profit exceeding that determined pursuant to the provision of Paragraph 1. Such decision may constitute part of the Permit for the establishment of the Company.

5. The foreign Shareholder may, subject ot Paragraph 6, freely use his zloty profit in the domestic market of the Polish People's Republic, without a separate foreign exchange permit.

6. The purchase of real estate from the Shareholder's profit requires a separate foreign exchange permit.

Article 21

1. Shareholders have the right to use their part of the profit to increase a Company's equity, without a separate permit, provided that there is no change in the ratio of equity holdings set in the Permit for the establishment of a Company.

2. The foreign Shareholder has the right to transfer abroad, without a separate foreign exchange permit, proceeds from the sale of his shares or ownership interests, and money due him, after tax, in connection with the dissolution of a Company.

3. In those cases where the amounts referred to in Paragraph 2 are received in zlotys, their transfer abroad may take place 10 years from the date of the registration of the Company.

4. The Minister of Finance may agree, in specially justified cases, to an earlier transfer of the amounts referred to in Paragraph 3.

Article 22

1. The Companies deposit their money into their accounts in the Polish foreign exchange banks of their choice.

2. Banks referred to in Paragraph 1 may open and maintain zloty and foreign currency accounts at the request of the Company and may extend loans to it.

3. The Company may, after it obtains a foreign exchange permit, maintain accounts in foreign banks.

4. The Company may secure foreign loans without a foreign exchange permit.

5. Banks referred to in Paragraph 1 may guarantee liabilities of the Company in accordance with applicable regulations.

6. The Minister of Finance, upon the application of the foreign Shareholder, issues him with a compensation payment guarantee to the amount equal to the value of the Company's assets due him, in the event of a loss resulting from a decision of any State authorities in respect of nationalization, expropriation, or from other actions having a result similar to that of nationalization or expropriation.

Article 23

1. The Company may purchase goods and services for foreign currency on the domestic market from licensed entities.

2. The Company may sell goods and services, within the scope of its business, on the domestic market wholly or partially for foreign currency, after it obtains a foreign exchange permit.

3. Companies may sell foreign currencies at the foreign exchange auctions, conducted on the basis of separate regulations.

Article 24

Procurement of raw materials and supplies in the domestic market by Companies is effected in accordance with the regulations applicable to socialized economic entities.

Article 25

State owned enterprises may sell fixed assets to Companies or may grant them limited rights in rem in respect of such assets.

Article 26

1. Companies:

- may be granted State land in perpetual use in accordance with the regulations applicable to the administration of State land or
- may lease such land.

2. Companies may, subject to existing laws, acquire and lease land and other real estate not owned by the State.

CHAPTER 4

TAXES AND FEES

Article 27

1. The company shall pay the following taxes: turnover tax, corporate tax, agricultural tax, wage tax, real estate tax and local taxes, as well as stamp duty and community and city fees. It is entitled to relief and exemptions therefrom in accordance with the principles applicable to non-socialized economic entities enjoying legal personality, however:

(1) corporate tax is 40 per cent of the taxable income;

(2) the following are deducted from the taxable income;

a)investment outlays, as defined in the decree of the Council of Ministers;

b)donations for socially beneficial purposes, including social organizations and foundations with their seats in Poland;

(3) the corporate tax rate decreases by 0.4 per cent for each percentage point of the share of export sales in total sales. The corporate tax, thus decreased, cannot be lower than 10 per cent of taxable income.

2. Donations referred to in Paragraph 1, clause 2(b) may not exceed 10 per cent of income.

Article 28

1. The Company is exempt from corporate tax during the first three years of its business activity. The date of the commencement of business is the date of the first invoice.

2. The Company may be granted an additional period - of up to three years - of tax exemption when it engages in the preferred sectors, as determined by the Council of Ministers, specified by the President of the Agency in the Permit.

Article 29

The income of the foreign Shareholder is subject ot an income tax of 30 per cent, unless international agreements concluded by the Polish People's Republic provide otherwise. The tax is withheld by the Company upon the distribution of profit as required by separate provisions. Tax on income paid out in foreign currency is collected in zlotys from a documented exchange of such currency.

Article 30

1. Customs duties and other fees of similar effect will not be levied on:

(1) items constituting in-kind contributions by Shareholders to the Company's equity, such as machinery and equipment as well as other items required for the conduct of business activity specified in the Permit; and

(2) machinery, equipment as well as other items required for the conduct of the business activity specified in the Permit, purchased by the Company on entities commissioned by it, within three years of its establishment.

2. Exempt from the export duty are items falling to the foreign Shareholder upon the dissolution of the Company.

3. The Company is entitled to a refund of import duty on export sales in accordance with the principles applicable to State-owned enterprises.

CHAPTER 5

EMPLOYMENT

Article 31

1. Polish law applies to employment, labor relations and work conditions in the Company, social benefits for the employees as well as the trade union activity.

2. The Company can employ persons without Polish citizenship or a Polish permanent residence card with the consent of the regional State administrative authority of specific competence of the voivodship level.

3. The permission described in Paragraph 2 is not required for persons although not employed by the Company, but acting in its production facilities on the assignment from the foreign partner, agreed upon by the Company.

Article 32

1. The principles for the remuneration of Company employees are laid down either in the Company's founding act or in the Company's resolutions.

2. The remuneration of Company employees shall be set and paid in zlotys, subject to Paragraph 3.

3. Remuneration of the employees, held to be foreign persons under the Foreign Exchange law, may be partially paid in foreign currency from the foreign currency revenues of the Company. This part of the remuneration may be transferred abroad, upon the request of the employee, without a separate foreign exchange permit.

4. The remuneration of employees, held to be foreign persons under the Foreign Exchange Law, is subject to 30 per cent tax in the currency in which the payment is affected, unless international agreements concluded by the Polish People's Republic provide otherwise. The tax is withheld by the Company upon the remuneration payment, according to separate provisions. Tax on remuneration paid in foreign currency is collected in zlotys from a documented exchange of such currency.

5. Remuneration of the Polish employees of the Company is subject to tax applicable to employees of non-socialized entities.

CHAPTER 6

TRANSFER OF RIGHTS RESULTING FROM PARTICIPATION IN THE COMPANY, AND THE DISSOLUTION OF THE COMPANY

Article 33

1. If the sale of shares or ownership interests is to be made pursuant to a judicial execution, the Company may, within two months from the date of receiving notice of such a sale being ordered, name a party who will purchase the shares or ownership interest at a price to be set by the court upon application by the Company and after consultation with experts.

2. If a request for a price determination was not filed or a person named by the Company fails to pay the price to the court officer, within a month of the date of the notification of the Company of the price determination or of the approval for the replacement of partner, whichever expires later, the shares of ownership interests will be sold according to the rules of judicial execution, with reservation of Article 5, Paragraph 3, Clause 2.

Article 34

In the case of dissolution of the Company, the Polish Shareholder shall have a pre-emptive right to purchase the items and rights constituting the assets of the Company, unless the Company's founding act provides otherwise.

Article 35

If the Company is dissolved during the corporate tax exemption period or within three years after it expires (Article 28, Paragraphs 1 and 2), the Company shall pay the tax for the exemption period. In such a cases the tax liability arises upon the notification of the dissolution of the Company.

CHAPTER 7

SPECIAL, TEMPORARY AND FINAL PROVISIONS

Article 36

The regulations pertaining to socialized economic entities are not applicable to the Companies, unless this Law states otherwise.

Article 37

1. Companies may associate in the Chamber of Industry and Commerce of Foreign Investors and other Polish economic chambers.

2. The Polish-Polonian Chamber of Industry and Commerce established under the law of July 6, 1982 on Principles of Conduct of Business Activity in Small Industry by Foreign Corporate Bodies and Natural Persons on the territory of the Polish People's Republic (*Dziennik Ustaw* No.13/85, item 58), hereby becomes the Chamber of Industry and Commerce of Foreign Investors, hereinafter referred to as the "Chamber". Former foreign members of the Polish-Polonian Chamber of Industry and Commerce may within three months from the date of the effectiveness of this Law confirm their membership of the Chamber.

3. The President of the Agency supervises the Chamber and approves its charter. The President of the Agency may refuse to approve the charter if its provisions infringe the law.

4. The responsibilities of the Chamber include, in particular:

(1) to represent the business interests of its members and to undertake actions to protect their interests;

(2) to assist its members in solving their business, management and legal problems of the commencement and conduct of their business activity.

5. The specific responsibilities of the Chamber, the principles of its activities, governing bodies, procedures for its establishment, the scope of its activity and its finances shall be set forth in its charter.

6. The Chamber has legal personality.

7 In the event that any activity of a governing body of the Chamber is in violation of law or the Chamber's charter, the authority that supervises the Chamber may set a date by which such violations must be corrected, or may request a change in the composition of that governing body of the Chamber within a specified period. If such a period expires without effect, the supervising authority may suspend the governing body of the Chamber and establish an appropriate provisional body until a new governing body is established in accordance with the procedures of its charter.

Article 38

1. This Law does not apply to international enterprises subject to compliance with the provisions of Paragraphs 2 - 4 unless an international agreement provides otherwise.

2. If an international agreement provides that an international enterprise, or its branch with its registered seat on the territory of the Polish People's Republic, has legal personality, the enterprise, or its branch, should be registered in the commercial register.

3. The registration in the commercial register is effected with an application from the appropriate authority of the international enterprise or its branch. The registration is made on the basis of a certified copy of the Polish text, or a certified translation into Polish, of the agreement establishing the international enterprise or its branch. The agreement should be accompanied by a list of the members of the Board of Directors and the plenipotentiaries of such enterprise or of its branch.

4. The regulations governing the commercial register on the limited liability companies are applied respectively to the registration of international enterprises, or of branches thereof, subject to the provisions of international agreements.

Article 39

1. Foreign entities, conducting business activity under the law referred to in Article 37, Paragraph 2, may, upon obtaining a permit, contribute their enterprises, or parts thereof, as well as items, rights and money from this activity to Companies established under this Law.

2. The permit referred to in Paragraph 1 may be issued after the requirement of minimum investment of US$ 50,000 in convertible currency in contributed enterprise or part thereof has been complied with.

3. The application for a permit should set forth the methods by which the creditors of the foreign entity will be satisfied in respect of the liabilities incurred in connection with the operation of its enterprise. The issuance of the permit may be conditional on the establishment of a proper security for the creditors' claims.

Article 40

1. Limited liability companies and joint stock companies established pursuant to the law referred to in Article 37, Paragraph 2, may obtain a permit to reorganize themselves into Companies established pursuant to this Law.

2. The permit may be issued after the requirement of Article 39, Paragraph 2, has been met.

Article 41

Foreign entities may, after obtaining a permit, purchase shares of, or ownership interests in, existing companies established under Polish law, which do not constitute companies with foreign capital participation, provided that the foreign entities thereby increase the equity of these companies. After such an increase in the company equity is properly registered, the provisions of this law shall apply to these companies.

Article 42

1. The permits referred to in Article 39, Paragraph 1, Article 40 Paragraph 1 and Article 41 are issued by the President of the Agency.

2. The application for the issuance of any of the permits referred to in Paragraph 1 is governed respectively by Articles 6 and 10 of this Law.

3. If the location and subject of business activity are the same as in the existing permit, permits referred to in Article 39, Paragraph 1 and in Article 40, Paragraph 1 are issued when the applicant complies with the condition of Article 39, Paragraph 2 and submits the draft of the founding act of the Company, in line with the provisions of this Law.

Article 43

The provisions of Article 28, paragraph 1, do not apply to companies established pursuant to the provisions of Articles 39, 40 and 41.

Article 44

1. Companies with foreign capital participation established under the Law of April 23, 1986 on Companies with a Foreign Capital Participation ("Dziennik Ustaw", No. 17/86, item 88 and No. 33/87, item 181), operating at the time this law is effective become Companies under the provisions of this Law.

2. The President of the Agency will adapt the permits already issued to the requirements of this Law within 3 months after the Law becomes effective.

Articles 45 - 52 [17]

Article 53

The Law of April 23, 1986 on Companies with Foreign Capital Participation (Dziennik Ustaw No. 17/86, item 88 and No. 33/87, item 181) is hereby null and void.

Article 54

This law becomes effective on January 1, 1989.

[17] These Articles set forth changes in the various laws already in force pertaining mostly to foreign business activity already conducted in small industry.

ROMANIA

DECREE No. 424
ON CONSTITUTION, ORGANIZATION AND OPERATION OF JOINT COMPANIES IN THE SOCIALIST REPUBLIC OF ROMANIA

(Published in the Official Bulletin of the Socialist Republic of Romania, No. 121/1972)

The State Council of the Socialist Republic of Romania decrees:

Chapter One

GENERAL PROVISIONS

Art. 1. Joint Companies with foreign participation may be set up in the Socialist Republic of Romania in the fields of industry, agriculture, construction, tourism, transport, scientific and technological research, with the object of producing and marketing material goods, performing services or carrying out work.

The object of activity of the Joint Company is set in the Company's Contract of Association and the Statutes. Economic and social developments of Romania shall be taken into account when establishing the object of activity.

Art. 2. The constitution of Joint Companies in the Socialist Republic of Romania has in view:

- To implement certain objectives which contribute to the development of national economy; to extend, modernize, and re-equip certain existing objectives; to accelerate the introduction of certain modern technologies; to raise the technical quality level of production and services; and to ensure a raised productivity of labour.
- To promote exports, to expand markets, to diversify products for export, and to develop collaboration activities in third markets.
- To promote and develop scientific research activities.
- To introduce modern methods of enterprise management and production organization.
- To train specialists for production, enterprise management and organization, trading activities included.

Art. 3. Joint Companies are Romanian corporate bodies and carry out their activities as prescribed by the laws of the Socialist Republic of Romania and the conditions set forth in the present decree.

Art. 4. The Romanian share in the registered capital shall be of at least 51 per cent.

Art. 5. The parties entitled to participate in the constitution of Joint Companies include:

- One or more Romanian economic units with legal status including Industrial Centrals or units assimilated to such centrals - combines, trusts, groups of enterprises, factories or works - and economic units which are entrusted under the law with foreign trade activities and economic collaboration with foreign countries.
- One or more foreign economic organizations, companies or enterprises carrying out business in trade, finance and banking, construction, transport, performance of services, foreign naturel persons included.

Art. 6. The duration of the Joint Companies shall be agreed upon by the parties and specified in the Contract of Association.

Art. 7. The Romanian State vouches for the transfer abroad through the Romanian Foreign Trade Bank or other authorized institutions, in favour of the foreign partners, of all profits made, of the value of share quotas transferred to the Romanian party, or of dues resulting from the distribution of assets following upon dissolution and winding up or of other dues, under the conditions stipulated in the Contract of Association and in the Statutes, after deduction of taxes and contributions to social insurance and the fulfilment of other obligations under the law and the contract.

Art. 8. Joint Companies shall work out annual and five-year programmes of economic and financial activity which are to have the approval and stipulated in the Company's Statutes.

Chapter Two

CONSTITUTION AND ORGANIZATION OF JOINT COMPANIES

Art. 9. Joint Companies shall be constituted as joint stock companies or as limited liability companies. The organization and operation of these companies are set up in the company's Contract of Association and Statutes.

Art. 10. The Contract of Association and Statutes shall stipulate for: the contracting parties, the legal form, the name, object, registered office, and duration of the company; the capital and ways for its subscription and for the transfer of the shares or parts of the capital, the number and value of the shares or parts of the capital; the rights and obligations of the partners; the first management bodies as well as other clauses which the parties may have agreed upon.

The Statutes, which are an integral part of the contract shall also include provisions referring to the organization and operation of the joint company: the general meeting, its attributions and organization, the exercise of the voting right in the general meeting; attributions and organization of the board of directors, the method by which these bodies are to adopt decisions - whether by simple majority or unanimity - the appointments attributions, remuneration and responsibility of the managers, directors, and auditing body of the company, the method of writing off fixed assets, drawing of the balance sheet and of the profit and loss account, the calculation and distribution of profits; the method of settlement of disputes between the partners concerning the company; cases of dissolution and methods of winding up of the Company as well as any other provision that would follow from the present decree and from an agreement between the contracting parties.

Art. 11. The partners may agree, by the Statutes of the Company, to take decisions with the unanimity of the votes of the members present at the legally constituted general meeting of the partners in matters concerning the programme of activity, the approval of the balance sheet and of the profit and loss account, the distribution of profits, the appointment of the executive bodies of the company and establishment of their competence, the proportion in which the parties are to be represented in the management bodies, the appointment, remuneration and dismissal of the executive bodies as well as any other matters expressly mentioned in the Statutes.

Art. 12. Assets initially contributed by the parties when the company is formed as well as those subsequently acquired shall be included in its patrimony with the title and effets laid down in the Company's Contract and Statutes.

Art. 13. Shares or capital quotas can be transferred only with the approval of the general meeting of the partners in keeping with the provisions of the Company's Contract and Statutes.

Art. 14. The contribution of the parties to the subscribed capital may consist of a financial contribution, a contribution in goods required for carrying out the investments and activities in which the company is currently engaged and a contribution in industrial property rights or other rights; it is established by the Company's Contract and Statutes.

The contribution of the Romanian party may also include the equivalent of the right of use of the ground which the Romanian States will make available to the Joint Company for its whole operating lifetime. If the equivalent of the right of use of the ground has not been included in the contribution of the Romanian party, the Joint Company shall pay a rent to the State to be established for this use.

Art. 15. The contribution of the parties to the constitution of the Joint Company shall be assessed in the currency agreed upon by the Company's Contract and Statutes.

The value of the goods contributed by each party to the company is to be established by the Company's Contract and Statutes, in the currency and at the foreign trade price agreed upon. The financial contribution of the parties shall be placed in an account with Romanian banking institutions in the name and at the disposal of the Joint Company.

Art. 16. In order to form a Joint Company, the partners shall draw up the Memorandum of Association, in Romanian, the Study of Technico-Economic Efficiency, the Contract of Association and the Statutes.

Before signing these documents, the Romanian partner shall obtain the unique advice of the State Planning Committee, the Ministry of Finance, the Ministry of Foreign Trade and International Economic Cooperation, the Ministry of Labour, the Romanian Foreign Trade Bank and other Romanian financing banks, and this advice is to consider the economic efficiency and the opportunity.

In order to obtain the approval for the constitution of the Joint Company, the partner shall take the duly signed documents mentioned in paragraph 1 of this article, together with a request, to the Ministry of Foreign Trade and International Economic Cooperation, where they will be checked from the point of view of the compliance with the law and then submitted to the Council of Ministers.

Art. 17. The constitution of the Joint Company, the Contract of Association, and the Statutes will receive the approval of the Council of States, by Decree, at the proposal of the Council of Ministers.

As a consequence of the approval by the Council of States, the organization, the whole activity of the Joint Company as well as its dissolution and winding up will be ruled for the whole duration of the company, in addition to the stipulations of the present Decree, by the provisions of the Contract of Association and the Statutes.

Art. 18. The Joint Company shall be registered with the Ministry of Foreign Trade and International Economic Cooperation and with the Ministry of Finance. It will become legally constituted on the date of registration with the Ministry of Finance.

The approval for the constitution and an extract from the Company's Contract of Association and Statutes shall be published in the Official Bulletin of the Socialist Republic of Romania.

Art. 19. Alteration of the Contract of Association and of the Statutes shall be submitted for approval to the Council of State, with adequate application of the provisions of articles 16-18 inclusive.

Chapter Three

ACTIVITY OF JOINT COMPANIES

Art. 20. Joint Companies are formed to achieve economic objectives whose production is particularly intended for export.

Art. 21. Expenses of Joint Companies are made in the currency agreed under the Contract of Association and the Statutes. For petty expenses and supplies with products for which no prices can be established in foreign currency, payment shall be carried out from the account in lei (Romanian currency) opened with the Romanian Foreign Trade Bank, in compliance with article 28.

Art. 22. Joint Companies provide themselves with raw materials, various supplies and other commodities under conditions of competitivity. Supply can be taken from this country, in the currency agreed upon, or can be imported.

Art. 23. The output of Joint Companies shall be traded in the home market with payment in the currency agreed under the Contract of Association and the Statutes, and in foreign markets either directly or through the agency of organizations entrusted with foreign trade activities.

Art. 24. All payments in foreign currency of the Joint Companies shall be made only out of their own foreign currency availabilities or from loans.

Art. 25. Economic and financial transactions of the Joint Company shall be booked in the currency agreed upon between the partners, under the conditions set up by the Statutes.

Art. 26. Reserve funds shall be formed from the profit made by the Joint Company under the conditions set up by the Statutes.

The benefit remaining after deduction of the reserve funds and legal taxes shall be distributed among the partners in proportion to their contribution to the subscribed capital, a part being set aside for future development requirements of the Joint Company.

Art. 27. Joint Companies will calculate and include in their costs the depreciation pertaining to the elements of the Company's assets which, according to Romanian Law, are considered fixed funds, until their value is fully written off.

The writing-off periods and depreciation annuities of the fixed funds are established by the Statutes or failing this by the general meeting of the partners. Writing off periods shall not be longer than the standard operating lifetime specified by the Romanian Law. That part which has not been written off as a result of the breaking or destruction of such fixed funds, or because of calamities or accidents shall be included in the production costs or the selling costs, to the extent to which it is not recuperated by insurance.

Art. 28. Joint Companies shall open accounts with banks in Romania through which all sums of money in foreign currency and in lei (Romanian currency) are to be collected and paid, having the right to dispose freely of the balances of these accounts. Interest shall be paid for the sums of money deposited in account with the banks.

The transfer of sums from the foreign currency account to the lei (Romanian currency) account and from this to the foreign currency account shall be done on the basis of the rate of exchange established for non-commercial transactions.

Art. 29. The Joint Company shall transfer to its bank the sums of money resulting from the application of tariffs in foreign currency, corresponding to the work performed by the Romanian personnel employed by the Company. The Bank will hold at the Joint Company's disposal the amounts of money in lei (Romanian currency) corresponding to the sums of money due to the Romanian personnel.

Chapter Four

CONTROL OF THE ACTIVITY OF JOINT COMPANIES

Art. 30. In order to be able to exercise their right of control, the partners shall be given, on request, information concerning the Company's activity, the state of assets, the profits and losses, under the conditions provided in the Statutes.

Art. 31. A number of 1-2 delegates from the Ministry of Finance shall belong to the Joint Company's body controlling its accounting activity.

Chapter Five

RIGHTS AND OBLIGATIONS OF JOINT COMPANIES

Art. 32. The Romanian personnel of Joint Companies shall enjoy the rights and obligations provided by the legislation in force for the personnel of state enterprises.

Tariffs in foreign currency according to skills and positions shall be established through the Contract of Association and the Statutes.

Art. 33. The rights and obligations of the foreign personnel of the Joint Company shall be established by the board of directors or by the managing committee as the case may be.

Within the framework of the Joint Company, the foreign personnel may be employed in managing positions.

The foreign personnel of a Joint Company shall be entitled to the transfer of their wages abroad, through the Romanian Foreign Trade Bank. The part of the wages which can be transferred shall be established by the management of the Company.

Art. 34. Provisions of the Romanian Law referring to the constitution and functioning of the working people's general meetings shall be applied correspondingly in the case of Joint Companies.

The general meetings of the working people shall appoint their representatives on the board of directors or on the managing committee of the Company, as part of the representatives of the Romanian party, according to the Statutes.

The working method of the collective managing bodies of the Joint Company shall be agreed upon by the parties and shall be provided in the Company's Statutes.

Art. 35. The contribution to social insurance due by Joint Companies for their whole personnel shall be paid in foreign currency, the amount being established by the legal provisions in force.

For the foreign personnel ordinarily residing in another country, the Joint Companies will deduct from the contribution for social insurance the quota that is to go to the superannuation fund; in this case, the foreign personnel shall derive advantage from all othe the other social insurance services.

The foreign personnel of the Joint Companies is entitled to renounce the Romanian social insurance services, in which case the Joint Company will cease to pay the social insurance contribution for this personnel.

Chapter Six

DISSOLUTION AND WINDING UP OF JOINT COMPANIES

Art. 36. Cases and procedure for the dissolution and liquidation of Joint Companies, obligations and responsibilities of the liquidators and the distribution among partners of the assets resulting after liquidation are established by the Statutes.

Art. 37. The documents of dissolution and winding up of Joint Companies shall be registered, with the Ministry of Foreign Trade and International Economic Cooperation and with the Ministry of Finance and published in the Official Bulletin of the Socialist Republic of Romania.

Chapter Seven

FINAL STIPULATIONS

Art. 38. Litigations between Joint Companies and Romanian natural persons or corporate bodies shall be brought before the law courts.

If the parties agree, litigations arising from contractual relations between Joint Companies and Romanian corporate bodies can also be solved by arbitration. In this case the parties may also fix upon the competence of the Arbitration Commission under the Chamber of Commerce and Industry of the Socialist Republic of Romania.

DECREE No. 425

REGARDING TAX ON PROFITS OF JOINT COMPANIES CONSTITUTED IN THE SOCIALIST REPUBLIC OF ROMANIA

(Published in the Official Bulletin of the Socialist Republic of Romania, No. 121/1972.)

The State Council of the Socialist Republic of Romania decrees:

Art. 1. Profits made by Joint Companies constituted in the Socialist Republic of Romania, with Romanian and foreign participation, are subject to an annual tax of 30 per cent.

Art. 2. The tax shall be computed on the annual profits before their distribution among the partners.

The taxable profits shall be established as the difference between the total amount of incomes collected and the amount of the expenses incurred to achieve the incomes, according to legal stipulations and the Company's Contract and Statutes.

The reserve fund to be considered in determining the taxable profits shall be allowed for deduction within the limit of five per cent of the profits of each year until the total reserve fund comes to represent 25 per cent of the invested capital.

Art. 3. For the tax established according to the provision in article 1, the Council of Ministers may grant a tax exemption for a period up to the end of the year when the taxable profits begin to be made, and a reduction of the tax by half for the following two calendar years.

In the event that the Joint Company begins to make profits during the second half of the year, the tax exemption may also be granted for the profits made in the first half of the following year.

Art. 4. The tax due for that part of the profits which is reinvested for a period of at least five years in the same Company or in other Joint Companies with Romanian participation shall be reduced by 20 per cent.

Non-observance of the conditions in terms of which the tax reduction has been granted leads to a cancellation of the facilities and application of the delay increases stipulated in the last paragraph of article 9.

Art. 5. The taxation of the current year shall be computed by the Joint Company within five days since drawing the balance sheet for the previous year and provisionally on the basis of the profits stipulated in the activity programme.

Final taxation for the previous year shall be established concurrently with the provisional taxation.

Art. 6. The provisional taxation for the current year and the final taxation for the previous year shall be announced within the term stipulated in art. 5, by a taxation statement filed, together with a copy of the balance sheet, with the Financial Department of the Executive Committee of the People's Council of the district or of the City of Bucharest on whose territory the Joint Company has its registered office.

The organs of the Financial Department will check the tax computation and establish possible differences which will be notified to the Joint Company within 15 days from the filing date of the taxation statement and balance sheet.

Art. 7. The provisional tax for the current year will be turned over to the budget in equal quarterly instalments through the banking unit where the Joint Company keeps its account, before the end of each term.

Taxation differences established for the previous year will be paid within ten days from the date of receipt of the notification from the financial organs. Any sums of money paid over and above those due will be charged to the tax account for the current year or returned on demand.

Art. 8. Joint Companies can appeal against tax differences established by Financial Departments within 20 days from receipt of the notification.

Appeals shall be filed in the first instance with the Financial Department which has established the differences and which will notify the solution to the Joint Company within 30 days.

Against the solution given by the Financial Department, Joint Companies may appeal to the Ministry of Finance. Appeals will be solved by a committee consisting of delegates of the Ministry of Finance and of the Chamber of Commerce and Industry presided over by a judge from the Supreme Court.

Art. 9. Joint Companies are responsible for the exactness of the data regarding the tax computation and for turning it over within the prescribed term. Eluding taxation in any form shall be sanctioned with a fine of 25 per cent on the eluded tax.

For exceeding the payment term of the tax, an increase of 0.05 per cent will be applied for every day of delay, but not more than double the tax due.

Art. 10. The Ministry of Finance and the financial departments of the executive committees of the districts or of the City of Bucharest have the right to order the banking unit where the Joint Company keeps its account to transfer to the budget the taxes that have not been paid at the established terms, the fines and the legal increases.

Art. 11. The control of the computation of the tax and its turning over to the budget within the prescribed term as well as of the way in which the books, records, and vouchers are kept, the finding of infringements of the provisions of the present decree, and the application of administrative sanctions shall be carried out by the organs of the financial departments of the executive committees of the people's councils of the districts or of the City of Bucharest, as well as by the organs of the Ministry of Finance.

Art. 12. Taxes or tax differences can be established for no more than two years previously to the year when a tax omission has been found or when tax alterations are requested.

Prosecution of due taxes shall be prescribed after five years have passed as reckoned from the last decree of prosecution bearing a definite date.

Any money collected as taxes over and above those due shall be returned if requested within a year from the date of payment.

Art. 13. Profits remaining for the partners after payment of taxes shall be taxed at a rate of ten per cent if transferred abroad.

The taxation of incomes from wages and other forms of remuneration of the employees and collaborators of Joint Companies as well as the establishment and payment of other taxes and duties shall be made according to the legal stipulations in force in the Socialist Republic of Romania.

Art. 14. Joint Companies shall be registered with the Ministry of Foreign Trade and International Economic Cooperation and with the Ministry of Finance on the basis of the Contract of Association and Statutes duly approved as stipulated by the law. The registration fee shall be 5,000 lei, payable in the currency provided in the Contract of Association.

SOVIET UNION

DECREE No. 6362-XI

OF THE PRESIDIUM OF THE USSR SUPREME SOVIET

ON QUESTIONS CONCERNING THE ESTABLISHMENT IN THE TERRITORY OF THE USSR AND OPERATION OF JOINT VENTURES, INTERNATIONAL AMALGAMATIONS AND ORGANIZATIONS WITH THE PARTICIPATION OF SOVIET AND FOREIGN ORGANIZATIONS, FIRMS AND MANAGEMENT BODIES

(13 January 1987)

The Presidium of the USSR Supreme Soviet decrees:

1. Joint ventures established in the territory of the USSR with participation of Soviet and foreign organizations, firms and management bodies shall pay tax on profit at the rate and in the order provided for by the USSR Council of Ministers. Tax shall be appropriated to the USSR national budget.

Joint ventures shall be exempt from tax on profit for the two initial years of their operation.

The USSR Ministry of Finance shall be authorized to reduce the tax rate or to completely exempt from tax individual payers.

2. Collection of the sums of the tax not paid in time shall be carried out conformably to the procedure prescribed in regard of foreign legal persons by the Rules on Collection of Delayed Taxes and Non-tax Payments, endorsed by the Decree of the Presidium of the USSR Supreme Soviet of January 26, 1981 (Vedomosti Verkhovnogo Soveta SSSR, 1981, No. 5, Art. 122).

3. Unless otherwise provided for by a treaty between the USSR and respective foreign state, the part of the profit due to a foreign partner in a joint venture shall be taxed, if transferred abroad, at the rate stipulated by the USSR Council of Ministers.

4. Land, entrails of the earth, water resources, and forests may be made available for use to joint ventures as for payment as well as free of charge.

5. Disputes of joint ventures, international amalgamations and organizations with Soviet state-owned, cooperative and other public organizations, their disputes among themselves, as well as disputes among partners in a joint venture, international amalgamation or organization over matters related to their activity shall be considered by the USSR courts or, upon agreement of the parties, by an arbitration tribunal, and in cases stipulated by the USSR legislation - by tribunals of state arbitration.

In this connection Article 9 of the USSR Law of November 30, 1979 "On State Arbitration in the USSR" *(Vedomosti Verkhovnogo Soveta SSSR,* 1979, No. 49, Art. 844) shall be amended to include after the words "and organizations" the words "joint ventures, international amalgamations and organizations of the USSR and other CMEA member-countries."

DECREE No. 49

OF THE USSR COUNCIL OF MINISTERS

ON THE ESTABLISHMENT IN THE TERRITORY OF THE USSR AND OPERATION OF JOINT VENTURES WITH THE PARTICIPATION OF SOVIET ORGANIZATIONS AND FIRMS FROM CAPITALIST AND DEVELOPING COUNTRIES [18]

(13 January 1987)

For the purpose of further development of trade, economic, scientific and technical cooperation with capitalist and developing countries on a stable and mutually beneficial basis, the USSR Council of Ministers hereby decrees:

I. GENERAL PROVISIONS

1. Joint ventures with the participation of Soviet organizations and firms of capitalist and developing countries (hereinafter "joint ventures") shall be established in the territory of the USSR on the basis of agreements concluded by partners therein.

Joint ventures shall be governed in their activities by the Decree of the Presidium of the USSR Supreme Soviet of January 13, 1987, "On Questions Concerning the Establishment in the Territory of the USSR and Operation of Joint Ventures, International Amalgamations and Organizations with the Participation of Soviet and Foreign Organizations, Firms and Management Bodies", by this Decree and other legislative acts of the Union of Soviet Socialist Republics and Union Republics with exceptions provided for by interstate and intergovernmental agreements, which the USSR is a party to.

2. Proposals in respect of the establishment of joint ventures with feasibility studies and draft foundation documents annexed thereto shall be submitted by Soviet organizations concerned to Ministries and government agencies, under which they operate. Ministries and government agencies of the Union Republics shall submit such proposals to the Councils of Ministers of their Republics. [19]

Decisions on questions regarding the establishment on the territory of the USSR of joint ventures with firms from capitalist and developing countries will be made independently by the ministries and government agencies of the USSR and the councils of ministers of the of the Union republics. [20]

3. Ministries and government agencies, within the system of which Soviet partners in joint ventures operate, shall set up joint ventures with the purpose to satisfy more fully domestic requirements for certain types of manufactured products, raw materials and foodstuffs, to attract advanced foreign equipment and technologies, management expertise, additional material and financial resources to the USSR national economy, to expand the national export sector and to reduce superfluous imports.

---

18 SP SSSR 1987, No. 9, page 40. The text includes the amendments relative to joint ventures, contained in the Decision of 17 September 1987 of the CPSU Central Committee and the USSR Council of Ministers, entitled "On Additional Measures to Improve the Country's External Economic Activity in the New Conditions of Economic Management". The amendments were incorporated in Decree 49 through Decree No. 352 of 17 March 1988 of the USSR Council of Ministers.

19 See para. 35 of the Decree of the USSR Council of Ministers of 2 December 1988, entitled *On the further development of the external economic activities of state, co-operative and other public enterprises, amalgamations and organizations* (hereinafter "Decree of 2 December 1988"). See pp. 151-152 below.

20 Id.

II. PARTNERS, PROPERTY AND RIGHTS OF JOINT VENTURES

4. One or more Soviet enterprises (amalgamations and other organizations) which are legal persons, and one or more foreign firms (companies, corporations and other organizations) which are legal persons, may be partners in a joint venture.

5. The share of the Soviet side in the authorized fund of a joint venture shall be not less than 51 per cent. [21]

6. Joint ventures are legal entities under Soviet law. They may, in their own name, contract, acquire proprietary and non-proprietary personal rights, undertake obligations, sue and be sued in courts of justice and in arbitration tribunals. Joint ventures shall have an independent balance and operate on the basis of full cost accounting, self-support and self-financing.

7. A joint venture shall have a statute approved by its partners. The statute shall specify the nature of the joint venture, the objectives of its operation, its legal address, the list of partners, the amount of the authorized fund, the shares of partners therein, the procedure for raising the authorized fund (including foreign currency contents), the structure, composition and competence of the venture's management bodies, the decision-making procedure, the range of issues to be unanimously [22] settled, and the joint venture liquidation procedure. The statute may incorporate other provisions related to the specific character of the joint venture's operations unless these are contrary to Soviet law.

8. The period of operation of a joint venture shall be specified by its partners in an agreement on the establishment thereof or in the joint venture's statute (hereinafter "foundation documents").

9. As soon as the foundation documents come into force, joint ventures established in the territory of the USSR shall be registered with the USSR Ministry of Finance and acquire the rights of a legal persons at the time of registration. A notification on the establishment of joint ventures shall be published in the press.

10. The authorized fund of a joint venture is formed from contributions made by the partners. It can be replenished by using profits derived from business operation of the joint venture and, if necessary, through additional contributions by the partners.

11. Contributions to the authorized fund of a joint venture may include buildings, structures, equipment and other assets, rights to use land, water and other natural resources, buildings, structures and equipment, as well as other proprietary rights (including those to work inventions and use know-how), money assets in the currencies of the partners' countries and in freely convertible currencies.

12. The contribution of the Soviet partner to the authorized fund of a joint venture is evaluated, in agreement with the foreign partner, either in Soviet or in foreign currency, on the basis of agreed prices with due regard to world market prices. The contribution of the foreign partner is evaluated in the same manner, with the value of the contribution being converted to rubles at the official exchange rate of the USSR State Bank as of the date of signing the joint venture agreement or as of any other date agreed by the partners. In the absence of world market prices the value of contributed property is agreed by the partners.

13. Equipment, materials and other property imported into the USSR by foreign partners in a joint venture as their contribution to the authorized fund of the venture are exempt from custom duties. [23]

14. The property of a joint venture is subject to compulsory insurance with USSR insurance agencies. [24]

---

21 See para. 31 of the Decree of 2 December 1988.

22 See para. 31 of the Decree of 2 December 1988.

23 Id.

24 See para. 33 of the Decree of 2 December 1988.

15. A joint venture is entitled under Soviet legislation to own, use and dispose of its property in accordance with the objectives of its activities and the purpose of the property. The property of a joint venture shall not be requisitioned or confiscated in the administrative order.

The property rights of a joint venture shall be protected under Soviet legislation protecting state-owned Soviet organizations. Execution can be applied to the property of a joint venture only by a decision of bodies empowered under USSR legislation to hear disputes involving joint ventures.

16. Partners in a joint venture shall have the right to assign, by common consent, their shares in the joint venture fully or partially to third parties. In each particular case the assignment is effected with an endorsement of the ministry, government agency or Council of Ministers of the Union Republic which made the decision concerning the establishment of the joint venture. [25]

Soviet partners have the priority right to acquire shares of foreign partners. [26]

If a joint venture is reorganized its rights and obligations shall pass to the beneficiaries.

17. Industrial property rights, belonging to joint ventures are protected by the Soviet law, including protection in the form of patents. The procedure for the assignment of industrial property rights to a joint venture by partners therein and by a joint venture to partners therein, as well as for commercial exploitation of those rights and their protection abroad is defined by the foundation documents.

18. A joint venture shall be liable on its obligations in all of its property.

The Soviet State and the partners in a joint venture shall not be liable for its obligations, nor shall a joint venture be liable for the obligations of the Soviet State and of the partners in the venture.

Affiliates the of joint venture established in the territory of the USSR, which are legal persons, shall not liable for the obligations of joint ventures, nor shall joint ventures be liable for the obligations of such affiliates.

19. Joint ventures established in the territory of the USSR may set up affiliates and representation offices provided their foundation documents stipulate their right to do so.

Affiliates of joint ventures set up with the participation of Soviet organizations in other countries shall be established in the territory of the USSR in accordance with the rules which apply to the establishment of joint ventures.

20. Disputes between a joint venture and Soviet state-owned, cooperative and other public organizations, disputes among joint ventures, and disputes among partners in a joint venture over matters related to its activities shall be settled according to the legislation of the USSR either by the USSR courts or, by common consent of both sides, by an arbitration tribunal.

III. OPERATION OF JOINT VENTURES

21. The governing body of a joint venture is the Board consisting of persons appointed by the partners. Its decision-making procedure is defined by the foundation documents. [27]

The operational activities of a joint venture are governed by the Management consisting of Soviet and foreign citizens.

The Chairman of the Board and the Director-General shall be citizens of the USSR. [28]

22. A joint venture shall enter into relations with the central state authorities of the USSR and of the Union Republics through authorities superior to the Soviet partner in the

[25] Id.

[26] Id.

[27] See para. 31 of the Decree of 2 December 1988.

[28] Id.

joint venture. Its contacts with local government authorities and other Soviet organizations shall be direct.

23. A joint venture is independent in developing and approving its business operation programmes. State bodies of the USSR shall not fix any mandatory plans for a joint venture nor shall they guarantee a market for its products.

24. A joint venture is entitled to transact independently in export and import operations necessary for its business activities, including export and import operations in the markets of CMEA member-countries.

The aforementioned export and import operations may also be effected through Soviet foreign trade organizations or marketing networks of foreign partners under contractual arrangements.

Shipping into and out of the USSR by a joint venture of goods and other property is effected under licences issued according to legislation of the USSR.

A joint venture is entitled to maintain correspondence, as well as telegraph, teletype and telephone communications with organizations in other countries.

25. All foreign currency expenditures of a joint venture, including transfer of profits and other sums due to foreign partners and specialists shall be covered by proceeds from sales of the joint venture's products on foreign markets.

26. The principles regarding the sales of products of a joint venture on the Soviet market, and the supplies to the joint venture from this market of equipment, raw and other materials, components, fuel, energy and other produce, as well as the kinds of currencies to be paid in settlement for the products sold and goods purchased, shall be determined by the joint venture in agreement with Soviet enterprises and organizations.

27. If necessary, a joint venture may use credits on commercial terms:

in foreign currency - from the USSR Bank for Foreign Trade[29] or, with its consent from foreign banks and firms;

in rubles - from the USSR State Bank or the USSR Bank for Foreign Trade.

28. The USSR State Bank or the USSR Bank for Foreign Trade shall be authorized control that credits extended to a joint venture are used for their specified purposes, are secured and repaid in due time.

29. The monetary assets of a joint venture shall be deposited on its ruble account or currency account with the USSR State Bank and the USSR Bank for Foreign Trade, respectively, and shall be used for the purposes of the joint venture's operations. The money on the accounts of the joint venture shall bear interest:

in foreign currency - depending on the world money market rates;

in rubles - on terms and according to the procedure specified by the USSR State Bank.

Exchange rate fluctuations regarding foreign currency accounts of joint ventures and their operations in foreign currencies shall be carried to their profit-and-loss accounts.

30. A joint venture shall form a reserve fund and other funds necessary for its operation and for the social needs of its personnel.

Deductions from profits shall be added to the reserve fund until the latter totals 25 per cent of the authorized fund of the joint venture. The amount of annual deductions to the reserve fund shall be defined by the foundation documents.

The list of other funds and the way they are formed and used shall be specified by the foundation documents.

31. The profits of a joint venture, less the amounts to be appropriated by the USSR national budget and sums allocated to form and replenish the joint venture's funds shall

---

29 Now called the USSR Bank of External Economic Relations.

be distributed among the partners in proportion to each partner's share in the authorized fund.

32. Foreign partners in a joint venture are guaranteed that amounts due to them as their share in distributed profits of the joint venture are transferable abroad in foreign currency.

33. Joint ventures shall make depreciation payments under regulations applying to state-owned Soviet organizations unless a different system is stipulated by the foundation documents. The sums thus accumulated shall remain at the joint venture's disposal.

34. The design and construction of joint venture's facilities, including those intended for social needs, shall be effected through contractual arrangements and paid for with the joint venture's own or loan money. Prior to approval, designs shall be agreed upon under the procedure established by the USSR State Building Committee. Orders from joint ventures shall receive priority both as regards limits on construction/assembly work to be carried out by Soviet construction/assembly organizations and as regards material resources required for the construction. [30]

35. Cargoes of joint ventures shall be transported under the procedure established for Soviet organizations.

IV. TAXATION OF JOINT VENTURES

36. Joint ventures shall pay taxes at the rate of 30 per cent of their profit remaining after deductions to their reserve and other funds intended for the development of production, science and technology. Sums paid in taxes shall be appropriated to the USSR national budget.[31]

Joint ventures shall be exempt from taxes on their profits during the first two years from the moment when profits are declared. [32]

The USSR Ministry of Finance shall be authorized to reduce the tax rate or to completely exempt from tax individual payers.

37. The assessment of the profit tax shall be effected by a joint venture.

The amounts of the advance tax payment for a current year shall be declared by a joint venture on the basis of its financial plans for a current year. The assessment of the final tax amount on the profit, actually made during the expired financial year, shall be effected by a joint venture not later than March 15 of the year, following the year under review.

38. Financial authorities are empowered to verify tax calculations prepared by joint ventures.

Overpaid taxes for the expired year can either be set off against current tax payments, or refunded to the payer at the latter's request.

39. The amount of the profit tax declared for the current year shall be transferred to the budget by equal instalments not later than 15 days before the end of each quarter. The final amount shall be paid not later than April 1 of the year, following the year under review.

Delayed payments shall be charged at the rate of 0.05 per cent for every day of delay.

Collection of the sums of the tax not paid in time shall be carried out in conformity with the procedure prescribed in regard of foreign legal persons by the Rules on Collection of Delayed Taxes and Non-tax Payments, endorsed by the Decree of the Presidium of the USSR Supreme Soviet of January 26, 1981 (*Vedomosti Verkhovnogo Soveta SSSR*, 1981, No. 5, Art. 122).

40. A joint venture has the right to appeal against actions of financial authorities in regard to tax collection. An appeal is filed with the financial authority which verifies the tax calculation. Each case shall be decided within one month from the day the appeal is filed.

---

30 See para. 35 of the Decree of 2 December 1988.

31 See para. 31 of the Decree of 2 December 1988.

32 See para. 31 of the Decree of 2 December 1988.

A joint venture is entitled to appeal against this ruling before a superior financial authority within one month from the day of the ruling.

The filing of an appeal does not releave from paying the tax.

41. Unless otherwise provided for by a treaty between the USSR and respective foreign state, the part of the profit due to a foreign partner in a joint venture shall be taxed, if transferred abroad, at the rate of 20 per cent. [33]

42. The aforementioned taxation procedure is applied to income made by joint ventures established in the territory of the USSR and by in the USSR affiliates of joint ventures set up with the participation of Soviet organizations in other countries, as a result of their operations both in the territory of the USSR, on its continental shelf, in the USSR economic zone, and in the territory of other countries.

43. Regulations regarding the taxation of joint ventures shall be issued by the USSR Ministry of Finance.

V. SUPERVISION OF JOINT VENTURES' OPERATIONS

44. In order to enable partners in a joint venture to exercise their supervision rights, the foundation documents shall stipulate a procedure for providing partners with information related to the operation of the joint venture, the state of its property, its profits and losses.

A joint venture may set up an auditing service to be formed in a manner defined by the foundation documents.

45. Joint ventures shall maintain business, bookkeeping and statistical accounting in accordance with the standards established in the USSR for state-owned Soviet enterprises. The forms of such accounting and bookkeeping shall be jointly specified by the USSR Ministry of Finance and the USSR Central Board of Statistics.

Joint ventures shall be held responsible under Soviet law for complying with the accounting and bookkeeping procedure and for the correctness thereof.

Joint ventures shall not submit any accounting or business information to the state or other authorities of foreign countries.

46. The auditing of finance, business and commercial activities of joint ventures shall be carried out for a consideration by the Soviet auditing organization operating on a self-supporting basis.

VI. PERSONNEL OF JOINT VENTURES

47. The personnel of joint ventures shall consist mainly of Soviet citizens. The management of a joint venture shall conclude collective agreements with trade union organization formed at the enterprise. The contents of these agreements including provisions for the social needs of the personnel are defined by Soviet legislation and by the foundation documents.

48. The pay, routine of work and recreation, social security and social insurance of Soviet employees of joint ventures shall be regulated by Soviet legislation. This legislation shall also apply to foreign citizens employed at joint ventures, except for matters of pay, leaves, and pensions which are stipulated by a contract signed with each foreign employee. [34]

The USSR State Committee for Labour and Social Affairs and the All-Union Central Council of Trade Unions shall be authorized to adopt special rules for the application of Soviet social insurance legislation to foreign employees of joint ventures.

49. A joint venture shall make contributions to the USSR national budget for state-sponsored social insurance of Soviet and foreign employees, as well as payments for pen-

---

33 See para. 32 of the Decree of 2 December 1988.

34 See para. 31 of the Decree of 2 December 1988.

sions for Soviet employees in accordance with rates established for state-owned Soviet organizations. Contributions to cover foreign employees' pensions shall be transferred to respective funds in the countries of their permanent residence (in these countries' currencies).

50. The pay of foreign employees of a joint venture is subject to income tax at the rate and in accordance with the procedure set up by the Decree of the Presidium of the USSR Supreme Soviet of May 12, 1978 "On the Income Tax Levied on Foreign Legal and Physical Persons" (*Vedomosti Verkhovnogo Soveta SSSR*, 1978, No. 20, Art. 313). The unutilized portion of foreign employees' pay may be transferred abroad in foreign currency.

VII. LIQUIDATION OF JOINT VENTURES

51. A joint venture may be liquidated in cases and in the manner stipulated by the foundation documents, and also by a decision of the USSR Council of Ministers if the activities thereof are not consistent with the objectives defined by these documents. A notification of a liquidation of a joint venture shall be published in the press.

52. In the case of liquidation of a joint venture or upon withdrawal from it, the foreign partner shall have the right to return his contribution in money or in kind pro rata to the residual balance value of this contribution at the moment of liquidation of the joint venture, after discharging his obligations to the Soviet partners and third parties.

53. The liquidation of a joint venture shall be registered with the USSR Ministry of Finance.

DECREE

OF THE USSR COUNCIL OF MINISTERS

ON THE FURTHER DEVELOPMENT OF THE EXTERNAL ECONOMIC ACTIVITIES OF STATE, CO-OPERATIVE AND OTHER PUBLIC ENTERPRISES, AMALGAMATIONS AND ORGANIZATIONS

(2 December 1988)

Excerpts

QUESTIONS CONCERNING THE ORGANIZATION AND ACTIVITIES OF JOINT VENTURES, INTERNATIONAL AMALGAMATIONS AND ORGANIZATIONS

31. In order to activate the work on the establishment in the territory of the USSR of joint ventures with the participation of foreign organizations and firms it is decreed that:

- shares of the Soviet and foreign participants in the authorized fund of a joint venture shall be as agreed between them;
- a foreign citizen may act as Chairman of the Board or Director-General of a joint venture;
- fundamental questions regarding the activities of a joint venture shall be decided at meetings of the Board on the basis of unanimity of all Board members;
- matters of recruitment and dismissal, forms and amounts of pay, and of material incentives in Soviet roubles for the employees of a joint venture, shall be decided by the joint venture;
- goods imported in the USSR by a joint venture for production purposes may be subject to minimal customs duties or be exempted from duties;
- payments by foreign employees of a joint venture for housing and other services shall be made in Soviet roubles, with the exception of cases defined in decisions of the USSR Council of Ministers.

In order to further stimulate the establishment of joint ventures in the Far Eastern economic region it was deemed necessary to exempt these enterprises from taxes on their profits during the first three years from the moment of declaring profits.

The USSR Ministry of Finance is instructed:

- to work out and have approved, within a period of three months, a procedure for determining the taxable income of joint ventures, based on the practice adopted in foreign countries;
- to reduce to 10 per cent tax on the profit of joint ventures in the Far Eastern economic region.

32. It is considered expedient to give the USSR Ministry of Finance the right to exempt from taxation, for a definite period of time, part of the profit due to the foreign partner in a joint venture, when the profit is transferred abroad, or to reduce the rate of the tax, if not otherwise provided for in a treaty between the USSR and the respective country. This right is to be used primarily in respect of joint ventures producing consumer goods, medical equipment and medicin and high-technology products which are of priority importance to the national economy, as well as to joint ventures established in the Far Eastern economic region.

33. It is decreed that the transfer of shares in a joint venture, insurance of joint venture risks and auditing of its financial-economic activities shall be effected as agreed between the partners.

34. The Main State Customs Control Department at the USSR Council of Ministers jointly with the USSR Ministry of External Economic Relations and the USSR Ministry of Finance shall ensure that a preferential customs regime is accorded to foreign employees of joint ventures.

35. State enterprises, amalgamations and organizations are given the right to make decisions on the establishment of joint ventures, international amalgamations and organizations with foreign organizations and firms with the consent of the respective superior administrative organ.

Production co-operatives shall establish joint ventures, international amalgamations and organizations with foreign organizations and firms with the consent of the Council of Ministers of a Union Republic which has no provincial *('oblast')* structure, or the Council of Ministers of an Autonomous Republic, or the Regional *('Kraevoj')* Executive Council, or Provincial *('Oblastnoj')* Executive Council, or the Moscow City Executive Council, or the Leningrad City Executive Council, respectively, depending on the domicile of the co-operative, or with the consent of the Ministry (or department) that supervises the enterprise (organization, institution) where the co-operative has been established.

New construction or large-scale reconstruction when founding joint ventures, international amalgamations or organizations shall be made with the consent of the territorial administrative organs.

In other cases Soviet participants in joint ventures, international amalgamations and organizations shall submit to the territorial administrative organs the respective information.

Direct production and scientific-technical ties of production co-operatives with enterprises and organizations of socialist countries, as well as coastal and frontier traffic (performed by such co-operatives) with the respective countries shall be carried out with the consent of the Council of Ministers of a Union Republic with no provincial *('oblast')* structure, or the Council of Ministers of an Autonomous Republic, or the Regional *('Kraevoj')* Executive Council, or the Provincial *('Oblastnoj')* Executive Council, or the Moscow City Executive Council, or the Leningrad City Executive Council (depending on the domicile of the co-operative), taking into account the existing regulations covering these ties.

The USSR Chamber of Trade and Industry jointly with the Ministry of Foreign Affairs and the Ministry of External Economic Relations shall submit, within a period of three months and in accordance with the established procedure, proposals on direct economic relations of enterprises, amalgamations, production co-operatives and other organizations of the Far Eastern economic region with firms and organizations from countries of the Asian Pacific region.

The USSR Chamber of Trade and Industry, with the participation of interested enterprises, amalgamations, organizations, ministries and departments, shall organize, beginning from 1989, international tenders to attract foreign firms and organizations as well as Soviet enterprises, amalgamations, production co-operatives and other organizations, to co-operation projects in the Far Eastern economic region.

REGULATION No. 224[35]

THE USSR MINISTRY OF FINANCE

CONCERNING THE PROCEDURE OF REGISTERING JOINT VENTURES, INTERNATIONAL AMALGAMATIONS AND ORGANIZATIONS ESTABLISHED IN THE TERRITORY OF THE USSR WITH THE PARTICIPATION OF SOVIET AND FOREIGN ORGANIZATIONS, FIRMS AND AUTHORITIES

(24 November 1987)

I. GENERAL

1. These Regulations shall determine the procedure of registering the establishment and the liquidation of joint ventures, international amalgamations and organizations established in the territory of the USSR in accordance with Decree No. 48 of the Council of Ministers of the USSR of 13 January 1987 "On Procedures Governing the Establishment in the Territory of the USSR and the Activities of Joint Ventures, International Amalgamations and Organizations of the USSR and Other CMEA Member-Countries", the Decree of the Council of Ministers of the USSR of 13 January 1987 No. 49 "On Procedures Governing the Establishment in the Territory of the USSR and the Activities of Joint Ventures with the Participation of Soviet Organizations and Firms from Capitalist and Developing Countries", and the Decree of the CPSU Central Committee and the Council of Ministers of the USSR of 17 September 1987 No. 1074 "On Additional Measures of Improving the External Economic Activities in the New Economic Conditions".

2. Joint ventures, international amalgamations and organization established in the territory of the USSR with the participation of Soviet and foreign organizations, firms and authorities as well as affiliates of joint ventures and organizations shall be subject to registration.

3. State-owned, cooperative and other public enterprises and economic organizations shall be prohibited from entering into any transactions or contracts with joint ventures, international amalgamations and organizations before to the latter's registration.

Banks of the USSR shall open payment and current accounts for joint ventures, international amalgamations and organizations, grant money thereto and carry out operations of crediting and settling payments therewith only after the latter's registration has been properly effected.

4. Registration shall be effected by the Administration of State Revenues of the USSR Ministry of Finance.

5. Registration shall be effected on the basis of a written application by one of the participants in a joint venture, international amalgamation or organization.

The application for registration shall be accompanied by:

(a) when establishing a joint venture, international amalgamation or organization;

- a copy of the decision of a ministry or department of the USSR or the Council of Ministers of a Union Republic concerning the establishment in the USSR of that joint venture, international amalgamation or organization;
- notarized copies of the articles of establishment;

(b) when establishing an affiliate of a joint venture or organization - notarized copies of the articles of establishment of the joint venture or organization, and a copy of the Statute of the affiliate, approved by the highest body of the joint venture or organization.

---

35 Annexes referred to these Regulations are not included in this Guide.

Joint ventures, international amalgamations and organizations shall be obliged to submit, upon request from the Administration of State Revenues of the USSR Ministry of Finance, other documents certifying the information entered into the Register as well.

When registering the opening in the USSR of affiliates of joint ventures or organizations established in the territory of other countries with the participation of a Soviet organization, the general procedure of registration shall apply.

6. Each joint venture, international amalgamation and organization shall be obliged to inform the Administration of State Revenues of the USSR Ministry of Finance in a timely manner about any amendment in its articles of establishment or about any other amendments and additions which are subject to registration.

7. The Administration of State Revenues of the USSR Ministry of Finance shall inform the fiscal body exercising control over payments between the joint venture and the budget about the registration of the joint venture within 5 days following the date of such registration.

8. Provisions of these Regulations shall be extended to affiliates of joint ventures and organizations as well as to joint ventures, international amalgamations and orgãnizations established in the territory of the USSR with socialist countries other than CMEA members (subject to the particuliarities of application of the Decrees mentioned in para. 1, above, of the Council of Ministers of the USSR, as determined by the State Foreign Economic Commission of the Council of Ministers of the USSR).

II. REGISTRATION PROCEDURES

9. After checking the completeness and compliance with existing requirements of the documents submitted for registration, the Administration of State Revenues of the USSR Ministry of Finance shall effect the registration of a joint venture, international amalgamation or organization. For each of them a separate sheet in the Register shall be opened, into which the information specified by the columns of the Register (Annexes 1, 2, 3 and 4 to these Regulations) shall be issued to the registered joint venture, international amalgamation or organization.

A certificate of registration attested by the signature of the director of the Administration of State Revenues of the USSR Ministry of Finance or his deputy and by the stamp of the Administration of State Revenues (Annex 5 to these Regulations) shall be issued to the registered joint venture, international amalgamation or organization.

On the basis of the said certificate the joint venture, international amalgamation or organization shall publish a communication concerning its establishment. The information entered into the Register and published shall be regarded as known to third parties, and no disputes concerning this issue shall be considered by the USSR Ministry of Finance.

Amendments subject to registration shall be entered into the Register according to the general procedure.

Each entry in the Register as well as amendments or additions made thereto shall be attested by the signature of the director of the Administration of State Revenues of the USSR Ministry of Finance or by his deputy and by the stamp of the Department of State Revenues.

10. All pages in the Register Book should be numbered stringed through, sealed with the stamp of the Administration of State Revenues of the USSR Ministry of Finance, and signed by the director of the Administration of State Revenues or his deputy.

Entries in the Register shall be made in a shortened form accompanied by references to documents on the basis of which the respective entry has been made. Corrections to entries should be endorsed.

11. There shall be separate Register Books for joint ventures, international amalgamations and organizations. Thus, in the first book joint ventures involving Soviet and foreign organizations shall be registered; in the second one international amalgamations of the USSR and other CMEA member-countries; in the third one joint organizations of the

USSR and other CMEA member-countries; and in the fourth one affiliates of joint ventures and organizations.

12. The USSR Ministry of Finance shall have the right to suspend or refuse registration of a joint venture, international amalgamation or organization, where documents submitted do not comply with the USSR legislation concerning the establishment and activities of joint ventures, international amalgamations and organizations with the participation of Soviet and foreign organizations, firms and authorities within the USSR.

13. In case of liquidation, a joint venture, international amalgamation or organization shall be obliged to file a statement to this effect with the Administration of State Revenues of the USSR Ministry of Finance. Accordingly, the registration shall be effected on the basis of an excerpt from the minutes of the meeting of the highest body of the entity in liquidation or an excerpt from the resolution of the Council of Ministers of the USSR.

14. All documents submitted for registration shall be kept in a separate file at the Administration of State Revenues of the USSR Ministry of Finance.

The contents of documents submitted for registration may be disclosed to third parties only with the consent of the registered joint venture, international amalgamation or organization.

15. With the entry into force of these Regulations, the Regulations of the USSR Ministry of Finance of 12 February 1987 No. 34 "On the Procedure Governing Registration of Joint Ventures, International Amalgamations and Organizations Established in the Territory of the USSR with the Participation of Soviet and Foreign Organizations, Firms and Authorities" shall become null and void.

REGULATION No. 124

OF THE USSR MINISTRY OF FINANCE

ON TAXATION OF JOINT VENTURES

(4 May 1987)

I. GENERAL PROVISIONS

1. These Regulations define the procedure for settling taxes with the USSR State budget by joint ventures as well as by foreign partners in joint ventures set up in the USSR territory in compliance with the Decree of the USSR Supreme Soviet Presidium of 13 January 1987 "On Questions Concerning the Establishment in the USSR Territory and Operation of Joint Ventures, International Amalgamations and Organizations, Firms and Management Bodies", as well as with Decree No. 48 of the USSR Council of Ministers of 13 January 1987 "On the Establishment in the USSR Territory and Operation of Joint Ventures, International Amalgamations and Organizations of the USSR and other CMEA Member Countries", and Decree No. 49 "On the Establishment in the USSR Territory and Operation of Joint Ventures with the Participation of Soviet Organizations and Firms from Capitalist and Developing Countries".

2. These Regulations cover the taxation procedure of profits made by joint ventures set up in the territory and situated in the USSR and by branches of joint ventures set up with the participation of Soviet organisations and management bodies in other countries from their activities both in the USSR territory, on its continental shelf, in the USSR economic zone, as well as in the territory of other countries. The Regulations also extend to the taxation of profits made by branches of joint ventures situated in the USSR and which are legal entities.

3. Profit tax is paid by joint ventures operating on a profit-and-loss basis and maintaining independent balance-sheet and a current account with a bank.

4. A joint venture shall pay taxes amounting to 30 per cent of taxable profits according to the procedure stipulated in Para. 6 of this Regulation.

5. Calculation of sums due as profit taxes and payment thereof shall be made by a joint venture. A joint venture is liable for accurate calculation, timely payment of taxes to the budget and timely provision to finance bodies of prescribed reports.

II. CALCULATION AND PAYMENT TO THE BUDGET OF TAXES ON PROFITS

6. Profits of a joint venture liable to a tax shall be calculated as the difference between the balance profit and deduction to the joint venture's reserve fund and those other funds intended for the development of production, science and technology.

The amount of annual deductions to the reserve fund shall be defined in the foundation documents. Deductions to the reserve fund shall be limited to 25 per cent of the authorized fund of a joint venture.

The list of other funds intended for the development of production, science and technology, as well as the procedure for raising and spending them shall be stipulated in the foundation documents of a joint venture.

7. The amounts of advance tax payment for a current year shall be determined by a joint venture on the basis of its fiscal plan for the current year.

The amount of profits under the plan for the current year and amounts of advance payments in accordance with the specific dates of payment are notified by a joint venture to its local finance body not later than 15 January of the current year.

Profit tax under the plan for the current year shall be paid to the USSR State budget by equal instalments or 25 per cent of their annual amount due not later than 15 days prior to the expiry of each quarter, that is say before 15 March, 15 June, 15 September and 15 December.

8. The calculation of profit tax actually paid for an expired calendar year shall be effected by a joint venture not later than 15 March of the year following the year of account, on the basis of an accounting report (balance) for the expired year. The amount of any additional payment as a result of the recalculation is paid to the USSR budget prior to 1 April following the year of account.

When as a result of auditing a joint venture by a finance body or auditing firm the latter recalculates the profit tax, the additional amount of profit tax due shall be paid to the budget within 5 days after the date of receipt of the notification from the finance body.

An overpayment of tax can either be deducted from the current year's tax payments, or returned within 5 days to the payer at the latter's request.

9. A joint venture shall be obliged prior to 15 March following the year of account to submit to its local finance body the annual accounting report (balance), calculation of taxes according to the form attached thereto as Annex 1, as well as any other materials requested by finance body which are necessary to calculate profit tax.

10. The tax on joint venture profits shall be paid in roubles; the amount of tax is to be allocated to the USSR budget under Section 12, Para. 25 entitled Other revenues. of the classification of revenues and expenses.

When a profit tax is transferred to the budget the following record should be made in the column Type of payment on the face page of the payment order: Tax on profits of joint venture.

11. If the payment of profit tax to the budget is overdue a joint venture shall pay a fine amounting to 0.05 per cent per day of the overdue sum, for every day following the assigned date of payment until the date of actual payment of the tax.

Overdue payments shall be exacted in accordance with the procedure specified for foreign legal entities by the Rules for Exacting Overdue Taxes and Non-tax Payments of 26 January 1981, endorsed by the Decree of the Presidium of the USSR Supreme Soviet (1981 r., No. 4, CT 122).

III. TAXATION OF THE FOREIGN PARTNER'S SHARE OF PROFITS WHEN TRANSFERRED ABROAD

12. If transferred abroad, the part of the profit due to a foreign partner in a joint venture shall be liable to a tax equal to 20 per cent of that part unless a different arrangement is stipulated by an agreement between the USSR and the partner's country.

13. A joint venture files simultaneously with the USSR Bank for Foreign Trade an application for the transfer abroad of the part of profits together with the payment order to the USSR budget of the tax in the currency of transfer.

The tax on the foreign participant's share of profits of a joint venture to be transferred abroad is to be allocated to the USSR budget under Section/12, Para. 25 entitled Other revenues of the classification of revenues and expenses.

When the tax on the part of profits to be transferred abroad is carried to the budget, the following record should be made in the column Type of payment on the face page of the payment order: tax on profits of foreign partner in the joint venture.

14. A foreign partner in a joint venture who can benefit under international agreements signed by the USSR from the right to have taxes mentioned in Para. 12 of these Regulations reduced must file with the Administration for State Revenues of the USSR Ministry of Finance an application for the return of the amount of tax, or a part of it, in accordance with the form attached as Annex 2 hereto. Such an application should be accompanied by a copy of the document testifying the payment of taxes when profits due to a foreign partner in a joint venture have been transferred abroad.

An application should be filed within one year of the date when the tax was exacted. Applications filed upon expiry of this period will not be considered.

The USSR Ministry of Finance shall on the basis of filed documents take a decision on the return of the tax or a part of it to a foreign partner in a joint venture according to the established procedure.

IV. EXEMPTIONS FROM TAXATION OF JOINT VENTURES

15. A joint venture shall be exempt from profit tax during the first two years of operation.

16. The USSR Ministry of Finance is authorized to reduce the amount of tax payments, or completely exempt individual joint ventures from taxes. To enjoy such an exemption a joint venture shall submit to its local finance body together with the documents enumerated in Para. 9 of these Regulations in an application for the extension of the tax exemption substantiating the necessity to obtain such exemption.

Upon the receipt of this application the finance body shall check whether it is well founded and send the submitted materials as welll as its decision to the USSR Ministry of Finance.

A decision on this issue is made by the USSR Ministry of Finance within one month of receipt of all documents mentioned thereabove.

V. AUDITING BY FINANCE BODIES OF ACCURATE CALCULATION AND TIMELY PAYMENT TO THE BUDGET OF PROFIT TAX BY A JOINT VENTURE AND OF TAX ON THE PART OF PROFITS OF A FOREIGN PARTNER IN A JOINT VENTURE WHEN TRANSFERRED ABROAD

17. Local finance bodies are obliged:

- to audit accurate calculation, timely and full payment to the budget of profit taxes as well as timely reporting by taxpayers in the prescribed manner;
- to audit accurate and timely payment to the budget of taxes on a foreign partner's share of profits in a joint venture when they are transferred abroad;
- to instruct employees of enterprises subject to auditing and payment of profit taxes to the budget on issues pertaining to payments to the budget by joint ventures.

On the basis of information received from a joint venture on the amount of profit under the plan for the current year and the amounts of advance tax payments in conformity with the dates of payment, a finance body shall open a personal account where all advance amounts of tax are set down and carried to, as well as where all the results of recalculations are fixed.

Finance bodies have the right to require additional materials from taxpayers when auditing payments of profit tax.

18. On the receipt from a joint venture of an annual accounting report (balance) and tax calculation a finance body must audit the accuracy of the calculated and paid sums of profit tax and where there are mistakes in the tax calculation - notify the joint venture on the results of its audit within 15 days of receipt of the above materials.

Additional tax payments, deduction of overpaid taxes from the current year payments or returning such payments are carried out according to Para. 8 of these Regulations.

VI. APPEALING AGAINST THE ACTIONS OF FINANCE BODIES

19. A joint venture has the right to appeal against actions of finance bodies in connection with charging tax. An appeal must be lodged with the finance body auditing the tax calculation within one month of receipt by a joint venture of notification of the auditing results by the finance body. Where a joint venture fails to notify its disagreement with the

auditing results within the prescribed period on the amount of taxes shall be considered as final and actions of finance bodies cannot be claimed.

A finance body must pass a judgement on the appeal of a joint venture within one month of the date of application.

A joint venture is entitled to appeal against the judgement of a finance body to the USSR Ministry of Finance within one month.

Lodging an appeal does not mean that the appellant may refrain from paying the tax.

USSR MINISTRY OF FINANCE

USSR BOARD OF STATISTICS

ACCOUNTING AND BOOKKEEPING OF JOINT VENTURES, INTERNATIONAL AMALGAMATIONS AND ORGANISATIONS ESTABLISHED IN THE USSR TERRITORY

(27 February 1987)

The two Decrees of the USSR Council of Ministers of 13 January 1987 No. 48 "On the Establishment in the USSR Territory and Operation of Joint Ventures, International Amalgamations and Organisations of the USSR and other CMEA Member Countries" and No. 49 "On the Establishment in the USSR Territory and Operation of Joint Ventures with the Participation of Soviet Organisations and Firms from Capitalist and Developing Countries" stipulate that joint ventures, international amalgamations and organisations undertake operational accounting and bookkeeping in accordance with the procedure in force in the USSR for Soviet state-owned enterprises. Forms for such accounting and bookkeeping shall be approved by the USSR Ministry of Finance together with the USSR Central Board of Statistics.

The above-mentioned Decrees specify that joint ventures, international amalgamations and organisations are liable under the USSR legislation for accurate and authentic accounting and bookkeeping.

In conformity with the aforegoing the USSR Ministry of Finance and the USSR Central Board of Statistics set out the following:

1. When organising primary costs and financial accounting joint ventures, international amalgamations and organisations must use model forms of primary documents, approved in accordance with the procedure established in the USSR for relevant Soviet state-owned enterprises.
2. Accounting is carried out at joint ventures, international amalgamations and organisations according to the forms and methods in force in the USSR for Soviet state-owned enterprises.
3. Accounting and bookkeeping at joint ventures, international amalgamations and organisations will be carried out by accountants directed by the accountant general, whose activities are governed by the Statute on Accountants General approved by the Decree of the USSR Council of Ministers No. 59 of 24 January 1980.
4. Joint ventures, international amalgamations and organisations when recording economic operations in keeping accounts should do so in conformity with the Plan of bookkeeping accounts of production and economic activities of amalgamations, enterprises and organisations and its operative regulations approved by the Directive of the USSR Ministry of Finance No. 40 dated 28/March 1985 upon agreement with the USSR Central Board of Statistics.

The following specific activities of joint ventures, international amalgamations and organisations should be taken into account when applying the above-mentioned Plan of accounts:

- income derived from selling products, labour and services shall be recorded in account 46 Sale;
- payments of profit tax and salary tax shall be recorded in account 68 Payments to the budget;
- payments in connection with the compulsory insurance of joint ventures' property made to USSR insurance offices shall be recorded in account 69 Insurance payments;
- partners' contributions in joint ventures, international amalgamations and organisations shall be recorded in account 85 Authorised fund. These contrib-

utions should be recorded in the analytic account in respect of every partner in roubles and in foreign currency;

- assets of the reserve and other funds necessary for the operation of a joint venture and elevation of social level of its personnel shall be recorded in account 88 Special-purpose funds. Movement of assets in regard to each separate fund shall be recorded in similar sub-accounts;
- movement of monetary assets (including payments) in foreign currency shall be recorded in the framework of cost accounting.

5. Accounting of export and import operations shall be carried out in accordance with the procedure established for foreign trade associations of ministries and agencies.
6. Book-keeping and statistical reports must be filed by joint ventures, international amalgamations and organisations in accordance with the procedure established in the USSR for relevant Soviet state-owned enterprises.

DECREE NO. 74

OF THE STATE COMMITTEE FOR SUPPLIES

SUPPLIES OF MATERIALS AND EQUIPMENT TO JOINT VENTURES ESTABLISHED IN THE USSR TERRITORY WITH THE PARTICIPATION OF OTHER COUNTRIES AND FOREIGN FIRMS AND MARKETING OF THEIR PRODUCTS

(4 June 1987)

Note: *By the Decree of the USSR State Committee for Supplies of 4 November 1987 Sections 1 and 3 of this document were made applicable to joint ventures established in the USSR territory with participation of firms from capitalist and developing countries so as to allow joint ventures to choose different forms of marketing their products on the Soviet market and of obtaining deliveries of goods from that market.*

1. Supplies of material and technological resources produced in the USSR to joint ventures of the USSR and other CMEA member countries established in the Soviet Union territory shall be effected through the Soviet system of supplies of materials and technical means by way of wholesale trade on the basis of agreements with territorial agencies of the USSR State Committee for Supplies or through the interested ministries and government agencies founders in accordance with the established procedure for them.

Supplies of material resources produced in the USSR for joint ventures set up by the USSR ministries and government agencies and Councils of Ministers of Union Republics, whose enterprises and organisations now come under the system of supplies on the basis of wholesale trade, shall be effected in conformity with the Statute on Wholesale Trade in Industrial and Engineering Products approved by the Directive of the USSR State Committee for Supplies No. 85 of 13 June 1986, except for some specific types of products which are identified by the USSR State Committee for Supplies and the USSR State Planning Committee which shall be supplied through the ministries and government agencies-founders.

Joint venture requirements in material resources produced in the USSR shall be met by the ministries and agencies-founders on the basis of orders from these ventures, drawn up in accordance with the pre-planned volume of production. Joint venture orders shall be taken into consideration by ministries and government agencies-founders when they develop supply plans for various branches of the economy. Such orders are executed according to the procedure established for supplies to enterprises of corresponding ministries and agencies.

Joint ventures shall pay for the supplied resources on the basis of wholesale or contractual prices.

2. Supplies of imported products to joint ventures of the USSR and other CMEA member countries established in the Soviet Union territory shall be carried out by way of purchases made by these ventures in external markets independently, or under agreements through relevant Soviet foreign trade associations for their own or borrowed foreign exchange on foreign trade prices.

Where joint ventures have no own or borrowed foreign exchange to buy the required imported products, corresponding ministries and government agencies shall provide for such products in accordance with the procedure established for importing products on wholesale or contractual prices.

3. The sale of products by joint ventures of the USSR and other CMEA member countries in the Soviet Union shall be effected in the framework of wholesale trade on wholesale or contractual prices in accordance with the Directive of the USSR State Committee for Supplies No. 85 of 13 June 1986, or through relevant Union Administrations for Supplies.

Such ventures shall market their products in external markets either independently, or under agreements through relevant Soviet foreign trade associations on foreign trade prices.

4. Supplies to joint ventures established in the Soviet Union territory with the participation of firms from capitalist and developing countries shall be effected:

- with regard to commodities, materials and engineering goods produced in the USSR - on the basis of contracts to be concluded with relevant Soviet foreign trade organizations in the framework of the range of goods and commodities allotted thereto; in accordance with USSR legislation, products shall be paid for in roubles on contractual prices with regard to world market prices;
- in respect of local materials and services - under agreements with territorial agencies of the USSR Committee for Supplies system and other local economic organisations, products and services shall be paid for in roubles on wholesale and contractual prices;
- in respect of imported products - by way of purchases made by joint ventures independently in external markets or under agreements through relevant Soviet foreign trade associations for their own or borrowed foreign exchange on contractual prices with regard to world market prices.

5. The sale of products from joint ventures set up with the participation of capitalist and developing countries in the Soviet Union shall be effected under agreements to be concluded with Soviet foreign trade associations in the framework of the range of goods and commodities allotted thereto and in accordance with USSR legislation; products shall be paid for in roubles on contractual prices with regard to world market prices. Soviet foreign trade associations shall sell joint venture products either directly to customers, or in accordance with the prescribed procedure through corresponding Union Administrations of Supplies.

Joint ventures shall sell their products in external markets either independently, or under agreements through Soviet foreign trade associations on foreign trade prices.

EXECUTIVE ORDER

OF THE STATE BANK OF THE USSR AND THE BANK FOR FOREIGN TRADE OF THE USSR

ON THE PROCEDURE FOR CREDITING AND SETTLEMENT OF ACCOUNTS OF JOINT VENTURES, INTERNATIONAL AMALGAMATIONS AND ORGANIZATIONS OF THE USSR AND OTHER CMEA MEMBER-COUNTRIES, AS WELL AS OF JOINT VENTURES WITH THE PARTICIPATION OF SOVIET ORGANIZATIONS AND FIRMS FROM CAPITALIST AND DEVELOPING COUNTRIES

(22 September 1987)

In accordance with the Decrees of the Council of Ministers of the USSR of 13 January 1987 Nos. 48 and 49, and for the purposes of deepening the socialist economic integration, closer consolidating the scientific and technical potentials of the countries of the Socialist community, further developing the trade, economic, scientific and technological co-operation with capitalist and developing countries, joint ventures, international amalgamations and organizations of the USSR and other CMEA member-countries as well as joint ventures with the participation of Soviet organizations and firms from capitalist and developing countries (hereinafter referred to as "joint ventures") may be established in the territory of the USSR.

This procedure shall govern the mode of settlement of accounts and crediting in roubles and in foreign currency of production and marketing requirements of joint ventures, as well as the financing and crediting of capital investments.

Section 1. Short-term crediting in roubles

1.1 Working capital requirements of a joint venture shall be met from its own assets (authorized capital) or through short-term bank credits in roubles.

1.2 Rouble assets of joint ventures shall be held on their accounts opened in local offices where the respective ministries have their balance accounts.

In order to open a current account, a joint venture shall submit to the bank the following documents;

- an application of the joint venture for opening an account;
- notarized copies of the agreement between the parties on the establishment of the joint venture, and of its statutes;
- a notarized copy of the certificate issued by the Department of State Revenues of the USSR Ministry of Finance attesting the registration of the joint venture;
- a card with the notarized patterns of signatures and an impression of the stamp.

Interest at the rate of 0.5 per cent per annum shall be paid by the bank on the joint venture's current account.

1.3 Banks shall extend short-term credits in roubles to joint ventures to pay for, and against the remainder of, raw materials, uncompleted production, expenses of future periods, other stocks and expenditures; against domestically shipped goods in respect of which payment is not yet due, and for opening letters of credit.

A loan against inventories shall be secured by a lien.

1.4 Joint ventures shall pay interest to the banks for the use of a credit according to rates specified for the corresponding field of the economy.

1.5 Credits shall be extended from loan accounts. In order to open a loan account, a joint venture shall submit a statement of undertaking (Annex 1) and its opening balance-sheet to the bank.

1.6 For the purpose of determining the amount of the credit required, the enterprise shall submit to the bank a credit application for the coming year, subdivided into quarters (Annex 2).

The amount of credit determined by the bank and the enterprise shall be the limit of crediting.

In case of a change in the terms of manufacturing, raw material supplies, or marketing of products the enterprise shall submit an amended calculation to the bank.

Bank offices shall communicate the specified limits of crediting joint ventures for the coming year, subdivided into quarters, to the credit department of the higher-level bank.

1.7 Payment of invoices for inventories or services and opening letters of credit shall be effected, in the absence of funds on the current account, from the loan account within the limit of free crediting. Repayment of the loan shall be effected within the time limits determined in the agreed credit application or, before the expiration of same, upon instructions from the enterprise.

1.8 The credit security shall be checked monthly, according to the form given in Annex 4, on the basis of the balance sheet of the enterprise and accompanying information (Annex 3).

1.9 The following shall not be accepted for crediting:

- the remainder of finished goods intended for sale to the domestic market over and above the own sources allocated for same, except in cases of delays in deliveries of goods due to transportation difficulties or the termination of deliveries to unpunctual payers;
- goods shipped and services rendered where documents have not been presented to the bank for repayment of loans within the specified time limits, or not paid for by customers within the time limits;
- inventories in transit for more than 5 months.

1.10 Credits against a surplus of the security shall be extended within the limit of crediting and shall be used to settle overdue liabilities; its remainder, upon request from the enterprise, may be transferred to the enterprise's current account.

1.11 Any deficiency in the loan security shall be recovered from the enterprise's current account, and in the absence of funds on the account, the deficiencies shall be transferred to the overdue loan account.

1.12 No new loans shall be granted to enterprises having overdue debts on bank loans in excess of two months. The incoming receipts shall be used for settlement of overdue loan repayments.

In such cases extension of new credits to a joint venture may be resumed, on receipt by the crediting bank of a guarantee from a foreign bank to the effect that any amounts on repayment of credits overdue now or in the future shall be settled by the joint venture.

1.13 Crediting of a joint venture against export transactions in case of its direct operations in foreign markets (without co-ordination services of Soviet foreign trade organizations) shall be effected against export goods in transit within the USSR and abroad as well as against export goods stored at ports and warehouses in the USSR whether sold or not.

Periods for which export goods shall be accepted for crediting shall depend on the terms of payment specified in a contract between the joint venture and a foreign customer, or determined by agreement with the bank office.

1.14 Crediting of export transactions shall be effected from a separate unlimited loan account.

For the purpose of opening such an account the enterprise shall submit a statement of undertaking to its bank in accordance with the form given in Anenx 5.

1.15 To secure payment of goods sold abroad where payments are made by instalments, joint ventures should submit foreign bank guarantees (as a rule, those of correspondent banks of Vneshtorgbank, USSR, or, where this is impossible, guarantees from insurers, large firms or the founders of the joint venture.

1.16 Banks shall exercise control over the purposeful use of credits extended to joint ventures, securities and timely repayment of same with visits to certain locations, if necessary.

1.17 Banks may extend credits to Soviet participants in international amalgamations and organizations for the period of up to 3 years for the purpose of contributing to the financial fund of an international amalgamation (organization), created for financing its activities, including the cost of maintenance of its staff and expenses on business trips relating to items of joint activities. The said credits shall be extended against guarantees from respective higher-level organizations.

In order to obtain such credits, the Soviet participant in an international amalgamation (organization) shall submit to the bank a calculation of the credit requirement and its repayment with the indication of sources.

Section 2. Financing and crediting of capital investments

2.1 Designing and capital construction of joint ventures, including social projects, shall be carried out under contracts and from their own capital and loan capital. Prior to their approval by a joint venture, projects shall be subject to approval as prescribed by the USSR State Committee for Construction (Gosstroi).

2.2 Financing and settlement of accounts for capital investments from a joint venture's own capital shall be effected in the manner prescribed from its current account. Upon request from the enterprise a separate bank account may be opened for accumulating and spending funds for these purposes (it is opened with the same balance account that maintains the current account).

2.3 When carrying out construction work involving the drawing of a credit, a credit agreement (Annex 6) shall be concluded between the bank office and the joint venture. The credit requirement shall be determined according to a calculation of the credit necessary for capital investments (Annex 2a).

2.4 Bank offices shall extend credits in roubles to joint ventures for the purposes of:

- constructing industrial projects within the limits of the approved estimated costs for a period of up to 6 years following the date of granting the first loan, provided that the works will be carried out and the credit repaid within the specified period;
- developing the material and technical basis of the social sphere in the amount of up to 75 per cent of the cost of construction works for a period of up to 6 years following the date of completion of the work, subject to repayment of the credit from the total revenues of the joint venture.

The bank shall exercise control over the purposeful use of the credit. Where a credit is not used for the intended purposes, it shall be withdrawn before expiration of the time limit and the credit agreement shall be cancelled.

Credits for new projects shall not be granted where there are overdue repayments under previously granted loans.

2.5 For use of long-term credits joint ventures shall pay interest to banks at the rates fixed for the respective branches of the economy.

2.6 Upon completion of a project, separate liability notes shall be drawn up for repayment of arrears of the loan within specified time limits.

Bank officeers may allow deferred repayment of loan arrears within the total time limit for which the loan was granted.

Section 3. Crediting in foreign currency

3.1 A joint venture shall meet its foreign currency requirements in transactions with foreign contractors from its authorized capital.

A joint venture may use credits in foreign currency obtained on commercial terms from Vneshtorgbank, USSR, or by approval of the latter from foreign banks and companies. The source of repaying such credits shall be the revenue from export sales.

3.2 Short-term credits in foreign currency to purchase raw and other materials, components etc. shall be extended by the USSR Vneshtorgbank for a period of up to 2 years.

3.3 Joint ventures may be given medium-term and long-term credits to pay for imported equipment, machines, licenses and other goods as well as services, required for the modernization and expansion of production. The periods of repaying such credits shall be determined by the USSR Vneshtorgbank depending on the payback of the object of crediting.

3.4 Internationally accepted currency assets belonging to a joint venture may be used as credit securities.

In cases where the security is insufficient, a credit in foreign currency may be extended under guarantees of the founders of a joint venture or under guarantees of foreign banks and companies.

Where a joint venture has unsecured debt the USSR Vneshtorgbank shall be entitled to draw any currency reserves available on the account of the joint venture at the USSR Vneshtorgbank in order to redeem such debt.

3.5 Credits in foreign currency shall be extended by the USSR Vneshtorgbank on usual commercial terms and subject to charging an interest in foreign currency on the unpaid part of the debt under a credit.

The rates of interest shall be determined by the USSR Vneshtorgbank on the basis of existing world money market rates for the respective currencies.

3.6 When extending a credit in foreign currency, the USSR Vneshtorgbank shall charge a liability commission to the borrower at the rate of 0.5 per cent per annum from the unused part of the said credit.

The enterprise-borrower shall compensate USSR Vneshtorgbank for the commission paid by the latter, as well as any cable and other expenses in foreign currency relating to the drawing of the credit.

In cases where the exchange rate of the currency in which the foreign trade contract was concluded using the credit facilities is altered, the difference in the exchange rates shall be borne by the borrower.

The interests charged and the differences in rates of exchange arising while using a credit shall not be included in the overall limit of the credit extended in foreign currency.

3.7 In order to obtain a credit, the enterprise-borrower shall submit an application to the USSR Vneshtorgbank which should contain the following information:

a) the purpose for which the credit is requested, its amount, and the period over which the credit is required;

b) the specification of the goods purchased abroad and their value, the name of country where the purchase will be made, and the currency of payment;

c) the economic effect of using the machines, equipment materials, and other merchandise, licenses intended for purchase on account of the credit, and payback periods for projects which are to be carried out with the use of the credit.

The application of the enterprise-borrower shall be accompanied by documents made up in accordance with the forms contained in Annexes 8, 9 and/10.

The USSR Vneshtorgbank may require from the enterprise-borrower the submission of a report on the financial status of the enterprise as well as additional information concerning the purposes for which the credit was used, on the repayment of same, and on the performance of the equipment purchased with the credit.

3.8 When the extension of a credit is agreed to, the USSR Vneshtorgbank and the enterprise-borrower shall enter into a credit agreement governing the procedure of granting loans in foreign currency, the use of same, the manner of payments, the terms of calculating interests and of paying off the indebtness of the enterprise-borrower.

Such credit agreement shall be signed:

- for the Bank for Foreign Trade of the USSR: by the Chairman of the Board or his Deputy or other authorized persons;
- for the enterprise-borrower: by its director or his deputy.

The form of a credit agreement is contained in Annex 7.

3.9 Credits shall be obtained on the basis of remittance orders or orders for opening letters of credit, or on the basis of a communication from a foreign bank on the payment made to a foreign exporter on account of the credit extended by that bank to the USSR Vneshtorgbank.

3.10 Orders for remitting currency abroad (for opening letters of credit) submitted by an enterprise-borrower to the USSR Vneshtorgbank shall contain, in addition to the usual requisites, a note "on account of credit in foreign currency", and the number of the respective loan account of the enterprise-borrower.

3.11 Records on the use of credits in foreign currency extended to enterprises for opening letters of credit and for payments of imported goods shall be kept on separate loan accounts.

3.12 Where an enterprise-borrower fails to repay any outstanding credit amounts within the prescribed time limits, the USSR Vneshtorgbank shall consider the reasons for the delay in repaying the credit and shall have the right to redeem what is due from the enterprise-borrower of the credit in foreign currency (main debt and interest) by using the funds available on his foreign currency account.

3.13 Where there are no such funds available on the currency account of a joint venture, the amount not repaid in time shall be transferred to the account of overdue debt under credits in foreign curency with an additional interest of 3 per cent per annum in addition to the interest specified in the credit agreement. In such circumstances, the bank may declare the whole existing debt under a given credit as due for repayment and charge it with an additional interest of 3 per cent per annum; the bank shall also be entitled to take recourse against any other sources and channel all the incoming revenues for repayment of the credit.

3.14 The USSR Vneshtorgbank shall exercise control over the purposes and efficiency of using the credits extended in foreign currency. Such control shall be exercised, in particular, by carrying out on site inspections.

3.15 The on site inspections shall be carried out by the USSR Vneshtorgbank, as a rule, with representatives of the founders of the enterprise-borrower. Representatives of other Soviet banks may also be involved in such inspections.

3.16 Where an enterprise-borrower systematically fails to fulfil the terms of a credit agreement, or to comply with requirements and recommendations of the bank, the USSR Vneshtorgbank, in accordance with the terms of the credit agreement, shall have the right:

- to suspend further use of the credit;
- to demand from the enterprise-borrower repayment of all foreign currency credits extended earlier ahead of schedule.

3.17 The USSR Vneshtorgbank, upon application from joint ventures, may issue guarantees and warranties in accordance with its Statutes and existing bank rules.

Section 4. Settlement of accounts

4.1 Joint ventures involving Socialist countries, international amalgamations and organizations shall settle their accounts with Soviet suppliers and customers in the same manner as prescribed for internal settlement of payments.

The parties may provide by agreement for the following forms of payment:

- by payment orders (the acceptance procedure shall be outlined in the agreement; the corresponding endorsements shall be made on the payment orders);
- by payment instructions;
- by letters of credit;
- by limited book cheques.

In cases where supplies to the said joint ventures, international amalgamations and organizations, as well as sales of their products, are effected through foreign trade organizations, accounts shall be settled in the same manner stipulated for such settlements with Soviet exporters and importers.

Joint ventures involving Soviet organizations and firms from capitalist and developing countries shall settle their accounts with Soviet suppliers and customers through foreign trade organizations at world market prices; and where goods are purchased and services rendered at domestic market prices, settlements shall be effected in the manner provided for domestic payments.

4.2 Joint ventures, directly operating in foreign markets shall settle their accounts under export-import transactions in accordance with terms of contracts by methods of collection, documentary letters of credit, bank remittances and other methods accepted in international banking practice.

Joint ventures may enter foreign markets through Soviet foreign trade organizations, and those with participants from capitalist or developing countries additionally through sales network of foreign partners in the joint ventures.

4.3 For the purpose of keeping currency funds and settling international accounts, separate currency accounts shall be opened for joint ventures with the USSR Vneshtorgbank or its branches in accordance with procedures set out in Para. 1.2 of this document.

Interest at rates fixed by the USSR Vneshtorgbank shall be paid on such foreign currency accounts.

4.4 Cable and other expenses incurred in the course of executing instructions given by joint ventures shall be borne by them at their actual cost and shall be charged in the currency of payment. Banks shall collect a commission for rendering their services to joint ventures according to their tariffs.

This procedure shall also apply to crediting, and settlement of payments of joint ventures, international amalgamations and organizations with the participation of socialist countries other than CMEA members.

INSTRUCTIONS ON THE PROCEDURE GOVERNING THE INSURANCE OF THE ASSETS AND INTERESTS OF JOINT VENTURES

(5 June 1987)

I. GENERAL

1. These Instructions establish the procedure for insurance of joint ventures, international amalgamations and organisations set up in accordance with the Decree No. 48 of the USSR Council of Ministers of 13 January 1987 "On the Establishment in the Territory of the USSR and Operation of Joint Ventures, International Amalgamations and Organisations of the USSR and Other CMEA Member Countries", as well as with Decree No. 49 of the USSR Council of Ministers of 13 January 1987 "On the Establishment in the Territory of the USSR and Operation of Joint Ventures with Participation of Soviet Organisations and Firms from Capitalist and Developing Countries".

2. The assets and property interests of joint ventures, international amalgamations and organisations set up in the territory of the USSR with the participation of Soviet and foreign organisations, firms and management bodies and of the affiliates of joint ventures and organizations shall be insured.

3. The insurance of the assets and property interests of joint ventures shall be effected by the Insurance Company of the USSR (Ingosstrakh).

II. TYPES OF INSURANCE

4. Insurance cover shall be taken out in respect of the following types of joint venture assets and property interests:

4.1 Fixed assets owned or leased by the joint venture:

4.1.1 For the period of the construction of buildings, structures and installations of equipment - on all risks of construction and all risks of installation conditions;

4.1.2 after commencement of operations - against fire and natural hazards.

4.2 Parts of working assets, *viz.: stocks* of materials and finished stock in storehouses of an enterprise, semi-finished products of own making - against fire and natural hazards.

4.3 Losses due to a downturn in production or economic activities, resulting from a fire.

4.4 Civil liabilities of a joint venture:

4.4.1 for causing injury to health or property of Soviet workers and officers employed at the joint ventures during the performance of their professional duties;

4.4.2 for polluting the environment;

4.4.3 for causing injury to health or property of third parties;

4.4.4 in connection with the operation of motor vehicles owned by the joint venture.

5. In addition to the above types of insurance and depending on the nature of economic activities of the joint venture, the following types of insurance may be effected:

5.1 Insurance of the equipment and machinery against failure, and insurance against losses due to a downturn in production, resulting from a failure in machinery.

5.2 Goods-in-transit insurance.

5.3 Insurance of the property and stocks of commodities against burglary.

5.4 Property insurance against water damage.

5.5 Insurance of electronic equipment.

5.6 Insurance of animals.

5.7 Insurance of other risks connected with the specific economic activities of a joint venture, i.e., storing and transporting products under special circumstances, special types of civil liability, etc.

6. Insurance of the types stated in para. 5 shall be effected by a joint venture at its own discretion, depending on the specific requirements of its economic activities.

III. PROCEDURE FOR TAKING OUT INSURANCE

7. The insurance contract shall be concluded in the form of an insurance policy signed by the authorized representatives of the Ingosstrakh and the joint venture on the basis of a written application for insurance filed by the joint venture with Ingosstrakh within the following time limits:

7.1 in respect of insurance of the types stated in para. 4.1.1, not later than one month prior to the starting date of the construction work or installation of the equipment;

7.2 in respect of insurance of the types stated in paras. 4.1.2, 4.2, 4.3, 4.4.2, not later than one month prior to the date of putting the buildings and the equipment into operation;

7.3 in respect of insurance of the type stated in para. 4.4.4, not later than three days prior to the date of transfer of the motor vehicles for operation;

7.4 in respect of insurance of the types stated in paras. 4.4.1 and 4.4.3, within one month after the date of registration of the joint venture, international association or their affiliates.

8. Applications for insurance shall be drafted according to the prescribed forms contained in Annexes [....! to these Instructions and shall be integral parts of insurance contracts. Joint ventures shall be liable for the authenticity of the information given in insurance applications in accordance with the rules and conditions of insurance.

9. A joint venture shall be bound, upon request from Ingosstrakh, to submit schemes of layout of induvidual objects of the joint venture, information on fire-extinguishing systems or fire-alarm systems and any other information necessary for assessing the degree of risk.

10. Upon consideration of an application for insurance, Ingosstrakh shall send the joint venture a draft insurance policy which states the rules or conditions of insurance, the amounts of insurance, the liability limits of Ingosstrakh, the time limits, the cost of insurance (insurance premium), and other necessary information. A draft insurance policy shall be prepared within 14 days following the date of receipt of all necessary information from the joint venture and shall be signed by Ingosstrakh's authorized officers.

11. The joint venture shall send to the Ingosstrakh within 30 days following the date of receipt of a draft policy, one copy of that document signed by its authorized officers; the contract of insurance (insurance policy) being considered thereafter as having entered into force, or shall inform the Ingosstrakh of its observations and proposals concerning the draft policy.

12. In the latter case, upon the consideration of such observations, Ingosstrakh shall prepare and send to the joint venture an insurance policy to be signed by the authorized officers of the joint venture within a time limit of 30 days.

13. Insurance of the risks given in paras. 5.1 to 5.7 shall be effected on the basis of a written application for insurance (letter, telex, cable) with the indication of the data necessary for the preparation of an insurance policy. For example, while applying for goods-in-transit insurance (para. 5.2), the application shall indicate the type of cargo, its packing, the amount and weight, the place of loading and the place of destination of the cargo, the type of vehicle transporting the cargo, the number and date of the shipping document (bill

of lading, waybill, invoice of road haulage, etc.), the amount of insurance, and the conditions of insurance.

On the basis of this data Ingosstrakh shall prepare, within three days, a goods-in-transit insurance policy and shall send to the joint venture the original together with a debit note for payment of the insurance premium.

14. The joint venture shall be bound to inform Ingosstrakh of all significant alterations concerning insured objects, the sums of insurance and the degree of risk. Ingosstrakh shall be entitled to review the conditions of insurance or require payment of an additional insurance premium on the basis of such alterations.

15. The alterations of the signed contract of insurance shall be made in the form of an addendum signed by Ingosstrakh; such an addendum shall be an integral part of the insurance contract and the insurance policy.

16. Where the insurance premium is not paid within the time limits stipulated in the insurance policy, the insurance contract shall lapse with regard to the liabilities of Ingosstrakh.

17. The procedure for filing claims upon the insurance cover indicated in paras. 4 and 5 with Ingosstrakh and the procedure for Ingosstrakh to consider such claims and pay compensation shall be defined in the corresponding rules and conditions of insurance which are an integral part of the insurance contract. Compensation shall be paid in the same currency given in the insurance contract and used for the payment of the insurance premium.

PART THREE

MODEL DOCUMENTS

1. PRE-FEASIBILITY STUDY

A. OUTLINE OF A PRE-FEASIBILITY STUDY [36]

1. Executive summary - a synoptic review of all the essential findings of each chapter.[37]

2. Project background and history:

(a) Project sponsor(s);

(b) Project history;

(c) Cost of studies and/or investigations already performed.

3. Market and plant capacity:

(a) Demand and market

(i) The estimated existing size and capacities of the industry (specifying market leaders), its past growth, the estimated future growth (specifying major programmes of development), the local dispersal of industry, its major problems and prospects, general quality of goods;

(ii) Past imports and their future trends, volume and prices;

(iii) The role of the industry in the national economy and the national policies, priorities and targets related or assigned to the industry;

(iv) The approximate present size of demand, its past growth, major determinants and indicators;

(b) Sales forecast and marketing

(i) Anticipated competition for the project from existing and potential local and foreign producers and supplies;

(ii) Localization of market(s);

(iii) Sales programme;

(iv) Estimated annual sales revenues from products and by-products (local/foreign);

(v) Estimated annual costs of sales promotion and marketing;

(c) Production programme (approximate)

(i) Products;

(ii) By-products;

(iii) Wastes (estimated annual cost of waste-disposal);

(d) Determination of plant capacity

(i) Feasible normal plant capacity;

(ii) Quantitative relationship between sales, plant capacity and material inputs.

36 Source: Manual for the Preparation of Industrial Feasibility Studies (ID/206). United Nations Industrial Development Organization (UNIDO), Vienna, 1986, pp. 223-225. Additional information may be taken from the detailed check-list and schedules given in each chapter of the *Manual*.

37 See page 180 below.

4. Material inputs (approximate input requirements, their present and potential supply positions, and a rough estimate of annual costs of local and foreign material inputs):

(a) Raw materials;

(b) Processed industrial materials;

(c) Components;

(d) Auxiliary materials;

(e) Factory supplies;

(f) Utilities, especially power.

5. Location and site (preselection, including, if appropriate, an estimate of the cost of land).

6. Project engineering:

(a) Preliminary determination of scope of project;

(b) Technology(ies) and equipment;

(i) Technologies and processes that can be adopted, given in relation to capacity size;

(ii) Rough estimate of costs of local and foreign technology;

(iii) Rough layout of proposed equipment (major components);

a. Production equipment;

b. Auxiliary equipment;

c. Service equipment;

d. Spare parts, wear and tear parts, tools;

(iv) Rough estimate of investment cost of equipment (local/foreign), classified as above;

(c) Civil engineering works

(i) Rough layout of civil engineering works, arrangement of buildings, short description of construction materials to be used:

a. Site preparation and development;

b. Buildings and special civil works;

c. Outdoor works;

(ii) Rough estimate of investment cost of civil engineering works (local/foreign), classified as above.

7. Plant organization and overhead costs:

(a) Rough organization layout

(i) Production;

(ii) Sales;

(iii) Administration;

(iv) Management;

(b) Estimated overhead costs

(i) Factory;

(ii) Administrative;

(iii) Financial.

8. Manpower:

(a) Estimated manpower requirements, broken down into labour and staff, and into major categories of skills (local/foreign);

(b) Estimated annual manpower costs, classified as above, including overheads on wages and salaries.

9. Implementation scheduling:

(a) Proposed rough implementation time schedule;

(b) Estimated implementation costs given the implementation programme.

10. Financial and economic evaluation:

(a) Total investment costs

(i) Rough estimate of working capital requirements;

(ii) Estimated fixed assets;

(iii) Total investment costs, obtained by summing the estimated investment cost items from chapters II-X;[38]

(b) Project financing

(i) Proposed capital structure and proposed financing (local/foreign);

(ii) Interest;

(c) Production cost (summary of estimated production costs from chapters II-X,[39] classified by fixed and variable costs);

(d) Financial evaluation based on above estimated values

(i) Pay-off period;

(ii) Simple rate of return;

(iii) Break-even point;

(iv) Internal rate of return;

(e) National economic evaluation

(i) Preliminary tests:

a. Project exchange rate;

b. Effective protection;

(ii) Approximate cost-benefit analysis, using estimated weights and shadow-prices (foreign exchange, labour, capital);

(iii) Economic industrial diversification;

(iv) Estimate of employment-creation effect;

(v) Estimate of foreign exchange savings.

---

38 See corresponding chapters in the *Manual*.

39 *Id.*

B. OUTLINE OF AN EXECUTIVE SUMMARY [40]

A feasibility study should arrive at definitive conclusions on all the basic issues of a project after consideration of various alternatives. For convenience of presentation, these conclusions and recommendations should be summarized in the "Executive Summary" which should cover all critical aspects of the study.

Project background and history

State:

Name and address of project promoter
Project orientation: market or raw material oriented
Market orientation: domestic or export
Economic and industrial policies supporting the project
Project background

Market and plant capacity

List annual data on:

Demand
Project sales
Production programme
Plant capacity

Materials and inputs

Describe general availability of:

Raw materials
Auxiliary materials
Factory supplies
Utilities

List annual supply requirements of material inputs

Location and site

Describe location and state plant site

Project engineering

Describe layout and scope of the project
State technology finally selected
Summarize equipment selected
Describe required civil engineering works

Plant organization and overhead costs

Manpower

State selected type and size of labour force
State selected type and size of staff

Implementation scheduling

Duration of plant erection and installation
Duration of production start-up and running-in period

40 Source: Manual for the Preparation of Industrial Feasibility Studies (ID/206). United Nations Industrial Development Organization (UNIDO), Vienna, 1986, pp. 31-33.

Financial and economic evaluation

Total investment costs

List major investment data in local and foreign exchange, as needed, for:
Land and site preparation
\+ civil engineering works
\+ technology and equipment
\+ pre-production capital costs
\+ working capital

= total investment costs

Project financing (assumed)

Sources of financing
Impact of cost of financing and debt servicing on project proposals
Public policy and regulations on financing
Financing institutions
Required financial statements
Financial ratios

Total production or manufacturing costs (at feasible normal capacity)

List annual data for
Factory costs
\+ administrative overheads
\+ sales and distribution costs

= operating costs

\+ financial costs
\+ depreciation

= total production or manufacturing costs

Financial evaluation

Net present value
Internal rate of return
Pay-back period
Simple rate of return
Break-even analysis
Sensitivity analysis

National economic evaluation

Appraise the project proposal from the national economic point of view

Conclusions

Major advantage of project
Major drawbacks of project
Chances of implementing the project

2. *JOINT VENTURE CONTRACT*

ROMANIA

JOINT COMPANY CONTRACT OF ASSOCIATION

Between

The industrial central (works .... trust .... group of enterprises .... foreign trade company ....) with headoffice in .... street .... No. .... legally represented by .... as .... and .... as authorized by .... henceforth named the Romanian party (parties) on one side,

and

The firm (company) .... (legal form ....), with the headoffice in .... street .... No. .... legally represented by .... as .... and by .... as .... as authorized by .... henceforth named the foreign party (parties) on the other side,

Agree hereby to set up an (industrial, agricultural, constructions, transports, scientific and technological research) joint company, under the following conditions:

ARTICLE 1 -- Name, headoffice, nationality, and duration of the joint company

The name of the joint company is .... The headoffice of the joint company is in ....

The joint company has Romanian nationality. It is set up, organized and is functioning under the provisions of Romanian legislation.

The duration of the life of the joint company is .... years from the registration date of the joint company at the Finance Ministry; it may be extended according to the unanimous decision of the General Assembly.

ARTICLE 2 -- Legal form of the joint company

The joint company (name) .... is a limited liability company (or alternatively a joint stock company)

ARTICLE 3 -- Object of activity of the joint company

The joint company shall have the following objectives:

(a) the establishment (expansion, modernization) of a plant for the production of .... with a capacity of ....

(b) production of .... (name of product and main characteristics)

(c) marketing of these products ....

(d) carrying out of projects concerning ....

(e) carrying out of services in the field of ....

ARTICLE 4 -- Financing of an investment

The investment is estimated at a total value of .... from which .... shall be financed by registered capital and .... by suppliers' credits obtained by the joint company from Romania and from abroad.

ARTICLE 5 -- Implementation of the investment

The investment shall be implemented in the following stages:

- the construction shall be carried out between the dates of .... and ....
- the technical documentation shall be delivered between the dates of .... and ....

- the equipment, machines and tools shall be delivered between the dates of .... and ....
- construction and technological tests shall be carried out in the period ....
- start up of the unit (plant) shall be carried out in the period ....

(If the contribution of the registered capital is made in cash only, the joint company shall conclude contracts - under competitive conditions - for purchasing equipment, machines, and other assets.)

ARTICLE 6 -- Technical level and product competitiveness

In order to maintain quantitative technical levels of production corresponding to requirements of domestic and foreign markets, the joint company shall:

- carry out research work within its specialized department;
- avail itself of research results obtained by the individual research departments of the parties, under conditions agreed upon mutually;
- make available to the parties or to third parties results of its own research program, under conditions to be agreed upon;
- make a thorough analysis of the domestic and foreign market trends regarding supply and demand, product quality and appearance, etc., and implement necessary programs.

ARTICLE 7 -- Registered capital

The registered capital is fixed at the sum of .... (in the agreed currency) represented by .... registered shares (nominative stocks) each having the value of ....

The Romanian party (parties) has .... registered shares marked A (........ shares numbered from .... to ....) in value of .... representing .... per cent of the registered capital.

The foreign party (parties) has .... registered shares marked B (........ shares numbered from .... to ....) in value of .... representing .... per cent of the registered capital.

The registered capital has been entirely subscribed; out of it .... per cent shall be paid up by each partner from its participation quota by the registration date of the present contract and the rest shall be paid as follows ....

ARTICLE 8 -- Setting up of the capital of the joint company

The parties contribute to the capital of the joint company as follows:

The Romanian party (parties): (The industrial central .... enterprise ...., etc.)

(a) financial contribution in the amount of .... which shall be deposited on account with the Romanian Bank of Foreign Trade under the name and at the disposal of the joint company;

(b) complete plants, machines, equipment, tools, testing equipment, spare parts, materials, etc., in value of .... which include all and any associated expenses up to the time they are taken in receipt by the joint company. Appendix .... specifies the structure and delivery terms;

(c) constructions in value of ...., free of any commitments. Appendix .... specifies the characteristics of the terms under which they are made available to the joint company;

(d) licenses, know-how, in value of ...., free of any commitments. Appendix .... specifies the conditions under which they are made available to the joint company;

(e) trade marks having a value of .... as described in Appendix........;

(f) the equivalent of the right to use land having a surface area of .... hectares during the time the joint company is in operation as per Appendix .... having a value of ....;[41]

(g) other forms of contribution.

The foreign party (parties): ....(The Company ...., enterprise ...., etc.):

(The contribution is specified in conformity with the list outlined above for the Romanian party, except the items "c" and "f".)

The parties agree that the contributions to the registered capital be expressed in .... (the currency stipulated).

The parties state on their own liability that they hold all the necessary legal notifications and approvals from the competent authorities in their countries of origin concerning the contribution of each party to the registered capital.

The contribution in kind of the parties has been estimated on the basis of foreign market prices, considering the technical economic characteristic as well as the state of the respective goods as certified in the report of the experts (Appendix ....) appointed for this purpose by the parties and approved by the General Assembly.

The goods contributed to the registered capital shall be taken in receipt and registered by the joint company according to their intended aims.

The taking in receipt of the goods will be made by specialists appointed by the joint company.

In the event that a good is not accepted for receipt, it is kept at the disposal of the party which contributed it until it is upgraded, at the owner's exclusive expense, to the required quality parameters.

The goods contributed at the formation of the company as well as those obtained subsequently, become part of the joint company.

ARTICLE 9 -- Transfer of shares

Transfer of registered stock or shares can occur only on the basis of a decision by the General Assembly under the condition stipulated in the statute.

ARTICLE 10 -- The parties' (shareholders') rights and obligations

The parties (shareholders) derive their rights and obligations from the proportion of registered stock (shares) subscribed, according to the legal provisions of this contract and the statute. (The parties can stipulate in the contract specific clauses regarding their obligations, e.g. responsibility for design, engineering construction, outfitting of plants, provision of spares, real estate, training, etc.)

The parties cannot transfer and entrust to third parties their rights or obligations resulting from this contract, except by previous written agreement of the other party (parties).

ARTICLE 11 -- Working capital

At the start-up of the company's plant, the company will have working capital amounting to .... which will be financed through the registered capital and credits provided by Romanian Bank of Foreign Trade under current market conditions.

ARTICLE 12 -- The supply of raw materials and other materials; marketing of products and services

Supply to the joint company of raw materials and other materials and goods will be done under competitive conditions.

Supplying may be done domestically with payment in the agreed currency, or from abroad.

---

41 If this right is not included in the contribution of the Romanian party, the joint company shall pay to the State rent for the property.

The joint company will sell its products (services, and any such functions that it may perform as part of the company's objectives) as follows:

(a) on the domestic market under sale contracts and other specific contracts, at the prices and currency which will be agreed by the joint company together with its clients;

(b) on export markets through:

- the joint company's own marketing network;
- Romanian organizations (enterprises);
- the foreign party's marketing network.

The parties undertake to support the marketing efforts of the company in export markets (e.g. by establishing marketing territories, agreeing on competition avoidance, support services, commercial advertisements etc.).

ARTICLE 13 -- The joint company's accounts

The joint company will open accounts at the following banks in the Socialist Republic of Romania, through which it will carry out commercial banking operations ....

All payments in convertible currency of the joint company will be made from its convertible currency funds.

The persons which will sign in the name of the joint company the documents for banking operations, will be appointed by the Managing Committee (Administrative Council).

ARTICLE 14 -- Depreciation of fixed assets

The terms and quotas for funds derived by a joint venture from the yearly depreciation of its fixed assets,[42] will be established by the statute and will conform to Romanian legislation in force.

ARTICLE 15 -- Capital repairs

The joint company shall ensure the capital repairs of the fixed assets in order to keep them in operation during the established period.

The carrying out of capital repairs shall be decided by the General Assembly in conformity to the conditions provided under the statute.

ARTICLE 16 -- Drawing up of the balance sheet and of the income statement

The balance sheet and the income statement as well as the record of financial-economic activity of the joint company shall be kept, in (the agreed currency), according to the provisions of the statute.

ARTICLE 17 -- Management and administration of the joint company

The operational policies of the joint company are prescribed by the General Assemby of Shareholders which shall be empowered by and shall operate according to the provisions of the statute.

The General Assembly appoints the executive body of collective management (the Managing Committee for the limited liability company or the Administrative Council for the stock company, respectively) whose competencies and responsibilities it establishes.

At the setting up of the joint company the Managing Committee (the Administrative Council) is made up of ....

The Workers' Council shall appoint - according to the statute - its representatives to the Managing Committee (Administrative Council) of the joint company as part of the established number of Romanian representatives.

---

42 Funds derived by joint companies from inclusion in product prices of the depreciation component are fully retained by the company to finance new investment and or capital repairs.

ARTICLE 18 -- Activity program of the joint company

The joint company shall develop its activity according to five-year and one-year programs in conformity with the objectives set by the statute.

The joint company shall communicate yearly, in timely fashion (to the ministry which oversees the Romanian party) the main economic-financial aims provided under the activity program, in order to include them in the plan of economic-social development of the Socialist Republic of Romania.

ARTICLE 19 -- New investments

The joint company may undertake new investments with the approval of the General Assembly, according to the articles in the statute.

The joint company must secure the necessary approvals for the investment.

ARTICLE 20 -- Insurance

The joint company shall insure its goods against risk or fire, flood, storms, etc.

Assets shall be insured according to their value. The insurance premiums shall be paid by the joint company.

Insurance shall be underwritten by Romanian insurance organizations.

ARTICLE 21 -- Control of the joint company's financial operations

The joint company's financial operations shall be controlled by the parties (shareholders) and by the auditing commission.

The auditing commission is appointed and its activities are regulated by the provisions of the statute.

At the formation of the joint company, the auditing commission is composed of: .... (1-2 auditors will be named by the Ministry of Finance.)

ARTICLE 22 -- The personnel of the joint company

(a) The organizational structure of the joint company is stipulated in Appendix .... It can be modified on the basis of the decision of the General Assembly according to the statute.

Responsibility for the hiring of personnel by the joint company lies with the Managing Committee (Administrative Council) or its representatives, on the basis of individual labor contracts, through which the rights and obligations of the personnel in regards to the joint company are established.

(a) The Romanian personnel of the joint company has the same rights and obligations stipulated by legislation in force for personnel of state enterprises. The rights and obligations of the foreign personnel are established by the Managing Committee (Administrative Council).

(b) Salaries for the joint company's personnel are established in convertible currency according to their qualifications, categories and functions, according to Appendix .... The General Assembly examines and establishes periodically modifications of the salaries according to Romanian legislation.

(c) The foreign personnel of the joint company can transfer abroad, through the Romanian Bank of Foreign Trade, a portion of its salaries according to a quota approved by the Managing Committee (Administrative Council).

(d) The contribution to social insurance owed by the company for its personnel, will be paid in convertible currency, in the amount established by the legal provisions in force.

ARTICLE 23 -- Expenses for setting up the joint company

The expenses incurred by the parties as a result of establishing the joint company shall be recovered from the first profit registered by the joint company or shall be borne by each party. They will not be included as a contribution to the registered capital.

ARTICLE 24 -- Guarantees

The parties agree to provide guarantees concerning the fulfillment of the obligations assumed through the present contract, as follows:

(a) The Romanian party (parties) provides the following guarantees:

- the guarantee of the Romanian Bank of Foreign Trade for the fulfillment of the obligations of the Romanian party (parties), according to Articles 4 and 5 of the present contract.
- the guarantee by the Romanian Bank of Foreign Trade concerning the transfer abroad of the foreign party's (parties') profits; the value of the shares quotas transferred to the Romanian party; the dues resulting from the distribution of assets following dissolution and liquidation of the company and other rights due the foreign party (parties) as a result of conditions stipulated by the present contract and the statute of the joint company, after the payment of the taxes and contributions to social insurance and fulfillment of other legal and contractual obligations.

(b) The foreign party (parties) provides the following guarantee:

- the guarantee of a bank approved by the Romanian Bank of Foreign Trade for the observance of its obligations, according to Articles 4 and 5 of the present contract.

ARTICLE 25 -- *Force Majeure*

The parties are exonerated of obligations under the present contract, in case of *force majeure*.

By *force majeure* cases are meant unforeseen and unavoidable cases, like: wars, floods, earthquakes, fires, catastrophes and other similar cases independent of the will of the parties.

The party (parties) who find it impossible to fulfill their contractual obligations due to the appearance of *force majeure* events, will inform without delay, in writing, the other party (parties) about these occurrences in fulfillment of his contractual obligations. This communication has to include data concerning the appearance and the character of the occurrences and of their possible consequences. The affected party also has the obligation to inform in writing, without delay, the end of these occurrences.

In cases of *force majeure*, the term of fulfillment of contractual obligations by the affected party, is prolonged by the duration of these circumstances and their consequences.

Should these circumstances and their consequences last more than 8 months, each party has the right to renounce carrying out further the present contract.

In such case, neither party has the right to ask for damages from the other party; the parties shall then decide on the liquidation of their relations.

If the parties cannot reach an amicable agreement they may apply to the competent Court of Arbitration.

ARTICLE 26 - Disputes

Possible disputes arising between the parties concerning interpretation and carrying out of the present contract will be amicably settled. In case of disagreement, disputes will be settled by the Court of Arbitration of the Chamber of Commerce of the Socialist Republic of Romania, according to its regulations and according to Romanian law.

ARTICLE 27 -- Final provisions

(a) The present contract has the following Appendices:

....

....

All these Appendices form an integral part of the contract.

(b) Any documents signed by the parties or by one of them, prior to the signing of this contract concerning this joint company, are invalid as of the date of the formation of the company;

(c) The present contract has been drawn up and signed in Bucharest, today on ...., in two originals in Romanian language, each party having received one of the originals.

SOVIET UNION

MODEL CONTRACT CONCERNING THE ESTABLISHMENT AND ACTIVITY OF A SOVIET-..........(name of country) .... JOINT VENTURE

...........*(name)*..........

The enterprise (association) "............ (name) ...." of the USSR, being a legal person within the meaning of Soviet law, on the one hand, and the firm of "............ (name) ....", being a legal person within the meaning of .... (country) .... law, on the other hand, have agreed as follows:

Article 1

Name, location and period of activity of the Joint Venture

1. The enterprise and the firm shall establish a joint venture (hereinafter referred to as "the Joint Venture").

2. Name of the Joint Venture: in Russian: .... in ....: ....

3. Location of the Joint Venture: USSR ....(address) ...... (telephone number, telex) ....

4. Period of activity of the Joint Venture: up to .... (date) ....

The period of activity of the Joint Venture may be extended by decision of the Parties.

Article 2

Object and purposes of the Joint Venture

1. The object of the activity and the purpose of the Joint Venture shall be the production and sale of ...... (name of product) .... in order to satisfy consumer demand in the home and foreign markets and also to make profits in the interests of the Parties.

2. The sale of the products of the Joint Venture should ensure the inflow of foreign currency needed both for the Joint Venture's requirements and for the transfer of the foreign Party's profits.

3. The Joint Venture shall carry on its activities on the basis of full cost accounting, self-financing and self-support, also in foreign currency, in accordance with the current and long-term plans of the Joint Venture.

4. After the registration of the Joint Venture in the Ministry of Finance of the USSR, the Parties shall make every effort to ensure that an output volume of approximately .... is reached within not more than .... months. The Parties shall agree between themselves on the production programme and shall plan the further expansion of production.

5. The financial plans of the Joint Venture shall be drawn up for each calendar year. They shall show the income and expenditure of the Joint Venture in roubles and in foreign currency.

Article 3

Legal status

1. The Joint Venture shall be a legal person in accordance with the legislation of the USSR.

The Joint Venture shall be entitled, in its own name, to make contracts, to acquire property rights and personal non-property rights, to assume obligations, to act as plaintiff or respondent in a court of law, in arbitration proceedings or before an arbitration tribunal.

2. The Joint Venture shall acquire the rights of a corporation with effect from .... (insert the date, or the words "the time of registration")

The Joint Venture shall, save as may be otherwise provided by inter-State or intergovernmental treaties between the countries of the Parties, be guided in its activity by the legislation of the USSR and also by this Contract and the Joint Venture Charter.

Article 4

Establishment of affiliates and branches

1. The Joint Venture may establish affiliates and branches in the territory of the countries of the Parties and also in the territories of third countries. The affiliates shall operate on the basis of specially drafted Regulations adopted in accordance with the procedure laid down in the Charter.

2. The Regulations concerning an affiliate shall state whether the affiliate is a legal person.

Affiliates which are legal persons shall not be responsible for the obligations of the Joint Venture and the Joint Venture shall not be responsible for the obligations of affiliates.

3. Branches of the Joint Venture shall not be legal persons and shall operate in its name.

Article 5

General information on the Joint Venture

1. Aggregate volume of production on attainment of rated capacity:
in terms of range of products ....
in terms of value ....

2. Aggregate value of the Joint Venture on attainment of rated capacity: .... roubles.

3. Statutory Capital as a proportion of the aggregate value of the Joint Venture: .... roubles; .... per cent.

Article 6

Statutory Capital

1. A Statutory Capital shall be established in the Joint Venture by means of contributions from the Parties.

2. The amount of the Statutory Capital shall be:

SUR .... (in words: .... roubles), including .... in foreign currency.

3. Contributions of the Parties to the Statutory Capital:

Soviet Party: .... roubles .... in foreign currency

Foreign Party: .... roubles .... in foreign currency

Soviet Party's share of the Statutory Capital: .... per cent

Foreign Party's share of the Statutory Capital: .... per cent

4. The Soviet Party shall include in the calculation of its share: .... (right to use land, water and other natural resources; buildings, installations, equipment and other material values; use of rights in industrial property (transfer of technology); monetary resources in roubles and foreign currency) ....

5. The foreign Party shall include in the calculation of its share: .... (machinery, equipment, rights in industrial property, monetary resources in roubles and foreign currency) ....

6. The material values which the Parties in the Joint Venture include in the calculation of their contributions shall be assessed at contract prices taking into account world market prices (both in roubles and in foreign currency).

Payments into the Statutory Capital shall be made .... (indicate procedure and dates of payment) ....

7. Any change in the amount of the Statutory Capital shall be made by decision of the supreme organ of the Joint Venture, that is the Board. The Statutory Capital may be replenished by income from the Joint Venture's own economic activity and by additional contributions from the Parties.

Article 7

Conditions and procedure for raising loans

1. Having regard to the aggregate amount of expenditure necessary for the operation of the Joint Venture and to the amount of the Statutory Capital, the Parties have agreed to raise loan in the amount of .... in roubles and .... in foreign currency. The specific conditions of raising the loans, the selection of the banks which are to extend credit and the provision of guarantees for the loans raised shall be within the discretion of the Board.

Article 8

Export of products of the Joint Venture

1. In order to ensure self-sufficiency in foreign currency, the Parties intend to sell .... per cent of the output of products in the foreign market.

2. Incomes received in foreign currency shall be applied primarily to covering any expenditure of the Joint Venture.

3. In the export of products, the foreign Party shall place its sales network at the Joint Venture's disposal.

Article 9

Formation of funds

1. The Joint Venture shall establish out of its profits a reserve fund amounting to 25 per cent of the Statutory Capital. Allocations to the reserve fund shall be made for .... years at the rate of .... per cent of the amount of the reserve fund (Variant 1)/ of the profits (Variant 2).

2. In addition to the reserve fund, the Joint Venture may form other funds whose amounts, designated purposes, rates of allocation and procedures for use shall be determined by the Board.

Article 10

Taxation. Procedure for calculation and distribution of profits

1. The Joint Venture shall pay tax at the rate of 30 per cent of the profits remaining after allocations to the reserve fund and also to other funds connected with the development of production, science and technology.

2. The advance amount of tax on the profits of the current year shall be calculated by the Joint Venture on the basis of the financial plan for the current year.

3. After tax has been paid on the profits, the Joint Venture shall make allocations to special funds (for material incentives, social and cultural measures, etc.).

4. The remaining profits shall be divided between the Parties in proportion to their shares in the Statutory Capital.

5. The Parties agree to reinvest in production, for a period of .... years, the profits accrued to them.

Article 11

Assistance by the Parties in the activity of the Joint Venture

1. The Soviet Party shall assist by:

- securing the Joint Venture the access to the use of available infrastructure and gas, water and energy supply at contract prices;
- equipping the Joint Venture with a sufficient number of connections for telephones, telexes and telefaxes to enable it to maintain direct business communications;
- carrying out Customs procedures connected with export and import operations.

2. The foreign Party shall assist by:

- organizing the export of products of the Joint Venture through its own sales network;
- doing market research and transmitting to the Board information on opportunities to use the results of such research in production;

- supplying imported raw materials, components and semi-manufactures produced both by the foreign Party and by other foreign firms.

Article 12

Organs of management of the Joint Venture

1. One supreme organ, one executive organ and one supervisory organ shall be established in the Joint Venture. By decision of the supreme organ, other organs may also be established in the Joint Venture.

2. The supreme organ of the Joint Venture is the Board. It shall be composed of .... members appointed by the Parties in the Joint Venture. The Board shall have the right to take decisions by vote on any matter relating to the activity of the Joint Venture.

Variant 1

The number of votes of each of the Parties at the Board shall be determined according to the amount of its contribution to the Statutory Capital.

The Soviet Party/Parties shall have .... (state number) .... votes, including .... (state number of votes of each party) ....

The foreign Party/Parties shall have ..... (state number) ...... votes, including .... (state number of votes of each party) ....

Variant 2

Each of the Parties shall have one vote at the Board.

3. The current activity of the Joint Venture shall be directed and the decisions taken by the Board shall be carried out by the Management headed by a General Manager. The Management shall be composed of Soviet and foreign citizens.

The General Manager shall be appointed by the Board on the nomination of the .... Party; his deputy shall be appointed on the nomination of the .... Party. The General Manager shall direct the current activity of the Joint Venture on the principle of one-person management within the limits of the competence and rights defined by the Charter and the decisions of the Board.

4. The financial and economic activity of the Joint Venture shall be supervised by an Audit Panel appointed by the Board.

Article 13

Staff

1. The Joint Venture shall be staffed in the main by Soviet citizens. A specified proportion of the staff shall be foreign citizens.

2. The Joint Venture shall be under a duty to enter into a collective agreement with the trade union organization established within it. The contents of the said agreement, including the provisions concerning the social development of the workforce, shall be determined by Soviet legislation. Questions of labour, wages, principles regarding the utilization of working hours and rest, material incentives and occupational safety and health, shall constitute the essentials of the collective agreement.

3. The organs of management of the Joint Venture shall ensure transparency in giving effect to the collective agreement.

4. An agreement for a term of .... years shall be concluded with foreign citizens engaged for employment by the Joint Venture.

5. Employees of the Joint Venture who are foreign citizens shall be provided with living quarters, communal services and medical care under the conditions stated in the agreement with the foreign citizen.

6. The Joint Venture (Variant 1) /each of the Parties (Variant 2)/ shall arrange for specialists employed in the Joint Venture to upgrade their skills through training both at the enterprise of the Soviet Party and at that of the foreign Party.

Article 14

Procurement and sales

1. The Joint Venture shall procure Soviet-produced material resources through .... against payment in roubles (or in foreign currency) at contract prices taking into account world market prices, and material resources produced in other countries through .... against payment in foreign currency at world market prices.

2. The Joint Venture shall sell its products both in the USSR and abroad:

- on the home market through ....
- abroad both independently and with the aid of the foreign Party's sales network, Soviet foreign trade organizations and other organizations.

3. The Joint Venture may establish company stores to sell its products on the USSR territory by agreement with local authorities.

4. Goods produced on the designs and by the technology of the Soviet or the foreign Party shall bear that Party's trade mark; in other cases the Joint Venture may devise and use its own trade marks.

Article 15

Form of control and accounting

1. In order to exercise its rights of control, each Party shall be entitled to receive general and specific information on all matters connected with the activities of the Joint Venture. Each Party shall be entitled at any time to familiarize itself with the documents of the Joint Venture and its property values, and to check the same.

2. The Joint Venture shall be under a duty to submit to the Parties and to the Board reports on the financial and economic situation of the Joint Venture, including a balance sheet and profit-and-loss account with explanations.

3. The accounts shall be kept in roubles. All conversions of foreign currency into roubles and *vice versa* shall be effected at the official rate of exchange of the State Bank of the USSR on the date of completion of the transaction. The movement of resources in foreign currency shall be reflected in the record of operations.

4. The functions of audit shall be performed by ....

Article 16

Breach of the Contract

1. In the event that one of the Parties fails to comply, or to comply properly, with its obligations under this Contract, it shall be under a duty to compensate the other Party for any losses caused by such non-compliance or improper compliance.

2. The expression "compensation for losses" shall be understood to mean compensation for losses caused to a Party (production expenses; loss of or damage to property) by a breach of this Contract on the part of the other Party. Indirect losses and lost opportunities shall not be compensated.

Article 17

Force majeure

1. The Parties shall be exempt from the effects of partial or total non-compliance with their obligations under this Contract if such non-compliance was the consequence of circumstances of *force majeure* arising after the conclusion of the Contract as a result of extraordinary events which a Party could neither foresee nor avert by reasonable means.

The expression "circumstances of *force majeure*" applies to events which are beyond the Party's control and for whose occurrence it is not responsible, for example earthquake, flood, fire, government decisions or the orders of State authorities,

2. A Party pleading circumstances of *force majeure* shall be under a duty to notify the second Party in writing immediately of the occurrence of such circumstances. At the second Party's request, an attestation, issued by the Chamber of Commerce and Industry of the USSR or, as the case may be, a similar institution in the country where such circumstances occur, shall be supplied.

The notification shall contain particulars of the circumstances and, if possible, also an assessment of their effect on the compliance by the Party with its obligations under this Contract, and an estimate of the date when the Party will again be able to comply with its obligations.

3. A Party which is unable owing to circumstances of *force majeure* to comply with its obligations under this Contract shall make every effort, with due regard to the provisions of the Contract, to make up for such non-compliance as quickly as possible.

4. When the said circumstances cease to apply, the Party shall without delay notify in writing the other Party to that effect.

In so doing, the Party shall state the date on which it is proposed to comply with an obligation under this Contract. If the Party fails to send the necessary notice or to send it in good time, it shall be under a duty to compensate the other Party for any loss caused by such failure to notify or late notification.

5. If circumstances of *force majeure* arise, the date of compliance with the obligations under this Contract shall be postponed with a time corresponding to the duration of such circumstances and their consequences.

Article 18

Commercial secrecy

1. For a period of five years after the expiry of this Contract, and irrespective of the reason for the expiry, information relative to the activities of the Joint Venture may not be communicated to third parties, published or otherwise divulged, except with the written consent of the other Party.

2. The scope of the information not to be divulged shall be determined by the Board of the Joint Venture.

Article 19

Arbitration

1. The Parties shall endeavour to settle by negotiation all disputes arising in connection with this Contract.

2. In the event that disputes cannot be agreed upon through bilateral negotiations, they shall be finally settled in arbitration /in Moscow, USSR, by the Court of Arbitration of the Chamber of Commerce and Industry of the USSR in accordance with its Rules (Variant 1)/ in .... (insert name of town and country) .... by .... (specify court of arbitration) .... in accordance with .... (specify applicable rules) .... (Variant 2).

Article 20

Procedure for amendment of the Contract. Liquidation

1. Neither Party shall be entitled to transfer its rights under this Contract in whole or in part to any third party without the other Party's written consent.

2. Any amendment or addition shall take the form of an annex to this Contract and shall constitute an integral part thereof.

3. Either of the Parties can, by giving a .... months' advance notice, terminate the contract to expire on the 31 December of that year. However, the Contract cannot be terminated to expire before 31 December ... (insert year)....

4. If the Joint Venture is liquidated or one of the Parties leaves the Joint Venture, this Contract shall cease to have effect. The procedure for liquidation shall be laid down in the Charter of the Joint Venture.

Article 21

Entry into force

1. This Contract shall enter into force on the date of its registration.

2. The Soviet Party shall be under a duty to notify the other Party immediately of its registration or of any obstacle to its registration.

Done in Moscow, on .... 19..., in duplicate in the Russian and .... languages, both texts being equally authentic.

For the Soviet Party   For the foreign Party

3. JOINT VENTURE CHARTER

ROMANIA

JOINT VENTURE STATUTE

Sample Format for a Joint Stock Company

CHAPTER I

Name, Juridical Form, Objective, Location, Duration

ARTICLE 1 -- The name of the Company

The name of the company is ....

On all invoices, notices, publications, and other documents issued by the company, the name of the company will be preceded or followed by the words "joint stock company" or the initials "S.A.", by the registered capital and the registration number at the Ministry of Finance.

ARTICLE 2 -- The juridical form of the joint stock company

The .... (name) company has the status of a Romanian juridical person, with the juridical form of a joint stock company. It carries out its activities in accordance with Romanian laws, which are compatible with the operational aims of joint companies, under the conditions of Decree No. 424/1972, the contract, and this statute.

ARTICLE 3 -- The objective of the company's activities

The company will have as its objective:

(a) the establishment or modernization of a production facility for .... with a capacity of ....;

(b) the production of .... (the name of the product will be accompanied by a decision of its main features);

(c) the sale of these products under the conditions outlined in the company's contract;

(d) the execution of projects concerning ....;

(e) the carrying out of services in the field of ....

ARTICLE 4 -- Location of the company

The location of the company is in the Socialist Republic of Romania, at ...., street ...., number ....

The location can be changed to another place in the Socialist Republic of Romania by the decision of the General Assembly of Stockholders.

ARTICLE 5 -- The duration of the company

The duration of the life of the company is .... years, beginning with the date the company is registered with the Ministry of Finance, and can be extended on the basis of the decision of the General Assembly.

CHAPTER II

Registered Capital and Stocks

ARTICLE 6 -- The registered capital

The registered capital is fixed at the sum of .... The capital is divided into .... nominative stocks each having a value of ...., and entirely underwritten by the stockholders in the following manner:

Stocks numbers one through .... represent the contribution of the Romanian stockholder(s) at a value of ...., representing .... per cent of the registered capital.

Stocks numbers .... through number .... represent the contribution of the foreign stockholder(s) at a value of ...., representing .... per cent of the registered capital.

The stockholders' contribution to the registered capital will be constituted in the following manner:

The contribution of the Romanian stockholder(s):

(a) a financial contribution in the sum of .... deposited in an account at the Romanian Bank of Foreign Trade in the name of and at the disposal of the company;

(b) complex installations, machinery, equipment, spare parts, materials, etc., having a value of ...., including all their expenses up to the time they are taken in receipt by the company;

(c) buildings and facilities, free of any commitments, in the value of ....;

(d) licenses, know-how, free of any commitments, in the value of ....;

(e) trademarks (factory markings or brand names) having a value of ....;

(f) the equivalent of the right to use land having a surface area of .... hectares during the time the company is in operation, having a value of ....;

(g) other forms of contribution.

The contribution of the foreign stockholder(s):

(The contribution is specified in accordance with the above outlined listing for the Romanian stockholder(s), with the exception of items "c" and "f").

ARTICLE 7 -- The stock

The company will issue and turn over to the stockholders the certificates, including:

- The name and duration of the company;
- The date the company is established, the registration number at the Ministry of Finance and the issue of the Official Bulletin where this was announced;
- The registered capital, the number of shares and their numbering order, the nominal value of the shares, and the payments made;
- The name (first and last names) and residence of the stockholder.

A single certificate can be issued for more than one share.

Shares that represent contributions other than cash will bear the notice that they are not transferrable for a period of two years from the date the company is established.

The certificates will bear the special stamp of the company and will be signed by two administrators, one of which will represent the Romanian party.

The company will keep record of the shares in a register numbered, sealed, and initialed by the Ministry of Finance, which will be kept at the company headquarters.

ARTICLE 8 -- Increasing the capital

The registered capital can be increased on the basis of the decision of the General Assembly of Stockholders by issuing new shares that represent the financial or in kind contribution, or by including reserves or profits.

The newly issued stock must be completely underwritten, free of any commitments, with their value deposited .... days from the date of the decision of the General Assembly of Stockholders to increase the amount of the capital.

The capital can be increased partially or totally in kind by a decision of the General Assembly of Stockholders on the basis of an appraisal made by designated experts appointed by the stockholders.

Increasing the capital will not change the proportion of shares held by the stockholders, as established by Law No.1/1971.

ARTICLE 9 -- Reducing the capital

The capital can be reduced on the basis of a decision of the General Assembly of Stockholders.

Proposals to reduce the capital must be communicated by the Administrative Council to the Auditing Commission at least 30 days prior to the date of the General Assembly of Stockholders, which will decide upon the reduction. The Auditing Commission will have to describe the causes and conditions of the reduction.

ARTICLE 10 -- Rights and obligations derived from shares

Each share underwritten and deposited by the stockholders confers to them the rights of: having a vote in the General Assembly of Stockholders; electing and being elected to positions of leadership; participating in the distribution of profits or other rights in accordance with the provisions of this statute and legal dispositions.

Possession of shares implies full adhesion to the statute and all modifications therein.

The rights and obligations related to the shares go along with the shares in the event they are transferred to other persons.

Social obligations are guaranteed regarding social inheritance, and the stockholders are obligated only for the payment of their shares.

The company's property cannot be attached by the personal debts or obligations of the stockholders. A creditor of a certain stockholder cannot make claims except upon the portion of the company's profits assigned to that stockholder by the General Assembly of Stockholders or upon that amount due this stockholder upon the liquidation of the company, as carried out under the conditions of this statute.

ARTICLE 11 -- The transfer of shares

Shares are indivisible with regards to the company, which recognizes one owner for each share.

The partial or complete transfer of shares between stockholders or to third parties can be accomplished on the basis of the decision of the General Assembly of Stockholders, reached unanimously.

Transfer proposals must be announced by the ceding stockholder to the company and the stockholders, indicating the person to whom the shares are to be transferred, as well as the conditions of transfer.

The transfer of shares between stockholders or to a third party is valid only to the degree to which the Romanian party maintains a minimum of 51 per cent of the registered capital.

Transfers to a third party can be accomplished only after a period of 30 days from the date of receipt of notification of a transfer proposal, with the stockholders having the right to pre-empt the transfer.

The transfer is recorded in the register which lists the shares and is inscribed in the certificate.

ARTICLE 12 -- The loss of shares

In the event that a share is lost, the owner must notify the Administrative Council and make the fact known through the press. After six months, he can obtain a "duplicate" of the share.

CHAPTER III

The Administrative Council

ARTICLE 13 -- Membership and organization

The company is administered by the Administrative Council composed of (odd number) administrators who qualify as stockholders and are named by the General Assembly of Stockholders for a period of four years, with the possibility to serve for a new period of four more years.

The appointment of the administrators is done from among persons designated by the stockholders, in the same proportion as their contribution to the capital.

When a vacant position arises within the Administrative Council, the General Assembly of Stockholders name a new administrator to fill the vacant position. The General Assembly will name as the new administrator a person designated by the same stockholder who named the predecessor.

The length of time for which an administrator is named to occupy a vacant position will correspond to the period of time remaining until the expiration of the predecessor's term.

Also, as part of the Romanian representation, the Workers' Council (designated by the General Assembly of Workers) are members of the Administrative Council.

The Administrative Council is the company's executive body of collective leadership, with a deliberative role, which carries out its activities on the basis of guidelines and responsibilities established by the General Assembly of Stockholders.

The Administrative Council meets, at the company's headquarters, whenever it is necessary, when convened by the president or one-third of its members and reaches decisions by a simple majority vote from among the total number of members of the Council. For special problems, expressly outlined in this statute, decisions are reached by unanimous vote. The Administrative Council is presided over by the president, and in his absence, by one of the vice presidents designated by the president. The president names a secretary either from among the members of the Council or from outside the Council.

In order to reach a valid decision, at least two-thirds of the number of members of the Administrative Council must be present.

Discussions within the Administrative Council take place in accordance with the agenda established by the Council on the basis of the draft forwarded by the president at least 15 days prior to the meeting. They are recorded in the written minutes of the meeting, which are in turn recorded in a register signed and sealed by the Ministry of Finance. The written minutes bear the signature of the meeting's president and secretary.

The Administrative Council can delegate to one or a number of its members certain powers regarding limited problems that may arise and can call upon experts to study certain problems.

At its first session, the Administrative Council will elect from amongst its members a president and from one to three vice presidents.

The president also normally fills the position of director general. He ensures the current leadership of the company and sees to it that the decisions of the General Assembly and the Council are carried out within the limits of the objectives set for the company's activities. He must be a Romanian citizen with his residence in the Socialist Republic of Romania.

The other leadership positions can be filled by any stockholder representatives.

In its relations with third parties, the company is represented by the president of the Administrative Council on the basis and within the limits of the powers given him by the General Assembly of Stockholders or, in his absence, by one of the vice presidents designated by the Council. The company representative signs the documents contracted with third parties.

The members of the Administrative Council will operate, either collectively or independently, in accordance with the powers given them by the General Assembly of Stockholders. They can carry out any act that is related to the administration of the company in its interest, within the limits of the rights conferred upon them.

The president of the Administrative Council is obligated to place at the disposal of the stockholders and Auditing Commission, upon their request, all company documents.

The president, vice presidents, members of the Administrative Council, general directors and their deputies, managers and their deputies are responsible, either individually or collectively, as the case may be, to the company for damages resulting from their infraction or violation of legal dispositions, from violations of the statute, and for errors in the administration of the company. In these situations, they can be removed from their position by decision of the General Assembly of Stockholders.

ARTICLE 14 -- Tasks

The Administrative Council has the following tasks:

(a) hires and fires Romanian employees;

(b) hires and fires foreign employees, establishing their rights and obligations; establishes the portion of their income which can be transferred abroad;

(c) draws up and approves the company's internal regulations by which duties and responsibilities are established for the company's employees in various departments;

(d) approves financial operations and payments which exceed the sum of ....;

(e) approves operations for the purchase and sale of goods (except for fixed assets) whose value exceeds the sum of ....;

(f) approves the carrying out of capital repairs and investments with a value of, at the most, ...;

(g) approves financing plans;

(h) approves the conclusion of contracts for renting (either making or receiving rent payments) in cases where the yearly rent exceeds the sum of ....;

(i) establishes marketing tactics and strategies;

(j) approves the closing or cancelling of other contracts whose value exceeds the sum of ....;

(k) presents, yearly, three months from the closing out of the annual financial economic budget, the report to the General Assembly of Stockholders regarding the company's activities, the balance sheet and income statement for the preceding year, as well as the company's draft program for the next year's activities;

(l) resolves other problems established by the General Assembly of Stockholders.

In problems relating to letters ...., decisions will be reached by unanimous vote; the rest of the problems will be resolved by a simple majority vote.

CHAPTER IV

Control of the Company

ARTICLE 15 -- The Auditing Commission

The operation of the company is controlled by the stockholders and the Auditing Commission.

In order to exercise the right of control, information regarding the company's activities, the state of its property holdings, and the status of profits and losses will be presented, upon request, to the stockholders. The General Assembly of Stockholders names an Auditing Commission composed of .... persons, with one to two delegates coming from the Ministry of Finance.

The majority of the auditors must be Romanian citizens.

Likewise, the General Assembly of Stockholders can name one or two alternate auditors who can replace the regular auditors, if need be.

The Auditing Commission has the following main tasks:

- during the course of (yearly) financial accounting, it verifies the management of fixed assets and working capital, stock portfolios, petty cash and the bookkeeping register, and presents activity reports to the Administrative Council.
- at the end of the (yearly) financial accounting, it reviews the accuracy of the inventory, of the documents and information presented by the Administrative Council regarding the company's accounts, of the balance sheet and of the income statement; it presents a written report to the General Assembly of Stockholders in which it proposes the approval or modification of the balance sheet and the income statement;
- upon the liquidation of the company, it reviews the liquidation operations;
- presents its viewpoint to the General Assembly of Stockholders regarding proposals to reduce the amount of social capital or to modify the statute and objective of the company.

The Auditing Commission meets at the company headquarters and reaches its decisions by unanimous vote. If it does not reach unanimity, a report of disagreement is forwarded to the Central Service for Accounting Expertise of the Ministry of Finance, which will verify the grounds for the disagreement; the findings of the Service will be subjected to the decisions of the General Assembly of Stockholders.

The auditors are responsible to the company for damages caused by them through nonfulfillment or fulfillment in bad faith of the duties assigned to them, in accordance with this statute.

The Auditing Commission can convoke the General Assembly of Stockholders in the event the registered capital is diminished by a minimum of 10 per cent, with the exception of the first two years of the company's existence, or whenever it is considered necessary to review other problems.

Auditors are named for a maximum period of four years.

CHAPTER V

The General Assemby of Stockholders

ARTICLE 16 -- Duties

The General Assembly of Stockholders is the leadership body of the company which decides upon the company's activities and its economic and commercial policies.

The General Assembly of Stockholders has the following major duties:

(a) approves the organizational structure of the company and the number of positions;

(b) names the members of the Administrative Council and the Auditing Commission, including the alternative members; establishes their salaries; discharges them from duties; and dismisses them;

(c) names the general directors and their deputies and the managers and their deputies; establishes their salaries; discharges them from duties; and dismisses them. General directors and deputy general directors can also be selected from among the members of the Administrative Council and they may be one or two;

(d) establishes duties and responsibilities of the Administrative Council and the Auditing Commission and the proportion in which the stockholders are represented on these bodies;

(e) approves the company's program of activities;

(f) gives its approval to the collective work contract;

(g) makes decisions regarding the contracting of bank loans and the granting of guarantees;

(h) examines, approves or modifies the balance sheet and the income statement after listening to the reports of the Administrative Council and Auditing Commission; approves the distribution of profits among the stockholders;

(i) makes decisions regarding the establishment and closing of branch offices, subsidiaries, and agencies;

(j) makes decisions regarding increasing or reducing the registered capital, modifying the number of shares or the nominal value of these shares, as well as transferring shares;

(k) makes decisions regarding the adoption or modification of the statute, as well as changing the juridical form of the company;

(l) makes decisions regarding the merger, split-up or dissolution and liquidation of the company;

(m) makes decisions regarding the modification of charges in hard currency for services provided by company employees;

(n) makes decisions regarding the carrying out of capital repairs and the implementation of investments whose value exceeds the authority of the Administrative Council;

(o) makes decisions regarding the extension of the period established by contract for the operation of the company;

(p) makes decisions regarding legal actions undertaken against members of the Administrative Council, general directors and their deputies, managers and their deputies, and auditors for damages caused to the company;

(q) makes decisions in any other problems regarding the company.

The decisions in the problems outlined in letters "k" and "l" can be carried out only after they are approved by the State Council of the Socialist Republic of Romania, and, in those problems outlined under letter "i", only after the decisions are approved by the Ministry of Foreign Trade and International Economic Cooperation and the Ministry of Finance.

ARTICLE 17 -- Convening the General Assembly of Stockholders

Sessions of the General Assembly of Stockholders are of two types: ordinary and extraordinary. They are convened by the president of the Administrative Council or one of the vice president empowered by the president.

Ordinary sessions of the General Assembly take place once each year, three months after the close-out of the yearly economic budget, in order to examine the balance sheet and the income statement for the preceding year and to establish the program of activities for the coming year.

Extraordinary sessions of the General Assembly are also convened upon the request of the stockholders representing at least one-third of the registered capital, at the request of the Auditing Commission, as well as in the event where the registered capital has decreased by a minimum of 10 per cent, except during the first two years of the company's existence.

The General Assembly of Stockholders is convened by letters of recommendations or telex messages sent to the addresses indicated by the stockholders in the company's contract of association (or to those corrected addresses which were provided, in writing, at a later date) at least .... days prior to the fixed date, showing the meeting place, the date, and the draft agenda of the meeting.

The General Assembly of Stockholders meets at the company headquarters or at another place in the same locality.

For ordinary sessions of the General Assembly, upon convocation, the stockholders are sent copies of the balance sheet and income statement, the auditors' report, the report regarding the company's activities during the just concluded yearly budget, and the draft program of activities for the coming year. The inventory is placed at the disposal of the stockholders at the company's headquarters. The person who presides over the General Assembly or any stockholder can propose subjects for discussion other than those outlined in the agenda. These subjects can be discussed only with the unanimous approval of the General Assembly of Stockholders.

ARTICLE 18 -- The organization of the General Assembly of Stockholders

The General Assembly of Stockholders is presided over by the president of the Administrative Council and, in his absence, by one of the vice presidents designated by the president.

The person who presides over the meeting opens the session and closes it when discussions have ended, ensures that all items on the agenda have been discussed, that the session is led in an organized manner, that each representative of the stockholders is given a chance to speak.

From among its members, the General Assembly elects a secretary who will record the statements of the session. These minutes will be noted in a register signed and sealed by the Ministry of Finance. The minutes will be signed by the person who presided over the session and the secretary.

In ordinary and extraordinary sessions of the General Assembly of Stockholders, during which issues concerning work relations with the company's employees are discussed, the president of the company's trade union committee also participates, as part of the delegation representing the Romanian stockholder(s).

ARTICLE 19 -- Exercising the right to vote in the General Assembly of Stockholders

An ordinary session of the General Assembly is legally constituted and may reach decisions if, at the first session, those stockholders present or their representatives hold at least two-thirds of the registered capital, and, at the second session, if they hold at least one-half of the capital.

An extraordinary session of the General Assembly is legally constituted and can reach decisions if, at the first session, the stockholders present or their representatives hold at least three-fourths of the registered capital, and, at the second session, if they hold at least one-half of the capital.

The general assembly of stockholders, as constituted by the statute, reaches decisions by unanimous vote of those present or represented in those problems outlined in Article 16, letters ....

Other decisions are reached by a simple majority of votes of those present.

Stockholders normally vote by a raising of hands. Upon the proposal of the presiding officer or a group of stockholders present or represented at the session, who hold at least one-fourth of the registered capital, it can be decided to resort to a secret vote.

For those decisions where it is not necessary to have a unanimous decision, it is admissible to also accept absentee votes.

Decisions of the General Assembly are also binding upon those stocholders who are absent or not represented.

CHAPTER VI

The Company's Activities

ARTICLE 20 -- The financial economic budget

The financial economic budget begins on 1 January and ends on 31 December of each year. The first budget begins on the date the company is established.

ARTICLE 21 -- The company's employees

The leadership personnel of the company and the auditors are named by the General Assembly of Stockholders. The rest of the employees are hired by the Administrative Council.

The hiring of company employees is carried out within the framework of the organizational layout and on the basis of individual work contracts.

The hard currency salaries of the company's employees, classified according to qualifications and positions, are outlined in annex ....; the salaries being subject to modification by the General Assembly of Stockholders.

The Romanian employees of the company have the rights and obligations as outlined in the current legislation regarding employees in state units in the Socialist Republic of Romania.

The rights and obligations of foreign employees of the joint company are established by the Administrative Council.

The foreign employees of the joint company can transfer their salaries abroad, through the Romanian Bank of Foreign Trade, in the proportion established by the Administrative Council.

ARTICLE 22 -- The depreciation of fixed assets

In depreciating fixed assets the following will be taken in consideration:

Depreciation is established by applying the norms regarding depreciation as outlined in annex .... to the acquisition costs of fixed assets and is included, as the case may be, in the production cost, the cost of services rendered or other costs; it is used for the replacement of fixed assets and to meet other needs of the company.

The term acquisition cost is understood to mean the sum of money spent on purchases and other expenditures made in order to put each fixed asset into operation.

Depreciation is calculated from the date the fixed assets are put into operation for the period of time outlined in annex ....

ARTICLE 23 -- Capital repairs and investments

Capital repairs and investments with a value of over .... (the authority limits of the Administrative Council are outlined) will be carried out on the basis of the decisions of the General Assembly of Stockholders.

The funds necessary for capital repairs are ensured by including these respective costs, as the case may be, in the costs of production, those of services rendered or other expenditures, in the year during when they are made or in payments spread over a number of years.

The funds necessary to implement investments are ensured by the registered capital and or by credits, obtained by the company from abroad or from the Socialist Republic of Romania.

ARTICLE 24 -- Preparation of the balance sheet and of the income statement

The company will prepare on a yearly basis the balance sheet and income statement and will keep a record of economic-financial activities keeping in mind "The Methodological Standards Comprising the Principles Regarding the Organization and Management of Bookkeeping for Joint Companies Established in the Socialist Republic of Romania", as drawn up by the Ministry of Finance.

ARTICLE 25 -- Calculation and distribution of profits

The company's profit is established by the balance sheet approved by the General Assembly of Stockholders. The taxable profit is established as the difference between the total amount of income collected and the total sum of expenditures made to realize this income. In calculating this profit, a sum will be deducted from the yearly profit for the reserve fund; this sum will be, at the most, five per cent of the total profit as outlined in the yearly balance sheet. This deduction will be made until it reaches 25 per cent of the amount of the registered capital.

From the profit outlined in the balance sheet, legal taxes will be subtracted, providing the profit due the stockholders. This profit is distributed among the stockholders in a manner that is proportional to their contribution to the registered capital, as well as for other needs of the company (e.g., yearly bonuses).

Payment of profits to the stockholders is carried out by the company within at most two months from the approval of the balance sheet by the General Assembly of Stockholders.

In the event a loss is recorded, the parties are obliged to analyze the causes and to take the necessary measures.

CHAPTER VII

Modification of the Juridical Form, Dissolution, Liquidation and Litigations

ARTICLE 26 -- Modification of the juridical form

The company can be transformed into another form of company by the decision of the General Assembly of Stockholders and after obtaining legal approval.

The new company can be established with an amount of capital at least equal to the amount of the old company and with the participation of the same stockholders.

To be established, the new company will fulfill the legal formalities of registration and publication demanded for the establishment of joint companies.

ARTICLE 27 -- Dissolution of the company

The following situations lead to the dissolution of the company:

- expiration of the agreed period of operation of the company, if the General Assembly does not approve an extension;
- the impossibility of achieving the social objective;
- the loss of at least one-third of the registered capital, following the depletion of the reserve fund, if the General Assembly of Stockholders does not decide to restore the capital to the original level or to reduce its amount to the remaining balance;
- upon request of any stockholder, if circumstances of *force majeure* and their consequences last more than eight months, and the General Assembly of Stockholders finds that the continued operation of the company is no longer possible;
- in any other situations on the basis of the decision of the General Assembly of Stockholders, reached unanimously.

ARTICLE 28 -- Liquidation of the company

In the event of dissolution, the company will be liquidated.

The liquidation will be done by one or more trustees named by the General Assembly of Stockholders.

From the moment the trustees assume their roles, the term of office of the administrators and directors ends; these officers no longer are empowered to undertake new operations in the name of the company.

The trustees have the same responsibilities as the administrators. They, together with the company's administrators, are obligated to hold an inventory immediately after assuming their positions, and to evaluate the company's holdings and to conduct a financial review, for the purpose of determining the exact status of public assets and liabilities. The trustees are obligated to accept and preserve the company's holdings and records which are entrusted to them by the administrators, and to maintain a register with all operations of liquidation in chronological order.

The trustees carry out their mandate under the supervision of the Auditing Commission.

In accordance with the powers entrusted to them by the General Assembly of Stockholders, the trustees will take all necessary measures to carry out those operations already underway, to collect payments owed to the company and to pay company debts, as well as to carry out other operations in the interest of liquidating the company.

The trustees can appear before the courts and can conclude transactions and settle with the company's creditors.

The trustees will notify the company's creditors, through a public announcement, asking them to present their claims within a set time period. The company will send separate announcements to creditors known to it asking them to present their claims.

Trustees who carry out new operations which are not necessary to the liquidation process, are personally and collectively responsible for these actions.

From the sums resulting from liquidation, payments will be made first to the preferred creditors (salaries and other employee rights, duties and taxes, contributions to social security, credit rates and interest, etc.) and then to other creditors. After this, the trustees will prepare the liquidation balance sheet and will make proposals for the distribution of profits to the stockholders in proportion to their contribution to the registered capital.

The liquidation balance sheet as well as the proposals for distributing the holdings resulting from liquidation will be presented for approval to the General Assembly of Stockholders. After the approval of this balance sheet, it will be considered that the company has relieved the trustees of their duties.

On the basis of the liquidation balance sheet, the trustees will prepare, in original form, a record of findings which will be recorded at the Ministry of Foreign Trade and Economic Cooperation and Ministry of Finance and will be published in the Official Bulletin of the Socialist Republic of Romania.

ARTICLE 29 -- Litigations

The company's litigations with Romanian juridical or physical persons fall under the competence of the law courts of the Socialist Republic of Romania.

Litigations growing out of contractual agreements between the joint company and Romanian juridical persons can be resolved also through arbitration. In this case, the stockholders also can choose the services of the Arbitration Commission of the Chamber of Commerce of the Socialist Republic of Romania.

Litigations of Romanian employees hired by the company, resulting from disagreements with the company, are resolved in accordance with the labour laws of the Socialist Republic of Romania, and those cases involving foreign employees will be resolved in accordance with the provisions of their work contract.

Concluded in Bucharest on ...., in two original copies in Romanian.

SOVIET UNION

MODEL CHARTER

of the Soviet - .... (foreign party's country) .... Joint Venture ..... (name) ....

The Soviet enterprise (association) .... (name) .... and the firm .... (name of firm, country) .... (hereinafter referred to as "the Parties") hereby adopt the Charter of the Joint Venture .... (name)......... (hereinafter referred to as "the Joint Venture")

The Joint Venture is established by the Parties through the contract (hereinafter referred to as "the Contract") concluded at .... on ....19...., to which this Charter is annexed.

Article 1

1. The object of the activity and the purpose of the Joint Venture shall be the production and sale of .... (name of product) ....

Article 2

1. The Joint Venture shall be a legal person within the meaning of the laws of the USSR.

2. The Joint Venture shall be entitled, in its own name, to make contracts, to acquire property rights and personal non-property rights, to assume obligations and to act as plaintiff or respondent in a court of law, in arbitration proceedings or before an arbitration tribunal.

3. The Joint Venture shall, save as may be otherwise provided by inter-State or intergovernmental treaties between the countries of the Contracting Parties, be guided in its activity by the legislation of the USSR and also by this Contract and this Charter.

4. The Joint Venture shall have a seal, the model of which shall be approved by the Board.

5. Location of the Joint Venture: USSR, town of ....

6. The official languages of the Joint Venture shall be Russian and ....; its working language shall be ....

Article 3

The Parties to the Joint Venture shall be entitled:

- to participate in the management of the Joint Venture in accordance with the procedure laid down by this Charter;
- to participate in all forms of activity and in the division of the profits in the amounts and forms specified by this Charter;
- to receive information concerning the activity of the Joint Venture and the state of its property, profits and losses;
- to submit to the directing organs of the Joint Venture proposals for examination.

Article 4

The Parties to the Joint Venture shall be under a duty:

- to make contributions to the Statutory Capital in the amount and on the dates specified by the Charter;
- to comply with the decisions adopted by the Board and other organs of management of the Joint Venture;
- to supply information for the purpose of attaining the current and strategic objectives of the activity of the Joint Venture;
- to be of assistance to the Joint Venture in achieving the purposes stated in the Contract.

Article 5

The Joint Venture shall have an independent balance sheet, a rouble account at .... (name of bank) .... and a foreign currency account at .... (name of bank) .... The Joint Venture shall operate on the basis of full cost accounting, self-support and self-financing.

Article 6

1. The Statutory Capital shall be made up of contributions from the Parties.

2. The amount of the Statutory Capital shall be:

SUR .... (in words: .... roubles), including

.... in foreign currency.

3. Contributions of the Parties to the Statutory Capital:

Soviet Party: .... roubles .... in foreign currency

Foreign Party: .... roubles .... in foreign currency.

Soviet Party's share of the Statutory Capital: .... per cent

Foreign Party's share of the Statutory Capital: .... per cent

4. The Soviet Party shall include in the calculation of its share: .... (right to use land, water and other natural resources; buildings; installations, equipment and other material values; use of rights in industrial property (transfer of technology); monetary resources in roubles and foreign currency) ....

5. The foreign partner shall include in the calculation of its share: .... (machinery, equipment, rights in industrial property, monetary resources in roubles and foreign currency) ....

6. Payments into the Statutory Capital shall be made .... (indicate procedure and dates of payment) ....

7. The Board shall issue the appropriate documents (certificates, attestations or vouchers) in the amounts of the contributions made.

8. Any change in the amount of the Statutory Capital shall be made by decision of the supreme organ of the Joint Venture, i.e. the Board. The Statutory Capital may be replenished by income from the Joint Venture's own economic activity and by additional contributions for the Parties.

9. The Parties to the Joint Venture shall not have separate rights in individual objects forming part of the property of the Joint Venture even if they were brought in by a Party as a contribution.

Article 7

1. The Joint Venture shall be liable for its obligations in accordance with the laws of the USSR, including those relative to enforced collection against its property.

2. The Joint Venture shall not be liable for the obligations of the Parties and the Parties shall not be liable for the obligations of the Joint Venture.

Article 8

1. The Joint Venture shall establish out of its profits a reserve fund amounting to 25 per cent of the Statutory Capital. Allocations to the reserve fund shall be made for .... years at the rate of .... per cent of the amount of the reserve fund (Variant 1)/of the profits (Variant 2).

2. In addition to the reserve fund, the Joint Venture may form other funds, whose amounts, designated purposes, rates of allocation and procedures for use shall be determined by the Board.

3. The resources of the funds shall be entirely at the Joint Venture's disposal.

Article 9

1. The profits of the Joint Venture, after deduction of sums due to the State budget of the USSR and moneys used to establish and replenish the funds of the Joint Venture, shall be divided amongst the Parties in proportion to their shares in the Statutory Capital.

Article 10

1. The Joint Venture shall keep operational, bookkeeping and statistical records and accounts in accordance with the procedures in force in the USSR.

2. The financial year of the Joint Venture shall coincide with the calendar year. The first financial year shall end on 31 December 19.. .

Article 11

1. The organs of management of the Joint Venture shall be:

- the Board;
- the Management;
- the Audit Panel.

2. The supreme organ of the Joint Venture shall be the Board. The Board shall be composed of .... members, of whom ...... members, including the Chairman of the Board, shall be appointed by the .... Party and .... members, including the Vice-Chairman of the Board, shall be appointed by the .... Party.

3. The members of the Board shall serve for .... years unless recalled earlier by the respective Party. Each of the Parties may appoint one or more alternate members of the Board and shall be entitled to replace members of the Board at any time.

4. The appointment and removal of members of the Board shall be immediately notified to the other Party in writing, by telex or by telegram.

5. The Board shall determine its own structure and rules of procedure. It shall elect a Chairman and a Vice-Chairman from among its members.

6. A member of the Board may refuse at any time, without stating his reasons, to take any further part in the Board's work. In that event the alternate member of the Board designated by the Party concerned shall take his place.

7. Alternate members of the Board may take part, without a right to vote, in meetings of the Board.

8. When unable to take part personally in a meeting of the Board, a member of the Board may, on the basis of a proxy issued by him in writing, be represented at the meeting by another member of the Board or by a person who is not a member of the Board.

9. The right to submit items for examination by the Board shall be vested with the Parties, the members of the Board, the General Manager and the Chairman of the Audit Panel.

10. The Board shall be convened as and when necessary but not less often than once a year.

11. Extraordinary meetings of the Board shall be convened by the Chairman of the Board on his initiative and also upon the written request of either Party, any member of the Board, or the General Manager.

12. The meetings of the Board shall as a rule be held at the location of the Joint Venture.

13. On individual questions the Board may adopt decisions by consulting its members in writing.

14. The meetings of the Board and the decisions adopted thereat, together with decisions adopted outside the meetings by written consultation of the members of the Board, shall be recorded in writing and signed by the Chairman and the Vice-Chairman of the Board.

15. The Joint Venture shall not pay any fee to the members of the Board for the performance of their functions.

Article 12

The Board shall have competence to decide the following matters.

1. Amendment of the Charter, including an increase or reduction in the Statutory Capital of the Joint Venture, decreasing or increasing the period of activity of the Joint Venture, changes related with the purposes of the Joint Venture, and other changes;
2. Determination of the main lines of activity of the Joint Venture in accordance with its purposes and objectives as prescribed by the Contract concerning the establishment of the Joint Venture and by the Charter;
3. Annual approval of the balance sheet, the profit-and-loss accounts and the annual report of the Management and the Audit Panel;
4. Distribution of the profits of the Joint Venture and also determination of the procedure for the distribution of earnings in foreign currency;
5. Determination of the procedure for covering losses;
6. Adoption of decisions on obtaining long-term credits;
7. Determination of the purpose, amount, sources of formation and procedure for the utilization of funds of the Joint Venture;
8. Approval of the plans of production and sales activity (including determination of the proportion of exports) of the Joint Venture which are necessary to the achievement of its purposes and objectives, and also of reports on the fulfilment of those plans;
9. Liquidation of the Joint Venture, appointment of the liquidation committee and approval of the liquidation balance sheet;
10. Establishment and termination of the activity of branches and subsidiaries;
11. Approval of financial plans and of reports on their fulfilment;
12. Approval of the Rules of Internal Working Procedure for the staff;
13. Approval and amendment of the manning table;
14. Determination of the skills and number of foreign specialists and the conditions of their engagement;
15. Approval of plans and measures for the training of staff of the Joint Venture;
16. Appointment and dismissal of the General Manager of the Joint Venture and his deputies;

17. Approval of the Regulations on the Activity of the Audit Panel, appointment of its Chairman and members, hearing the reprots of the Audit Panel and the adoption of decisions tereon;
18. Adoption of decisions to hold extraordinary audits;
19. Decision-making on any other matters connected with the direction of the Joint Venture's activities;
20. Decisions on the matters referred to in subparagraphs .... shall be adopted unanimously. [43] Decisions on other matters shall be adopted by majority vote. If the vote is equally divided, the Chairman of the Board shall have a casting vote.

Article 13

1. The Board of the Joint Venture may refer to the Management for decision individual matters which under this Charter are within the competence of the Board.

Article 14

1. The Management shall direct the current activities of the Joint Venture in accordance with the instructions of the Board and the General Manager and under the General Manager's direct guidance and supervision.

2. The Management shall be composed of the General Manager and his deputies, who shall be appointed and dismissed by the Board.

3. The General Manager and his deputies shall be appointed for a term of .... years. Their powers may be revoked prematurely by the decision of the Board. The General Manager may be reappointed for additional terms.

4. If, during his term of office, the General Manager or one of his deputies should for any reason cease to perform his duties, the Board shall immediately replace him in accordance with the procedure set forth above.

5. The Management shall be accountable to the Board for its activities.

Article 15

The General Manager of the Joint Venture shall, within the limits of his powers, perform the following functions:

1. He shall operationally direct all the work of the Joint Venture in accordance with the plans drawn up in the Joint Venture.
2. He shall manage the property of the Joint Venture, including its financial resources, in accordance with the legislation in force and with this Charter.
3. He shall present for the approval of the Board the drafts of the plans provided for in this Charter, and reports on their fulfilment. No later than .... months after the end of the financial year he shall present the annual balance sheet, profit-and-loss account and annual report, together with a report on the fulfilment of the financial plan.
4. He shall, without a power of attorney, act in the name of the Joint Venture and represent it in all institutions and organizations both in the USSR and abroad.
5. He shall conduct all kinds of transactions and perform other legal acts, issue powers of attorney and open a current account and other accounts of the Joint Venture in banks.
6. He shall be responsible for drawing up the Rules of Internal Working Procedure and presenting them for the approval of the Board of the Joint Venture; he shall ensure compliance with those Rules.
7. He shall approve regulations concerning structural subdivisions and service instructions for employees of the Joint Venture.
8. He shall participate in the conclusion and termination of the collective agreement and individual agreements with the workers of the Joint Venture.

43 It is desirable to provide where possible for decisions to be taken unanimously only on the most important matters.

9. He shall apply incentive measures to the workers and impose penalties on them in accordance with the Rules of Internal Working Procedure.
10. He shall adopt decisions and issue orders on operational matters relating to the internal activity of the Joint Venture.
11. He shall participate in carrying out plans and measures for the training of staff of the Joint Venture.
12. He shall prepare materials and proposals for examination by the Board of the Joint Venture.
13. He shall perform any other actions necessary to achieve the purposes of the Joint Venture, with the exception of those measures that are directly assigned to the Board under the Charter.

Article 16

1. The Deputy General Managers shall perform the functions entrusted to them in connection with the activity of the Joint Venture.

2. The Deputy General Managers shall be responsible for the performance of the duties entrusted to them.

The Deputy Manager for Finance shall

....[44]

The Deputy Manager for procurement shall

....[45]

The Deputy Manager for Marketing shall

....[46]

etc. ... .

Article 17

1. Current supervision of the financial and economic activities of the Joint Venture shall be exercised by the Audit Panel.

2. The Audit Panel shall be composed of .... members appointed by the Board. .... members, including the Chairman of the Audit Panel, shall be appointed on the nomination of the Soviet Party and .... members shall be appointed on the nomination of the Foreign Party.

3. The members of the Audit Panel shall be appointed for a term of .... years. Their powers may be revoked before the end of their terms of office by a decision of the Board. Members of the Audit Panel may be reappointed for an additional term.

4. If, during his term of office, a member of the Audit Panel should for any reason cease to perform his duties, the Board shall immediately replace him in accordance with the procedure set forth above.

---

44 It is desirable to indicate all the functions of each of the deputies, e.g. Deputy Manager for finance, procurement, marketing, etc.)

45 *Id.*

46 *Id.*

Article 18

1. The Audit Panel shall each year carry out a regular audit and shall report thereof to the Board.

2. At the request of either Party or by decision of the Board, extraordinary audits may be held.

3. The General Manager and his deputies shall place at the Audit Panel's disposal all materials and documents needed for auditing and shall provide the necessary conditions thereof.

4. The Chairman and members of the Audit Panel shall be entitled to attend meetings of the Board and meetings of the Management of the Joint Venture with the right to speak but not to vote.

5. The Regulation concerning the Activities of the Audit Panel shall be approved by the Board.

Article 19

1. The Management shall conclude a collective agreement with the trade union organization active within the Joint Venture.

2. The contents of the said agreement, including the provisions concerning the social development of the workforce, shall be determined by Soviet legislation and also by the characteristics of the Joint Venture's activity.

Article 20

The property and property interests of the Joint Venture shall be insured at the *Strakhovoe aktsionernoe obshchestvo SSSR* (the Joint-Stock Insurance Company of the USSR) (Ingosstrakh).

Article 21

The Joint Venture shall be liquidated in the following circumstances:

1. On the expiry of the period of activity of the Joint Venture unless the said period is extended;
2. If the activity of the Joint Venture becomes unprofitable and the Joint Venture is not in a position to meet its obligations;
3. If the Contract concerning the establishment of the Joint Venture is terminated before the agreed date;
4. By decision of the competent State authority of the USSR, if the activity of the Joint Venture does not correspond to the purposes and objectives provided for in the Contract and the Charter.

Article 22

1. In the event of liquidation of the Joint Venture, the Board shall appoint a liquidation committee composed of equal numbers of representatives of the Parties.

2. The liquidation committee shall draw up the liquidation balance sheet and present it for the approval of the Board.

3. Upon the liquidation of the Joint Venture, its property shall be evaluated, taking into account wear and tear and obsolescence.

4. Such property of the Joint Venture as remains after the creditors' demands have been met shall be divided amongst the Parties in proportion to their shares in the Statutory Capital.

5. The Joint Venture shall forfeit its rights of an enterprise and shall be deemed to cease to exist at the time of the registration of its liquidation in the Ministry of Finance of the USSR.

Article 23

This Charter shall enter into force on the date of its approval at the assembly of members of the Board.

Article 24

Legal addresses of the Parties:

For the Soviet Party: For the foreign Party

....

.. .. *19...*